HUMAN AGGRESSION:
NATURALISTIC APPROACHES

HUMAN AGGRESSION: NATURALISTIC APPROACHES

Edited by:

JOHN ARCHER

School of Psychology,
Lancashire Polytechnic,
Preston, Lancashire, UK.

and

KEVIN BROWNE

Department of Psychology,
University of Leicester,
Leicester, UK.

ROUTLEDGE
London and New York

TO ODILE AND JUNE
FOR LOST WEEKENDS

First published in 1989
by Routledge
11 New Fetter Lane, London EC4P 4EE
29 West 35th Street, New York NY 10001

Printed and bound in Great Britain by
Mackays of Chatham PLC, Chatham, Kent

British Library Cataloguing in Publication Data

Human aggression: naturalistic approaches.
1. Man. Aggression, — Sociological perspectives
I. Archer, John, *1944–*   II. Browne, Kevin
302.5′4

ISBN 0–415–030366
ISBN 0–415–030374 pbk

Library of Congress Cataloging in Publication Data available

CONTENTS

Part One: Introduction

CONTENTS

Part Two: Naturalistic Methods:
Specific Examples

Part Three: Applications to Social
Problems Involving Aggression

CONTENTS

Part Four: Conclusions

FIGURES

ix

TABLES

ABBREVIATIONS

ADSS	Association of Directors of Social Services
BASW	British Association of Social Workers
DHSS	Department of Health and Social Security (UK)
FSW	Field social worker
HDHQ	Hostility and Direction of Hostility Questionnaire
NSPCC	National Society for the Prevention of Cruelty to Children
OED	Oxford English Dictionary
RSW	Residential social worker
SSD	Social services department

CONTRIBUTORS

John Archer: School of Psychology, Lancashire Polytechnic, Preston, Lancashire PR1 2TQ, UK.

Len Berkowitz: Department of Psychology, University of Wisconsin, Madison, Wisconsin, USA.

John Beynon: Department of Behavioural and Communication Studies, The Polytechnic of Wales, Pontypridd, Mid Glamorgan CF37 1DL, Wales, UK.

D. Caroline Blanchard: Department of Psychology and Bekesy Laboratory of Neurobiology, University of Hawaii, Honolulu, Hawaii, USA.

Robert J. Blanchard: Department of Psychology and Bekesy Laboratory of Neurobiology, University of Hawaii, Honolulu, Hawaii, USA.

Glynis Breakwell: Department of Psychology, University of Surrey, Guildford, Surrey, UK.

Kevin Browne: Family Violence Research Group, Department of Psychology, University of Leicester, Leicester LE1 7RH, UK.

Mervyn Eastman: Social Services Department, London Borough of Enfield, 1A Old Road, Enfield, Middlesex EN3 5XX, UK.

Kevin Howells: Department of Psychology, University of Birmingham, Birmingham B15 2TT, UK.

Colin Rowett: Department of Social Work, St. Luke's Hospital, Guildford, Surrey, UK.

Peter K. Smith: Department of Psychology, University of Sheffield, Sheffield, UK.

PREFACE

Human aggression is one of the most pervasive and serious problems facing modern societies. The quality of many people's lives is lessened by violence experienced in the home, at work, at school, and on the streets. However, the bulk of social psychological research has been concerned with solving rather general questions connected with the nature of aggressive motivation, and has primarily adopted a laboratory-based experimental approach which has at times seemed remote from real-life aggression. The psychological processes leading to violence in the community are still poorly understood. In *Human Aggression: Naturalistic Approaches* we explore alternatives to laboratory-based social psychological methods for studying aggression. We seek to demonstrate the importance of viewing it in the context of the interactions, relationships, and situations in which it occurs – features which are difficult to isolate and capture in laboratory experiments.

An understanding of human aggression in terms of its social context will require different methods of study from the testing of general hypotheses in the laboratory. In the first part of the book we explore some of these methods, and then consider specific topics to which they have been applied. The studies and methods discussed in the book come from a variety of disciplines in addition to psychology – anthropology, criminology, education, gerontology, law, medicine, politics, physiology, psychiatry, sociology, social policy, social work, and zoology. Some of these disciplines are primarily concerned with solving urgent social problems, and it is argued that the study of aggression by naturalistic approaches offers the best basis for designing more effective strategies for identifying, preventing, and treating violent behaviour.

We would like to thank Jo Swaby for constructing the Author Index, Marijke Veltman for her help in preparing some of the manuscript, and our colleagues at the University of Leicester and Lancashire Polytechnic for their comments and discussions of various chapters and issues.

John Archer
and Kevin Browne
October, 1988.

Part One

INTRODUCTION

Chapter 1

CONCEPTS AND APPROACHES TO THE STUDY OF AGGRESSION

JOHN ARCHER AND KEVIN BROWNE

This chapter provides a broad introduction to the subject-matter of the book, by concentrating on three issues: first, the different terminology used in research on aggression and violence; second, an overview of different theoretical approaches in terms of the level of analysis used; and third, how naturalistic methods of studying aggression relate to the level of analysis. We argue that the study of the social interactions of the participants in a naturalistic setting occupies a central place between the individual psychological and the broader societal levels. Naturalistic methods are seen as particularly appropriate for pursuing the investigation of aggression in this context.

TERMINOLOGY

The terms aggression, violence, and disruption have all been widely used in the behavioural sciences. Although several authors have attempted to formulate rigorous definitions, problems and disagreements over terminology are widespread. In this section, we explore some of the issues surrounding these terminological difficulties.

Aggression

Beginning with the term aggression, the *Oxford English Dictionary* (OED) defines it as either an unprovoked attack (i.e. the first attack in a quarrel, or an assault), or as the practice of making an attack or setting on a person. Aggressiveness is defined as the quality of being aggressive (OED 1933). These definitions refer

3

to the everyday uses of the terms, which were derived (in the seventeenth century) from the French 'agression', meaning an aggression, assault, or an encounter. This is the sense in which the word is often used in news reports of international events, for example, 'an act of aggression', meaning the first attack.

In psychology, the meaning of aggression is different (Supplement to the OED 1972), referring to a 'hostile or destructive tendency or behaviour'. This difference in meaning from the everyday one appears to be derived from the psychoanalytic writings of Freud and Adler, where 'aggression' is seen as a drive, and 'aggressive' is pertaining to such a drive. This use is reflected in the definition given by Dollard *et al.* (1939) in their famous book *Frustration and Aggression*, which formed part of a wider endeavour to operationalize psychoanalytic concepts by reformulating them in learning theory terms (see N.E. Miller 1979; P.H. Miller 1983). Dollard *et al.* defined aggression as 'any sequence of behaviour, the goal response of which is the injury of the person toward which it is directed'. Most subsequent definitions have adopted injurious intent as an essential feature of aggression (e.g. Berkowitz 1962; Feshbach 1964; Johnson 1972; Bandura 1973). Strictly interpreted, this assumes that *physical* injury is always the goal of aggressive behaviour, and therefore fails to include either verbal or symbolic forms of aggression, or aggression which is instrumental in obtaining other goals.

One of the first distinctions to be made between different types of aggression in psychological studies was between 'instrumental' aggression, which is directed towards the achievement of non-aggressive goals, and 'hostile' aggression, for which the goal response is injury to a person or object (Sears *et al.* 1957). Like all attempts at a rigid classification of aggression, this distinction is not entirely satisfactory, for, as Valzelli (1969) has pointed out, 'Aggressiveness should indicate a particular oriented behaviour, directed toward removing or overcoming whatever is menacing the physical or psychological integrity of the living organism.' It could be argued, on this view, that virtually all aggression is instrumental. However, such a view does not distinguish between the general goal-directedness of aggressive behaviour, which is concerned with overcoming an irritating or noxious event, and the learning of aggressive behaviour as an instrumental response in order to obtain a wider range of goals than the removal of such an event.

Buss (1961) sought to remove (or evade) the difficulties involved with 'goal direction' by resorting to a behaviourist approach, defining aggression as 'a response that delivers noxious stimuli to another organism'. This definition is, however, unsatisfactory since it omits intentionality, and to do so leaves out a central aspect of the meaning of aggression, and hence fails to exclude accidental damage. Other definitions, such as Kaufmann (1970), have sought to remedy this defect by adding the notion of expectancy to a behaviourally based definition, i.e. there must be a perceived chance of harm being done to the victim.

An alternative approach to seeking a tight definition of aggression is to explore the nature of the problem in trying to reach a consensus. Cognitive categories such as aggression are represented by instances on which there is good agreement (prototypical cases), together with those on which there is lesser agreement (Rosch 1978): this is sometimes depicted as a solid core surrounded by a fuzzy edge. If we apply this notion to psychological definitions of 'aggression', we can begin by identifying prototypical cases in terms of the features which are relevant for categorizing an act as one of 'aggression': there appear to be at least three of these features (Archer 1977). The first one is intent: this is often seen as the crucial defining feature and, as we have seen, it has led to many problems. Subjectively, the intent must be to harm by injury, ridicule, or by preventing access to a resource. In terms of a motivational system, these intentions can be shown as the desired end-points, specified as reference-values in the control system (see Toates and Archer 1978). In practice, we have to rely on verbal statements, inferences from actions, and contextual cues, to infer about intent.

The second feature is the presence of actions which cause damage or are likely to do so. Again, if we consider the prototypical case, physical damage would be inflicted; in addition, verbal aggression and non-verbal signals of hostility usually accompany damaging actions. In other cases, however, only verbal and non-verbal expressions of the intent to harm occur. Non-verbal human expressions of aggression, such as staring, and clench-fist gestures, can be compared with similar expressions in non-human primates (e.g. Jolly 1972), and verbal insults can be seen as symbolic challenges to status and sexuality, again with biological origins (Blanchard and Blanchard 1984).

The third feature relevant to categorization is emotional state. In making the distinction between 'hostile' and 'instrumental' aggression, Sears *et al.* (1957) were forshadowing a later distinction between angry aggression and instrumental (or manipulative) aggression (Feshbach 1964). This distinction recognizes the special case of 'cold' aggression, i.e. where the intent to harm and the actual injury are present without anger, the emotion. Returning to our prototypical case, the emotional state of anger (including the accompanying physiological changes) would be present. To complicate this picture, there are a number of other emotional states associated with aggression: a milder state may be referred to as 'irritation' and an extreme state as 'rage' (c.f. Averill 1983).

We therefore have three features – intent, injurious behaviour, and emotion – which, if all are present, would produce a prototypical case of aggression. If one or more of these is absent, or present to a lesser degree, there will be more disagreement about whether the category 'aggression' applies.

These three features are, of course, the ones which in more general terms characterize any behavioural output: affect, intent, and behaviour (Figure 1.1). They are best regarded as related but dissociable components characteristic of a particular motivational state.

Campbell *et al.* (1985a) used a multidimensional scaling technique to investigate common-sense distinctions between descriptions of aggressive incidents. This technique involves sorting out the degree to which items are similar or different from one another. They found that the subjects' classification reflected aspects of motivation, two aspects of the *form* of aggression (whether it was direct or indirect), and also the motive, whether hostile, instrumental, normative, or status-related. Although this was a preliminary study, involving only a small number of subjects, who were restricted in their choices, it does provide an interesting way of investigating common-sense distinctions about aggressive situations. In a follow-up study using different aggressive incidents, Muncer *et al.* (1986) found that the respondents' classifications reflected the verbal–physical

Figure 1.1 Three components characterizing any behavioural output

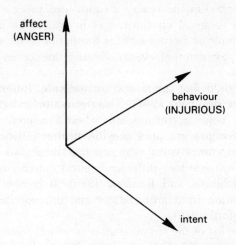

distinction, as well as the familiar or unfamiliar nature of the target, and a sense of equity as opposed to victimization. In these studies, we are moving from the psychologist's definition (supposedly as an outside observer) to the social perceptions people have about aggressive acts. Of course, this will influence the psychologist's definitions to the extent that he or she possesses shared cultural values about aggression, and incorporates these into psychological judgements.

In addition to naturalistic and laboratory research on human aggression, there is a vast amount of research on animal aggression, carried out from both a biological and a psychological standpoint (see Johnson 1972; Archer 1976, 1988). Here the problems of defining aggression are more pronounced since verbal statements of intent are absent. The three components we have just discussed, intent, injurious behaviour, and emotion, again enter into judgements about whether an act is aggressive or not, but the judgement is more difficult because intent must be inferred from behaviour.

Several attempts have been made to classify the different forms of animal aggression. Before describing these, it is necessary to point out the different criteria which can be used when considering and categorizing animal behaviour. On the one hand, a functional approach (Hinde, 1975) refers to the

7

consequences of behaviour which are crucial for the action of natural selection. On the other, a causal explanation refers to the immediate external circumstances in which the behaviour occurs, or to internal factors such as hormones or neural representations of past external events which influence an animal's responsiveness.

In seeking to define aggression in animals, Lorenz (1966) emphasized the situations in which aggressive behaviour occurs, distinguishing between intraspecific ('social aggression') and fighting between predator and prey. A further justification for this distinction comes from evidence that these two forms of behaviour may involve different neural mechanisms (for example, Hutchinson and Renfrew 1966). It is now usual to separate predation from antipredator and intraspecific aggression (Huntingford 1976).

An extensive list of the circumstances in which animal aggression occurs was given by Moyer (1968, 1976). He claimed that eight categories of aggressive behaviour, which are not necessarily mutually exclusive, differed in either the brain structures involved or in their dependence on external factors or hormones. Moyer's categories are summarized in Table 1.1.

A number of criticisms have been made of this scheme (e.g. Archer 1976; Huntingford 1976), for example (a) that so-called predatory aggression is so motivationally and neurally different from other forms of aggression that it is most usefully considered as a separate form of behaviour; (b) that Moyer's criteria for classifying the types of aggression were diverse and inconsistent; and (c) that the neural evidence did not support the division into inter-male, territorial, maternal, and irritable aggression (Archer 1976). Other criticisms are that paternal aggression and inter-female aggression are not considered. Whatever the detailed criticisms, such a multifactorial approach to aggression stands in contrast to the view, prominent in many discussions of human aggression, that aggression is a unitary category.

Another multidimensional approach to animal aggression was offered by Wilson (1975), who was viewing the problem from a functional evolutionary standpoint. He defined aggression in terms of competition as: 'A physical act or threat of action by one individual that reduces the freedom or genetic fitness of

Table 1.1 Moyer's (1968) classification of aggressive behaviour in animals

---

1. PREDATORY AGGRESSION: in response to a natural object of prey.
2. INTER-MALE AGGRESSION: in response to the proximity of an unfamiliar male.
3. FEAR-INDUCED AGGRESSION: shown by a confined or cornered animal, and preceded by escape attempts.
4. IRRITABLE AGGRESSION: in response to a broad range of external circumstances, such as pain, frustration, and deprivation, and shown towards inanimate as well as animate objects.
5. TERRITORIAL DEFENCE: in response to an intruder into an area in which the individual has established itself.
6. MATERNAL AGGRESSION: in response to the proximity of an animal which is perceived as threatening the young.
7. INSTRUMENTAL AGGRESSION: a learned response to obtain reinforcement.
8. SEX-RELATED AGGRESSION: in response to competition for a mate.

---

another'. He also recommended eight provisional categories of aggression – predatory, antipredatory, territorial, dominance, sexual, parental, disciplinary, weaning, and moralistic. We should note that in this case the criteria are consistently functional: the first five categories are similar to the situations covered by Moyer's categories (1, 3, 5, 2 and 8 in Table 1.1, respectively); the last three categories were concerned with aggressive interactions relating to the functional models of parent-offspring conflict and reciprocal altruism of Trivers (1971, 1974), which were not considered by authors such as Moyer, who used only causal criteria.

In any investigation of 'social' aggression, it soon becomes evident that aggressive behaviour directed towards another individual usually involves a risk of sustaining injury. Thus, an attack on a rival is often associated with self-protective behaviours, in which there are both elements of attack and withdrawal (Eibl-Eibesfeldt 1961, 1975). In descriptive accounts, it is generally considered useful to consider both aspects of fighting as a single category, which has been termed 'agonistic behaviour' (Scott and Fredericson 1951; Scott 1958). More recently, emphasis has been placed on the distinction between 'offensive' and 'defensive' forms of aggression, in terms of situational determinants, emotional and motivational state, and behavioural acts (for example, Adams 1979, 1980; Brain 1981; Blanchard and Blanchard 1984). Brain (1981) also suggests that these correspond to a functional distinction between aggression whose consequence is obtaining or retaining resources and that which protects the individual or its offspring. Archer (1985, 1988) has argued that although it is useful to divide aggression into functional or motivational categories, these do not always correspond with each other: for example, protective aggression may be offensive in form and competitive aggression may be defensive in form.

A further causal approach to classifying animal aggression is in terms of the context in which it occurs (Archer 1976) – for example, whether in response to pain, or frustration, or individual distance, or territorial intrusion, or in response to classical or instrumentally conditioned stimuli.

The discussions arising from these various attempts to classify animal aggression have produced some order into a diverse field, and have led to some general conclusions which are potentially transferrable to the study of human behaviour. These include the following: (1) that aggression may be distinguished on broad functional grounds; (2) that it may also be distinguished on motivational and physiological grounds (i.e., the extent to which it is motivated by fear or anger); and (3) that it can be further distinguished according to the context in which it occurs. Nevertheless, all these attempts to bring order to the field flounder if based on the assumption that aggression represents one or more logically distinct categories. As we indicated earlier, aggression is a cognitive category with a clear centre and fuzzy edges: it consists of a series of features which, when combined together, produce greater or lesser consensus as to whether the label 'aggression' is appropriate.

Violence and disruptive behaviour

The term 'violence' has had a longer history of everyday use than is the case with the term 'aggression'. From the Latin, *violentia*, meaning vehemence or impetuosity, it came to have several different meanings, all dating from the thirteenth or fourteenth century (OED 1933). The definition most relevant to our current discussion is the following: the exercise of physical force so as to injure or damage persons or property; otherwise to treat or use persons or property in a way that causes bodily injury and/or forcibly interferes with personal freedom. Alternative meanings include, first, force or strength of physical action or natural agents; and second, great force or severity or vehemence of personal feeling or action.

Current usage of the term 'violence' in relation to aggressive behaviour typically concerns a more societal level of analysis, and refers to acts of physical aggression within a social context. Physical harm is typically emphasized, but perhaps a more important aspect is the negative social judgement entailed by the term 'violence'. Whether referring to 'violence on the picket line' or to 'police violence' or to 'marital violence', the respondent is referring to the illegitimate and unlawful nature of the act. In contrast, the same acts of physical aggression may be referred to by different respondents as 'defence of trade union rights' or 'maintenance of law and order' or 'punishing an errant wife'.

'Violence' is typically the preferred word of the media when referring to criminal acts carried out by both individuals or a group, either in public or private. In the social science literature, for example, on physical aggression in domestic situations, 'marital violence' (Gelles 1987; Roy 1977) or 'intimate violence' (Gelles and Cornell 1985) refers to physically damaging assaults which are not socially legitimized in any way.

In some accounts there is a tendency to generalize from actual to metaphorical violence (for example, 'the violence of unemployment'), and this is particularly characteristic of approaches which seek to understand violence in terms of a wider social context. Gil (1978), for example, saw violence in families as rooted in wider societal violence, and he used a very broad definition which involved 'acts and conditions which obstruct the spontaneous unfolding of innate human potential, the inherent human drive toward the development of self-actualisation'. Such a definition is so wide as to include virtually any thwarting of wishes and activities, and is so vague as to be incapable of being operationalized.

A further term, which has been used in relation to aggression in schools, is 'disruptive behaviour' (Frude and Gault 1984a). It refers to behaviour which forcibly interferes with the usual behaviour appropriate in a particular context: it is therefore

11

defined in relation to the expected standards – for example, of the school or society. 'Disruptive behaviour' is used to refer to behaviour which is aggressive, but the emphasis is very much on its social consequences, and its implications for an issue which is defined in terms of public concern and media interest (Frude and Gault 1984b), and is part of a more general popular concern about a supposed decline in law and order.

As Frude and Gault (ibid.) pointed out, disruption is 'behaviour related to a context', i.e. the same physical action may constitute a disruption in one situation but not in another. This poses enormous problems of definition, since the term can only be socially relative in meaning.

Examining the derivation of the term disruption, it conveys the meaning of suddenly breaking or severing something which was orderly or calm. Originating in the seventeenth century, it referred to an act of rending or bursting asunder, a violent dissolution of continuity, or a forcible severance (as in the case of great earthquakes and disruptions). These earlier meanings have persisted as connotations of the current usage in the context of children's behaviour at school.

LEVELS OF EXPLANATION IN RELATION TO TERMINOLOGY

Throughout the preceding discussion of definitional problems, it was apparent that terminology reflects the way the researcher approaches the topic. This is shown in the use of the different terms aggression, violence, and disruption, and in the different definitions and classification of forms of aggression. How a researcher approaches a problem such as aggression or violence will reflect his or her theoretical background, and the particular method used will in turn affect how the subject is conceptualized.

Lystad (1975) has grouped 'theories of violence' into three categories, those involving psychological variables, those involving social structural ones, and those which seek the causes in contemporary society's fundamental cultural assumptions and values. Beginning with psychological explanations, these can be subdivided into ones which focus on the individual level and those which are more social and interactive in approach.

Individually-focused explanations may concentrate on personality characteristics, often of a psychopathological or deviant nature. This research tradition is characterized by the use of rating scales to measure aggressiveness and hostility (Buss and Durkee 1957; Edmunds and Kendrick 1980). Some individually oriented theorists have claimed that biological variables underlie a tendency to be violent. Perhaps the most extreme version of these was the work of Mark and Ervin (1970), who advocated widespread psychosurgery as a solution to violent behaviour.

Other research areas adopting this general approach include the attempt to establish a causal connection between gonadal hormone levels and violent crime (for example, Persky *et al.* 1971; Rada *et al.* 1976), and the identification of specific pathological conditions, such as alcoholism, which are likely to be predisposing or determining factors in violent behaviour (for example, Byles 1978; Gerson 1978).

Social learning provides an alternative form of within-individual explanation to biological determinism. Schultz (1960), for example, claims that the source of violence in a marital context is unfulfilled childhood experiences and deviant marital relationships. Gayford (1975), who carried out research in conjunction with Chiswick Women's Aid, attempted to show the learned character of domestic violence within the family of origin.

These approaches are all concerned with the perpetrators of violence. Other explanations concentrate on their victims. Gayford (1976) distinguished various types of victim of domestic violence, offering names and descriptions which imply that the cause of the behaviour lies with the victim. Others (for example, Walker and Browne 1985) have argued that such consistent response patterns are situationally determined. Experimental laboratory studies (see Chapters 2 and 3) also concentrate on the individual level, and generally seek to explain aggression in terms of situational variables.

A more interactive approach would include the social relationships of the participants, and their environmental setting, rather than seeking to isolate the person or situation. This entails a move from the individual psychological level to a social interactive approach. Toch (1969), for example, in his study entitled *Violent Men*, looked not only at the characteristics of these men

13

but also at the context of their violence and the characteristics of their victims. He concluded that aggressive behaviour was associated with 'machismo' and the maintenance of a particular personal identity in relation to others, an observation that supports Valzelli's (1969) definition of aggression referred to earlier. In a study which sought to measure the characteristics of aggressiveness, using psychometric techniques, Edmunds and Kendrick (1980) eventually concluded that a more interactive approach that took account of situational differences would be required to explain the lack of relationship between many of the personality measures and overt behaviour.

Campbell *et al.* (1985b) also noted the high degree of situational specificity in a study using a self-report technique: teenaged subjects (from New Jersey) were asked to report their predicted responses to twenty-four conflict scenarios involving male and female targets. Cross-situational consistency was found to be low, even controlling for the sex and social class of the subjects, and the authors remarked that there was little support from their findings for the notion of a generalized aggressive personality.

Such findings are in apparent conflict with studies showing developmental consistency in aggressive reactions (Olweus 1979, 1984). Olweus adopted a broad approach to assessing aggressiveness, rather than relying on measures applying to a limited number of settings. It seems, therefore, that there *is* evidence for developmental consistency in an overall trait which can be labelled 'aggressiveness', yet inconsistency is found across situations for measures of aggression taken at one particular time (Kaplan 1984).

Most of the authors of chapters in this book adopt an interactionist approach, viewing aggression or violence as the outcome of the relationship between the persons involved within a particular setting. Indeed, concentration on aggression occurring in naturalistic settings implies a dissatisfaction with approaches which isolate the individual from his or her social context. Naturalistic approaches widen the context of the investigation to include interactions with other people and with situations.

Theories which emphasize the importance of social structural factors are more sociological in approach and are generally concerned with explaining socially problematic forms of 'violence', rather than explaining 'aggression' in psychological terms. They can, however, be formulated in psychological terms: for example, Turner *et al.* (1984) sought to explain the link between the economic recession and criminal violence in young adults in terms of relative deprivation. At a more psychological level, this would involve an aversive response to perceived deprivation, which is also dependent on a variety of other factors such as aspiration level, alternative resources, specific environmental cues for aggression, and social learning in a criminal subculture. In relation to domestic violence, factors such as low wages, poor housing, overcrowding, isolation, and alienating work conditions are seen by Gelles (1987) and Gelles and Cornell (1985) as causing frustration and stress at the individual level, which in turn may lead to violence. Gelles concluded from his research that 'violence is an adaptation or response to structural stress'. However, since domestic violence is not confined to families in the lower socio-economic groups but is spread across the class spectrum, this view must be a limited one. (These limitations are discussed further in Chapter 9.)

Other attempts to explain domestic violence in wider social terms include the exchange theory of Goode (1971) and the general systems approach of Straus (1978, 1980).

Goode argued that the family, like all social institutions, rests to some degree on force or threat to maintain order. He postulated that the more alternatives (or 'resources') an individual can command, or perceive to command, the less he or she will use force (itself a 'resource') in an overt manner. Most people do not willingly use overt force when they command other 'resources' because the costs of doing so are high. Goode assumed that middle-class families have more 'resources', arising, for example, from their greater prestige and better economic position, and consequently will be less likely to resort to violence or threat. O'Brien (1971) showed a similar line of thought in his 'status inconsistency' hypothesis. He focused on the economic problems of the husband and the differential educational achievements between husband and wife that may result in his lower status in the family. Violence is seen as an option to be used in remedying the low-status position, and hence increasing self-esteem.

Straus (1978, 1980) explained the occurrence of domestic violence in the context of a general systems approach, in terms of 'deviant family structures'. He referred to deviant authority structures and claimed that the level of violence is likely to be greatest when the wife is dominant in decision-making.

These explanations all view violence within the family in terms of wider societal or structural variables. An alternative approach, but also couched in terms of the social position of the people involved, can be referred to as the micropolitical view. This holds that individual violence is a microcosm of the power relations in the wider society. For example, a common feminist explanation of violence towards women is to view it as a function of women's generally oppressed position in society. Within this framework, the purpose of male violence is seen as to control women. Hanmer (1977, 1978) has expanded this idea into a complete theory incorporating the whole state apparatus (which represents men), and in her view the policies of the Welfare State induce dependency in women. However, Dobash and Dobash (1979) are probably the most well-known theorists taking this general position. They stated: 'We propose that the correct interpretation of violence between husbands and wives conceptualises such violence as the extension of the domination and control of husbands over their wives' (p. 21).

Gil (1978) distinguished between 'structural' violence (violence at the institutional and societal levels), which is embedded in socially sanctioned practices, and personal violence, which usually involves acts which transcend social sanctions. As we noted earlier, Gil's definition of violence is a particularly wide one, which reflects his theoretical view that violence should be viewed in terms of the wider power relations in society. He therefore says that structural violence and personal violence should not be viewed as discrete phenomena: they are both symptoms of the same social context, i.e. the same values and institutions, and they interact and reinforce each other. He sees personal violence as being reactive, as being rooted in structural violence, since experiences which inhibit a person's development will often result in stress and frustration, and the urge to retaliate by inflicting violence on others. Domestic violence is reactive violence which originates outside the family but which cannot be discharged there. It can be

Figure 1.2   Integration of psychological and societal approaches

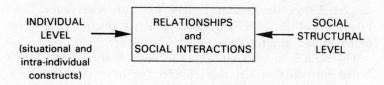

discharged within the family because the family is more informal, most time is spent there, and less punitive sanctions will result than from violence in other social situations.

This very brief overview shows the variety of different approaches which have been adopted in studying aggression. In considering the relationship between different levels of analysis in the social sciences, Hinde (1979, 1983) has identified the study of personal relationships as occupying a central and potentially integrating position in between the individual psychological level on the one hand, and the broader societal level on the other. A version of this view applied to aggression is shown in Figure 1.2.

In relation to the study of aggression, the level of analysis represented by the study of relationships – that which is intermediate between the study of broad societal processes and intra-individual ones – can also be seen as occupying a central and especially important place: by concentrating on this level of analysis, we can approach both the impact of the wider context and the part played by individual and situational aspects.

Studying aggression at the level of the social interactions and relationships of the people involved represents, as far as psychology is concerned, a move away from the traditions of psychometric testing and laboratory experiments, designed with an emphasis on analysing and controlling a small number of intra-individual and situational variables. Instead, the emphasis is shifted towards studying interactions between individuals in settings where aggression is likely to occur.

Within psychology, the analytical laboratory approach has dominated the study of aggression. In order to investigate the subject in more naturalistic settings, we have to seek non-laboratory methods of enquiry, some of which were developed early in the history of psychology, and have been relatively neglected since (for example, diary accounts, observations) and others of which have originated in other disciplines such as ethology and anthropology.

The book is divided into three sections. Section 1 provides a broad introduction. In this chapter we have considered the wider issues involved in aggression research. Chapter 2, by John Archer, is concerned with outlining some of the criticisms of the experimental social psychological approach, and to introducing in general terms the range of naturalistic methods which are available as alternatives. The question of laboratory vs. naturalistic approaches is continued from a different perspective in Chapter 3 where Len Berkowitz, an eminent researcher in the laboratory tradition, provides a reply to some of the criticisms which have been levelled at this tradition, including those presented in Chapter 2. In this way, we hope to capture the debate over the strengths and weaknesses of the two approaches, rather than presenting the issue in a one-sided way. Nevertheless, the remainder of the book is wholly devoted to a consideration of naturalistic methods of study.

In the second section, we present three widely different approaches to studying aggression in natural settings. In Chapter 4, Peter K. Smith describes the ethological approach which involves direct nonparticipant observations, often in natural settings, and aims for systematic, objectively defined categories of behaviour recorded by a detached observer. Ethologists have also been concerned with the question of biological function, thus linking human with animal behaviour. Most ethological observational research has involved children, especially preschool children, whose behaviour is particularly well-suited to this approach. Peter Smith traces the history and influence of the direct observation of aggression in psychology, and considers how modern ethological methods have been used to investigate a number of problems. These include the classification of aggression (discussed earlier in this chapter), the distinction between rough-and-tumble play and aggression, and environmental influences on aggression.

Continuing the ethological theme, the next chapter (by Caroline and Robert Blanchard) describes how a model of aggression derived from research on animal behaviour can be used to investigate human aggression under naturalistic conditions. They argue that examining a 'biological model' (used in the sense of a simpler system – in this case an animal) can be used as a starting-point for analysing and interpreting naturalistic accounts of human aggression. In particular, use of an *ethological* model encourages a great deal of description prior to the theory-generating stage. One important distinction to emerge from analysis of non-human mammalian aggression is between offensive (anger-motivated) and defensive (fear-motivated) attack. These differ in respect of antecedent conditions, motivational state, behavioural organization, and their consequences. Yet this fundamental distinction frequently goes unrecognized in accounts of human aggression under naturalistic conditions, despite the implications it has for many practical issues connected with human aggression and violence, such as the danger of tackling a cornered intruder, and passing judgement in cases where a murderer was in a highly fearful state at the time of the killing. In more general terms, this chapter also makes the case for the importance of animal research in psychology (see also Gray 1985; N.E. Miller 1985).

In Chapter 6, a very different form of naturalistic approach is considered. Here the emphasis shifts from behaviour or its motivational significance to the meaning of the acts in a social context. In the ethnographic approach (and also the ethogenic tradition – see Chapter 2), the accounts given by the participants to explain their actions are given prominence. As John Beynon indicates, ethnography was originally derived from an anthropological tradition but it has now become transposed to more familiar settings such as the school classroom.

In the third section of the book, naturalistic approaches are presented in relation to their application to some real-life problems rather than in connection with specific methodological traditions. The methods used cover diary accounts, ethological observations, and interviews, and the subject-matter includes anger management (Kevin Howells in Chapter 7), family violence and child abuse (Kevin Browne in Chapter 8), violence towards old people by their caregivers (Chapter 9 by Mervyn Eastman), and assaults on professional welfare workers (Chapter 10 by Glynis Breakwell and Colin Rowett).

Kevin Howells's chapter assesses the extent to which the anger-management approach pioneered by Novaco can be applied to different types of problems people may encounter with their aggression and violence. His assessment involves the use of various naturalistic methods including anger-inventories, diary accounts, and direct observations.

Chapters 8 and 9 cover the subject of family violence, which includes spouse abuse, child abuse, and elder abuse. Kevin Browne provides a broad overview of research into all three forms of violence in domestic situations, before considering the various explanations or models which have been put forward to account for them. He concludes that although structural factors such as bad housing and other stressors are important, they are mediated through the interpersonal relationships within the family, and it is therefore at this level that research aimed at the prevention, treatment, and management of family violence should concentrate. As an example, Browne describes the application of an ethological observational method to the study of parent–child relationships in child-abusing families.

In Chapter 9, Mervyn Eastman, a practising social worker in London, outlines the lack of research interest and public concern in the area of elder abuse – which provides a marked contrast with the areas of spouse violence and child abuse.

In Chapter 10, Glynis Breakwell and Colin Rowett describe a further area of current social concern, violence towards social service and health-care professionals in the course of their work.

REFERENCES

Adams, D.B. (1979) 'Brain mechanisms for offence, defence, and submission', *The Behavioral and Brain Sciences* 2: 201–41.
—— (1980) 'Motivational systems of agonistic behavior in muroid rodents: a comparative review and neural model', *Aggressive Behavior* 6: 295–346.
Archer, J. (1976) 'The organization of aggression and fear in vertebrates', in P.P.G. Bateson and P. Klopfer (eds) *Perspectives in Ethology, Vol. 2*, New York: Plenum Press.
—— (1977) 'The psychology of violence', *New Society* 42: 63–6.
—— (1985) 'Pain-induced aggression from an ethological perspective', *Bulletin of the British Psychological Society* 38: A99.
—— (1988) *The Behavioural Biology of Aggression*, Cambridge: Cambridge University Press.

Averill, J.R. (1983) 'Studies on anger and aggression', *American Psychologist* 38: 1145–60.

Bandura, A. (1973) *Aggression: A Social Learning Analysis*, New York: Prentice Hall.

Berkowitz, L. (1962) *Aggression: A Social Psychological Analysis*, New York: McGraw-Hill.

Blanchard, D.C. and Blanchard, R.J. (1984) 'Affect and aggression: an animal model applied to human behavior', in R.J. and D.C. Blanchard (eds) *Advances in the Study of Aggression, Vol. 1*, New York: Academic Press.

Brain, P.F. (1981) 'Differentiating types of attack and defence in rodents', in P.F. Brain and D. Benton (eds) *Multidisciplinary Approaches to Aggression Research*, Amsterdam: Elsevier/North Holland.

Buss, A.H. (1961) *The Psychology of Aggression*, New York: J. Wiley.

Buss, A.H. and Durkee, A. (1957) 'An inventory for assessing different types of hostility', *Journal of Consulting Psychology* 21: 343–9.

Byles, J.E. (1978) 'Violence, alcohol problems and other problems in disintegrating families', *Journal of Studies on Alcohol*: 551–3.

Campbell, A., Muncer, S., and Bibel, D. (1985a) 'Taxonomies of aggressive behavior: a preliminary report', *Aggressive Behavior* 11: 217–22.

Campbell, A., Bibel, D., and Muncer, S. (1985b) 'Predicting our own aggression: person, subculture or situation?', *British Journal of Social Psychology* 24: 169–80.

Dobash, R.E. and Dobash, R.P. (1979) *Violence Against Wives: A Case Against the Patriarchy*, London: Open Books.

Dollard, J., Doob, L.W., Miller, N.E., Mowrer, O.H., and Sears, R.R. (1939) *Frustration and Aggression*, New Haven: Yale University Press.

Edmunds, G. and Kendrick, D.C. (1980) *The Measurement of Human Aggressiveness*, Chichester: Ellis Horwood (Wiley).

Eibl-Eibesfeldt, I. (1961) 'The fighting behavior of animals', *Scientific American* 205: 112–22.

—— (1975) *Ethology, the Biology of Behavior* (2nd edn), New York: Holt, Rinehart, & Winston.

Feshbach, S. (1964) 'The function of aggression and the regulation of the aggressive drive', *Psychological Review* 71: 257–72.

Frude, N. and Gault, H. (1984a) 'Introduction', in N. Frude and H. Gault (eds) *Disruptive Behaviour in Schools*, Chichester: Wiley.

—— (1984b) 'Children's disruptions at school: cause for concern?', in N. Frude and H. Gault (eds) *Disruptive Behaviour in Schools*, Chichester: Wiley.

Gayford, J.J. (1975) 'Wife battering: a preliminary survey of 100 cases', *British Medical Journal* 1: 94–7.

—— (1976) 'Ten types of battered wives', *The Welfare Officer* 25: 5–9.

Gelles, R.J. (1987) *The Violent Home* (2nd edn), Beverly Hills: Sage.
Gelles, R.J. and Cornell, C.P. (1985) *Intimate Violence in Families*, Beverly Hills: Sage.
Gerson, L.W. (1978) 'Alcohol-related acts of violence', *Journal of Studies on Alcohol* 39: 1294–6.
Gil, D. (1978) 'Societal violence in families', in J.M. Eekelaar and S.N. Katz (eds) *Family Violence*, Toronto: Butterworths, pp. 14–33.
Goode, W.J. (1971) 'Force and violence in the family', *Journal of Marriage and the Family* 33: 624–36.
Gray, J.A. (1985) 'A whole and its parts: behaviour, the brain, cognition and emotion', *Bulletin of the British Psychological Society* 38: 99–112.
Hanmer, J. (1977) 'Community action, women's aid and the womens liberation movement', in M. Mayo (ed.) *Women in the Community*, London: Routledge-Kegan Paul, pp. 91–108.
—— (1978) 'Violence and the social control of women', in G. Littlejohn (ed.) *Power and State*, London: Croom Helm.
Hinde, R.A. (1975) 'The concept of function', in G.P. Baerends, C. Beer and A. Manning (eds) *Function and Evolution in Behaviour* Oxford: Clarendon.
—— (1979) *Towards Understanding Relationships*, London and New York: Academic Press.
—— (1983) 'The study of interpersonal relationships', in J. Miller (ed.) *States of Mind: Conversations with Psychological Investigators*, London: BBC.
Huntingford, F.A. (1976) 'The relationship between inter- and intra-specific aggression', *Animal Behaviour* 24: 485–97.
Hutchinson, R. and Renfrew, J.W. (1966) 'Stalking attack and eating behaviors elicited from the same sites in the hypothalamus', *Journal of Comparative Physiology and Psychology* 61: 360–7.
Johnson, R.N. (1972) *Aggression in Man and Animals*, Philadelphia: Saunders.
Jolly, A. (1972) *The Evolution of Primate Behavior*, New York: Macmillan.
Kaplan, R.M. (1984) 'The measurement of human aggression', in R.M. Kaplan, V.J. Konecni and R.W. Novaco (eds) *Aggression in Children and Youth*, The Hague: Nijhoff.
Kaufmann, H. (1970) *Aggression and Altruism*, New York: Holt, Rinehart, & Winston.
Lorenz, K. (1966) *On Aggression*, New York: Harcourt, Brace, and World.
Lystad, M.H. (1975) 'Violence at home: a review of the literature', *American Journal of Orthopsychiatry* 45(5): 328–45.
Mark, V.H. and Ervin, F.R. (1970) *Violence and the Brain*, New York: Harper & Row.
Miller, N.E. (1979) 'Dollard, John', in D.S. Sills (ed.) *International*

Encyclopedia of the Social Sciences, Vol. 18, New York: The Free Press.
—— (1985) 'The value of behavioral research on animals', *American Psychologist* 40: 423–40.
Miller, P.H. (1983) *Theories of Developmental Psychology*, San Francisco: Freeman.
Moyer, K.E. (1968) 'Kinds of aggression and their physiological basis', *Communications in Behavioral Biology A* 2: 65–87.
—— (1976) *The Psychobiology of Aggression*, New York: Harper & Row.
Muncer, S.J., Gorman, B., and Campbell, A. (1986) 'Sorting out aggression: dimensional and categorical perceptions of aggressive episodes', *Aggressive Behavior* 12: 327–36.
O'Brien, J. (1971) 'Violence in divorce-prone families', *Journal of Marriage and the Family* 33: 692–8.
Olweus, D. (1979) 'Stability of aggressive reaction patterns in males: a review', *Psychological Bulletin* 86: 852–75.
—— (1984) 'Development of stable aggressive reaction patterns in males', in R.J. and D.C. Blanchard (eds) *Advances in the Study of Aggression, Vol. 1*, New York: Academic Press.
Oxford English Dictionary (1933) London: Oxford University Press.
Persky, H., Smith, K.D., and Basu, G.K. (1971) 'Relation of psychological measures of aggression and hostility to testosterone production in man', *Psychosomatic Medicine* 33: 265–77.
Rada, R.T., Laws, D.R., and Kellner, R. (1976) 'Plasma testosterone levels in the rapist', *Psychosomatic Medicine* 38: 257–68.
Rosch, E. (1978) 'Principles of categorization', in E. Rosch and B.B. Lloyd (eds) *Cognition and Categorization*, Hillsdale, NJ: Erlbaum.
Roy, M. (1977) 'A survey of 150 cases', in M. Roy (ed.) *Battered Women: A Psychosociological Study of Domestic Violence*, New York: Van Nostrand.
Schultz, L.G. (1960) 'The wife assaulter', *Journal of Social Therapy*, 103–12.
Scott, J.P. (1958) *Aggression*, Chicago: Chicago University Press.
Scott, J.P. and Fredericson, E. (1951) 'The causes of fighting in mice and rats', *Physiological Zoology* 24: 273–309.
Sears, R., Maccoby, E.E., and Levin, H. (1957) *Patterns of Child Rearing*, Illinois: Row Peterson.
Straus, M.A. (1978) 'Wife-beating: How common and why?', in J.M. Eekelaar and S.N. Katz (eds) *Family Violence*, Toronto: Butterworths.
—— (1980) 'A sociological perspective on causes of family violence', in M.R. Green (ed.) *Violence and the Family*, New York: Bould & Westview.
Supplement to Oxford English Dictionary (1972) London: Oxford University Press.
Toates, F.M. and Archer, J. (1978) 'A comparative review of

23

motivational systems using classical control theory', *Animal Behaviour* 26: 368–80.

Toch, H. (1969) *Violent Men*, Chicago: Aldine.

Trivers, R.L. (1971) 'The evolution of reciprocal altruism', *Quarterly Review of Biology* 46: 35–57.

——— (1974) 'Parent-offspring conflict', *American Zoologist* 14: 249–64.

Turner, C.W., Cole, A.M., and Cerro, D.S. (1984) 'Contributions of aversive experiences to robbery and homicide: a demographic analysis', in R.M. Kaplan, V.J. Konecni and R.W. Novaco (eds) *Aggression in Children and Youth*, The Hague: Sijthoff.

Valzelli, L. (1969) 'Aggressive behaviour induced by social isolation', in S. Garattini and E.B. Sigg (eds) *Aggressive Behaviour*, Amsterdam: Excerpta Medica Foundation.

Walker, L.E. and Browne, A. (1985) 'Gender and victimization by inmates', in A.J. Stewart and M.B. Lykes (eds) *Gender and Personality: Current Perspectives on Theory and Research*, Durham, NC: Duke University Press.

Wilson, E.O. (1975) *Sociobiology: The New Synthesis*, Cambridge, Mass.: Harvard University Press.

Chapter 2

FROM THE LABORATORY TO THE COMMUNITY: STUDYING THE NATURAL HISTORY OF HUMAN AGGRESSION

JOHN ARCHER

LABORATORY STUDIES OF AGGRESSION

It is difficult to study human aggression directly, for it occurs sporadically and people often have reasons for not acknowledging or reporting it. Most forms of physical violence are illegal, so that their initiators are strongly motivated to evade the consequence of their actions, or to commit violent acts only within the safety of the closed world of the institution or the family.

Traditional social psychological research has often sought to overcome such problems by isolating variables which affect aggressive behaviour under controlled laboratory conditions. This approach as by now produced vast literature on the laboratory study of aggression, most of it explicitly or implicitly guided by theoretical positions derived from a behaviourist or social learning framework. The review of Baron (1977) deals almost exclusively with laboratory-based studies, aimed at testing a variety of hypotheses about how different variables affect human aggression under controlled conditions.

A recurrent problem encountered in these studies is that of chosing an appropriate aggressive 'response' and establishing conditions which will reliably lead to this response. Baron (1977) has listed the following laboratory measures of aggression: (1) verbal retorts to frustrating circumstances, including the opportunity to evaluate someone presumed to be involved in creating the frustration; (2) assaults against inanimate objects –

25

including the widely cited bobo doll experiment of Bandura *et al.* (1961); (3) noninjurious attacks on a confederate, for example, with a toy gun or a sponge-rubber brick. Konecni (1984) put forward a more detailed classification of the dependent variables used in these studies: essentially these were direct or indirect physical aggression, aggression towards inanimate objects, and direct or displaced verbal aggression.

Measures such as these appear artificial, and to an intelligent outside observer many of them may even look ridiculous. As Konecni (1984) put it: 'Many of the behaviours that have been used as dependent variables are so esoteric as to strain both credibility and the logic that links them to theoretical ideas being tested in the experiment in question' (p. 25). Nevertheless, their use reflects the dilemma in which aggression researchers are placed: on the one hand, they endeavour to chose actions which are clearly associated with aggressive impulses, and on the other they are constrained by ethical principles. Berkowitz and Donnerstein (1982) have addressed a variety of criticisms of laboratory studies of aggression. On this particular point, they argue that it is the meaning to the subject rather than the specific measure that is crucial. In other words, as long as the situation is perceived by the subject as one in which an aggressive response is appropriate, its actual form does not matter. However, the use of measures such as those referred to above are governed to such a large extent by ethical constraints that their meaning is severely prejudiced. Graebelein (1981) has argued that the context in which behaviour is performed affects its interpretation, and in laboratory studies the context can be altered by small procedural changes.

One way of addressing this dilemma is by becoming less ethically restrained, using deception and even the infliction of pain on subjects. Although Milgram's (1974) conformity studies are more dramatic and more widely cited than the laboratory studies of aggression carried out by Berkowitz, Buss, Taylor, and others (Baron 1977), they raise the same ethical issue: they all involve the subjects believing that they are administering electric shocks to another person as a way of motivating them in a learning task, or of evaluating their work, or in competitive tasks. In some of these procedures, the subjects themselves receive a series of painful electric shocks during the course of the sessions.

Some experimental social psychologists have been sufficiently dissatisfied with the laboratory to abandon it entirely, though seeking still to retain the experimental method. Procedures involving honking a car horn or queue-jumping are amongst the so-called naturalistic experimental methods used by some social psychologists in an attempt to avoid the artificiality of the laboratory (ibid.).

As Berkowitz and Donnerstein (1982) pointed out, there is increasing doubt about the validity of all experimental approaches to aggression even amongst researchers generally sympathetic to social psychological experiments. These authors have sought to refute some of the criticisms levelled against experimental studies of aggression, and Len Berkowitz continues to argue the case for laboratory studies in Chapter 3 of this volume.

One of the criticisms was that the subjects seek to comply with the demand characteristics of the experiment – in other words they behave according to their perception of the experimenter's wishes. This is, of course, a problem which is common to all laboratory studies. In relation to aggression, Berkowitz and Donnerstein argued against this criticism by pointing out that when the subject's comprehension of the experiment was manipulated, this did not affect the response.

Although I would accept their rebuttal of the criticism based on compliance to demand cues, the second major difficulty Berkowitz and Donnerstein dealt with is more problematic. It concerns the unrepresentative nature of the measures. They argued that the exact nature of the response measure is unimportant, as long as the subject's intention is to hurt another person: in other words, the aggressive motivation is crucial, but the precise form it takes is not. Adopting this view, one can argue that laboratory studies, notably those where deception is involved, may involve the same emotions and intentions to harm as a naturally occurring aggressive act. To demonstrate that the two are related then becomes, as Berkowitz and Donnerstein pointed out, an empirical question. Their evidence for such a link came from two sources: first, that angered subjects in laboratory studies are motivated to hurt the person who had offended them; and second, that laboratory measures of aggression are often correlated with other measures of

27

aggressiveness (derived from questionnaires and rating scales).

The first type of evidence relates to the construct validity of measures within laboratory studies, and the second to the relationship of laboratory measures to other measures of aggressiveness. In both cases, Berkowitz and Donnerstein cite some evidence for the supposed relationship, but they do not address the issue of how general such a relationship may be. Edmunds and Kendrick (1980) set out to validate several questionnaire measures of aggressiveness by using the Buss aggression-machine, a commonly used laboratory procedure involving the supposed administration of electric shocks to a confederate in a simulated learning task (for example, Buss 1971). They found no relationship between questionnaire measures of aggressiveness and hostility and the number of supposed shocks administered, a result which was also in accordance with two previous studies, which were not cited by Berkowitz and Donnerstein.

Another review of the evidence on this issue concluded that 'the number of empirical attempts to obtain correlations among even the most popular measures (not to mention systematic attempts to examine the external and construct validity of such measures) remains woefully small' (Konecni 1984). A similar conclusion is reached by Kaplan (1984), who remarked that Berkowitz and Donnerstein omitted to cite the evidence which opposed their own conclusion.

There is, however, a wider sense in which laboratory measures may be said to be unrepresentative of naturally occurring aggression, and this concerns their isolation from the social context in which aggression occurs. Laboratory studies may tell us about certain general features of aggression, but to seek to understand a specific form of aggression such as child abuse or violence by children at school through a laboratory model would be to divest it of its specific context and meaning. Real-life acts of violence are embedded in a web of social structures, relationships, and interactions that provide them with a setting which needs to be considered in understanding their meaning.

In conclusion, my main reservations about the laboratory approach are not that it has produced no useful findings at all but that it is limited to answering certain types of general questions about aggression. More specific questions concerning areas of social concern cannot be tackled in this way, and consequently, it is regrettable that a disproportionate degree of research effort has been focused in the direction of the laboratory.

NATURALISTIC STUDIES

In the light of the above conclusion, it seems reasonable to suggest that more prominence be given to alternative 'naturalistic' approaches to studying human aggression, broadly characterized by the following concerns: first, to study aggressive acts in the context in which they occur; and second, to understand them in relation to the wider social exchanges of the participants.

Naturalistic methods of studying aggression can be divided into the following categories: first, indirect methods such as crime statistics, large-scale surveys, official reports of incidents and injuries in institutions, and indirect data obtained from parents, teachers, or institutional staff; second, direct verbal or written accounts from participants – for example, those obtained from diaries, questionnaires, or interviews; and third, direct observations, involving methods derived from the ethological, the ethogenic, or the ethnographic traditions.

For many forms of aggression, particularly those which involve acts of criminal violence, official statistics are a primary source of indirect data for the social scientist. Thus, for example, the books on aggression by Goldstein (1975) and Johnson (1972) sought to integrate material from crime statistics (such as those for murder) with the results of social psychological experiments. More recently, there have been studies of violence in psychiatric hospitals or prisons which have used official reports of injury (Davies 1982; Drinkwater 1982), and of spouse abuse which have used statistics from Women's Aid Centres (Roy 1977).

Such reports should only be used as preliminary data since they suffer from many drawbacks. Although official statistics may appear to be an objective and quantified source of information, 'it is important to remember the complex and ambiguous judgemental processes that lie behind this precise presentation' (Archer and Lloyd 1985: 30). The issues involved in such judgemental processes include age, sex, and social class biases, the influence of selective crime reporting, and the degree of attention to law-enforcement (Kaplan 1984).

Another indirect method is to obtain accounts of aggressive acts – for example, from the staff of institutions, or from teachers or parents of their children. The classic study in this tradition was carried out by Goodenough (1931), who asked mothers to keep diaries of their children's angry outbursts, recording instigating circumstances and adult's responses. From these data, she traced developmental changes, documented sex and individual differences and studied parental control methods.

A more recent study using a similar method is that of Cummings *et al.* (1984) who trained mothers in the techniques of detailed reporting of behaviour in order to study children's reactions to anger in the home.

Teacher ratings and questionnaires have also been widely used to assess children's behaviour (see, for example, Maccoby and Jacklin's 1974 review of the findings for gender differences in aggression). Hinde *et al.* (1984) have recently reported overall agreement between teacher's ratings of aggression and observational data from a sample of pre-school children.

Moving on to more direct methods, written or verbal accounts of aggressive incidents by the participants have a long history in psychology. Questionnaire methods date back to 1899, when G. Stanley Hall asked a large number of people to describe various acts of anger in relation to facial expression, physical loss of self-control, and precipitating circumstances (Hall 1899). More recently the Buss–Durkee hostility inventory (Buss and Durkee 1957) and a number of other self-report measures of aggressive actions and thoughts have been used (see, for example, Frodi *et al.* 1977; Edmunds and Kendrick 1980). One of these is the Straus Conflict Tactics Scale, which has proved useful for studying violence in intimate relationships (Deal and Wampler 1986). It consists of three sub-scales (reasoning, verbal aggression, and violence), each comprising a series of specific items. For the violence sub-scale, the respondent is asked to rate how often he or she uses a series of acts against the partner and how often the partner uses them against the respondent. The scale has been used successfully to study topics such as spouse abuse in a more direct manner than is possible by relying on official statistics or reports from women's aid centres.

Anger is likely to occur more frequently than overt aggressive acts, but to be regularly associated with the impulse to aggress (Averill 1983). In Chapter 7 of this volume, Kevin Howells describes several recent inventories which have been used to assess anger. Diary accounts of anger have a long history. Richardson (1918) asked twelve people, mostly graduate students from Clark University, to note down instances of anger and fear they experienced each day over a three-month period. From their accounts, Richardson classified anger into three types according to its circumstances. The first type occurred after a period of irritable feelings (often associated with pain or frustration); the second was associated with feelings of self-humiliation; and the third was associated with notions of justice and fairness.

Gates (1926) sought to refine Hall's introspective method by asking the subjects to write a report of each event immediately after it had occurred and also to rate the severity of each event on a five-point scale. Meltzer (1933) used a similar method which less of an emphasis on description and more on adjustment. He used controlled diaries of anger experiences covering a week in the life of ninety-three men and women college students. Some thwarting of self-assertion accounted for most angry experiences and more than half of these incidents were reactions to other people. A verbal retort was the most common form of response associated with the angry feeling, and some respondents experienced the impulse to harm the other person physically.

The diary method has been taken up in recent times by Averill (1982, 1983), who studied both undergraduate students and people obtained at random from the telephone directory, using both diaries and questionnaires. Averill was more interested in anger in relation to theories of emotion than he was in aggression, but he was also concerned with the relation between the two. He collected valuable self-report data on the natural history of anger, which can provide us with a broader perspective on topics such as the consequences of anger and gender differences than can be obtained from experimental and questionnaire methods alone (Maccoby and Jacklin 1974; Frodi *et al.* 1977; White 1983). In relation to gender differences, women were reported as becoming angry as often as men, and as intensely, for much the same reasons.

Averill's account of these findings is described in terms of an approach which emphasizes cognitive and social aspects (a 'social constructivist' view). Averill also sought to deny the occurrence of emotions in animals, and to dismiss studies of animal aggression as irrelevant to human emotions. It could be argued instead that ever since the work of Darwin (1872), it has been apparent that one feature of our psychology that we do share with animals is our emotions. Admittedly the experience and meaning we attach to them is entirely different, but the area of the emotions and their expression is surely one where interspecific comparisons can enrich our perspective on human psychology.

A researcher who *has* taken a broadly evolutionary approach to human feelings is John Bowlby. One aspect of the research on human grief which has been stimulated by Bowlby's analysis of human attachment (Bowlby 1969) is the study of anger in the context of grief. Accounts of these experiences were collected by interviewing bereaved people. The studies of Parkes (1986) are the most comprehensive (others are reviewed by Bowlby 1980). From these we learn how often such feelings are accompanied by overt aggressive acts. In one case, for example, a widow attacked the doctor who broke the news of her husband's death (Marris 1958). In other examples, it is commonly doctors, nurses, or hospital authorities who are blamed for the loss. Parkes (1986) remarked that it is the frequency of the quarrels and the feelings of bitterness and irritability which accompany them that distinguishes them from anger experienced at other times. Anger has also been reported in studies of other forms of loss – for example, loss of mobility following an accident (Dlugokinski 1985) and loss of an established job (Archer and Rhodes 1987). It appears to be accentuated in the context of marital separation, where there is a clearly defined source to which feelings of bitterness can be attributed (Weiss 1976).

The third category of naturalistic methods is direct observation. One form arises from the comparative approach to human and animal behaviour provided by ethology. In addition to providing a wide variety of information on the range, variety, and characteristics of aggression in animals (for example, Archer 1976, 1988; Marler 1976; Geist 1978; Huntingford and Turner, 1987), some ethologists have applied their methods of observation to humans, in particular studying the social behaviour of pre-school age children (e.g. Blurton Jones 1972; Roper and Hinde 1978; Smith and Connolly 1980). Such work was forshadowed by observational studies of children carried out in the 1930s, and studies such as those of Dawe (1934) and Jersild and Markey (1935) applied the observational approach to aggressive interactions among young children.

Observational studies of aggressive behaviour in children have a number of advantages over laboratory studies. Attili (1985) lists these as follows: first, that they enable different types of aggressive behaviour to be recorded (experimental studies are often restricted to one category); second, that they can be analysed in interactionist terms; and third, that they record not only aggression but also behavioural acts which may be relevant to the context in which aggression occurs.

Ethological methods may have these advantages over laboratory studies and they have provided detailed data on topics such as individual and gender differences and the sequence of interactions in naturalistic contexts. Nevertheless, they are often criticized for their inability to deal with how the participants perceive their interactions. Perhaps for this reason, they have been used less frequently with older children (cf. Whiting and Edwards 1973; Archer and Westeman 1981) and with adults (cf. Grant 1968). A more detailed assessment of the ethological approach is provided in Chapter 4 of this volume by Peter K. Smith.

Alternative observational methods, which are rooted in different theoretical traditions, regard the intentions and meanings of human actions as being central considerations. The ethogenic approach (e.g. Marsh *et al.* 1978; Sluckin 1981; Marsh 1982) seeks to reveal the content and organization of the social knowledge which underlies actions and the accounts people give of such actions.

The ethnographic tradition, described in Chapter 6 of this volume, has been used in educational research (Beynon 1983; Delamont and Hamilton 1984). Originally, most ethnographers were anthropologists studying other cultures. The major impact of the approach in studying subjects such as classroom violence (Beynon and Delamont 1984) is in its attempt to challenge familiar ways of looking at the subject, by approaching it as if it occurred in a 'new culture'. Ethnography is characterized methodologically by the interactive nature of the investigation, subjects becoming informants, and the observer a participant (for example, Beynon and Atkinson 1984).

PROBLEMS ASSOCIATED WITH NATURALISTIC APPROACHES

There are a number of problems and difficulties with the naturalistic study of human aggression in the community. These include the accuracy of the data-base, the problem of obtaining a representative sample, the difficulty of constructing and testing hypotheses under naturalistic conditions, and the importance of context in studying aggression.

First, the potential difficulties in obtaining accurate information on all forms of human aggression and violence are enormous. As noted earlier, most forms of violence are illegal, may occur in private, and the aggressor (and sometimes the victim) will try to prevent knowledge of such acts reaching official agencies and even their own social network. There are therefore great problems in obtaining accurate accounts from those who have committed acts of domestic violence, or violence towards inmates of institutions. It is against such a background that we are forced to rely on indirect methods for studying these forms of violence. Such indirect methods may be supplemented by interviews with those participants who *are* willing to discuss what has happened: for example, information may be obtained on violence between married couples from women taking refuge in a Women's Aid Centre (Roy 1977). Such accounts raise problems of accuracy, of course, because they are obtained from an interested party.

Beynon (1983) made a similar point about the difficulties of studying violence in schools. His research involved him in witnessing violence between teachers and pupils, and his account of this research is sensitive to the political and moral issues it raises about the concealment of violence (see Chapter 6 this volume). Consider the far greater problems that are involved in, for example, attempting to include violence by prison staff towards prisoners in a study of 'violence in prisons'. The article by Davies (1982) on prison violence considered hostage-taking, violence by prisoners, and prison riots. The possibility of the staff being violent was not considered, thereby helping the institution, in Beynon's words, 'to conceal discreditable information and to promote an efficient and favourable image' (Beynon, Chapter 6).

A second and related issue concerns the representativeness of the sample. Although this is a potential problem in all studies of human aggression, it again poses a particular problem for the study of 'hidden' violence. How can we tell whether the cases of spouse abuse which have led to women seeking refuge in a Women's Aid Centre are representative of such violence in the general population? Some attempts have been made to address this problem: for example, the National Crime Survey obtained information from 60,000 households selected as a representative sample of the 1970 UK census data (Minchin 1982), and other studies have sought to obtain information on this subject from samples other than those who had been brought to the attention of the police or social work agencies (Gelles 1987; Steinmetz 1977). Surveys which rely on respondents replying to magazine advertisements again will have problems of bias, particularly if the specialist nature of the readership is likely to be relevant to the subject-matter, as for example when the readership of *Ms* magazine was used to study domestic violence (Minchin 1982).

Laboratory-based studies of human aggression are of course notorious for being studies of college students, and an additional reason for carrying out naturalistic studies is to move away from relying on this one subject group for information. In Averill's (1982) research on anger, he studied both students and community residents: the latter were obtained at random from the telephone directory and were then contacted by phone or letter. One practical problem was the much lower return rates obtained from the community sample.

A third issue concerns the difficulties in constructing and testing hypotheses under natural conditions. In contrasting the different approaches of 'basic' and 'applied' research, Fishman and Neigher (1982) characterized basic research as being concerned with, *inter alia*, testing theoretically derived

35

JOHN ARCHER

hypotheses. This is certainly an accurate description of
laboratory-based research on aggression (Baron 1977). Applied
research, on the other hand, 'focuses on dealing directly with
conditions in the real world' (Fishman and Neigher 1982: 541).
In view of these different aims, it is argued that applied research
should be more concerned with developing a systematic picture
of the social and psychological phenomena as they occur in the
community. Although the methods Fishman and Neigher
advocated to pursue this aim were rather limited, consisting of
surveys and tests, what they identify as the overall aims for
applied research is very much in accord with the aims of
naturalistic studies of aggression. They therefore differ from
laboratory studies not only in their methodology but also in
their aims. Although the 'pure' researcher may step out of the
laboratory when dissatisfied with traditional methods, he or she
will still tend to use a restricted set of measures such as car
horn-honking, and a continued 'experimental' set-up such as
queue-jumping (Baron 1977). The applied researcher, on the
other hand, will be pursuing different ends – what can be
characterized as developing a picture of the natural history of
aggression.

This brings us to the fourth issue, namely, the importance of
context in studying human aggression. Laboratory studies have
typically used simplified measures of aggression, in pursuit of a
readily quantifiable 'response'. Even to label a particular act as
aggressive constitutes a step away from viewing it as part of the
social interaction, and towards decontextualizing it as laboratory
researchers have done. In a way this mirrors the dominant
ideology in our society which seeks to isolate the violent act itself
as a legal, medical, or social problem. It is customary for politi-
cians and other public figures to condemn violence in general,
i.e. to seek to consider it as a series of deliberate acts rather than
as part of a network of social interactions. It can be argued that
the forms of violence which occur in our society are only understandable in terms of the social conditions and context in which
they arise: in order to study the natural history of human
aggression we must consider the social setting in which the
violent or aggressive act is embedded. As Attili (1985) stated in
relation to children, 'aggression is not an isolated phenomenon;
rather it is part of a child's social world that must be considered

in its totality' (p. 279). Such an approach has been adopted in studies of child abuse by investigating the interaction styles of abusing parents and their children (Gardner and Gray 1982; Browne and Saqi, 1987). This type of study can lead to a wider perspective than that obtained by focusing only on the immediate context and details of the violent or aggressive act.

CONCLUSIONS

In this chapter, laboratory-based studies of aggression were discussed in relation to two issues: first, the dilemma of devising an ethical yet realistic way of instigating an aggressive response; and second, the isolation of such studies from the social context of aggression. An overview of alternative naturalistic methods was then presented: first, indirect methods such as crime statistics, official reports, and data obtained from parents, teachers, or staff of institutions; second, direct verbal or written accounts from participants, such as diaries, questionnaires, or interviews; third, direct observations, using ethological, ethogenic, or ethnographic approaches. Finally, some problems arising from naturalistic methods are discussed – for example, the accuracy of the information, the representative nature of the sample, and the formulation and testing of hypotheses.

ACKNOWLEDGEMENTS

I thank Len Berkowitz and Kevin Browne for their discussion of issues raised in this chapter, and Derek Blackman and Peter Smith for their helpful comments on an earlier draft.

REFERENCES

Archer, J. (1976) 'The organization of aggression and fear in vertebrates', in P.P.G. Bateson and P. Klopfer (eds) *Perspectives in Ethology*, 2, New York: Plenum Press.
——— (1988) *The Behavioural Biology of Aggression*, Cambridge: Cambridge University Press.
Archer, J. and Lloyd, B.B. (1985) *Sex and Gender*, New York: Cambridge University Press.
Archer, J. and Rhodes, V. (1987) 'Bereavement and reactions to job loss: a comparative review', *British Journal of Social Psychology* 26: 211–24.

JOHN ARCHER

Archer, J. and Westeman, K. (1981) 'Sex differences in the aggressive behaviour of schoolchildren', *British Journal of Social Psychology* 20: 31–6.

Attili, G. (1985) 'Aggression in young children – introduction: some methodological issues related to the nature of aggression', *Aggressive Behavior* 11: 79–81.

Averill, J.R. (1982) *Anger and Aggression: An Essay on Emotion*, New York: Springer-Verlag.

—— (1983) 'Studies on anger and aggression', *American Psychologist* 38: 1145–60.

Bandura, A., Ross, D., and Ross, S.A. (1961) 'Transmission of aggression through imitation of aggressive models', *Journal of Abnormal and Social Psychology* 63: 575–82.

Baron, R.A. (1977) *Human Aggression*, New York: Wiley.

Berkowitz, L. and Donnerstein, E. (1982) 'External validity is more than skin deep: some answers to criticisms of laboratory experiments', *American Psychologist* 37: 245–57.

Beynon, J. (1983) 'Ways in and staying in: fieldwork as problem-solving', in M. Hammersley (ed.) *The Ethnography of Schooling*, Driffield: Nafferton.

Beynon, J. and Atkinson, P. (1984) 'Pupils as data gatherers; mucking and sussing', in S. Delamont (ed.) *Readings on Interaction in the Classroom*, London and New York: Methuen.

Beynon, J. and Delamont, S. (1984) 'The sound and the fury: pupil perceptions of school violence', in N. Frude and H. Gault (eds) *Disruptive Behaviour in Schools*, Chichester: Wiley.

Blurton Jones, N. (1972) 'Characteristics of ethological studies of human behaviour', in N. Blurton Jones (ed.) *Ethological Studies of Child Behaviour*, London: Cambridge University Press.

Bowlby, J. (1969) *Attachment*, London: Hogarth Press.

—— (1980) *Loss: Sadness and Depression*, London: Hogarth Press.

Browne, K. and Saqi, S.M. (1987) 'Parent–child interaction in abusing families: possible causes and consequences', in P. Maher (ed.) *Child Abuse: An Educational Perspective*, Oxford: Blackwell.

Buss, A.H. (1971) 'Aggression pays', in J.L. Singer (ed.) *The Control of Aggression and Violence*, London and New York: Academic Press.

Buss, A.H. and Durkee, A. (1957) 'An inventory for assessing different types of hostility', *Journal of Consulting Psychology* 21: 343–9.

Cummings, E.M., Zahn-Waxler, C., and Redke-Yarrow, M. (1984) 'Developmental changes in children's reactions to anger in the home', *Journal of Child Psychology and Psychiatry* 25: 63–74.

Darwin, C. (1872) *The Expression of the Emotions in Man and Animals*, London: Murray.

Davies, W. (1982) 'Violence in prisons', in M.P. Feldman (ed.) *Developments in the Study of Criminal Behaviour, Vol 2: Violence*, Chichester: Wiley.

38

Dawe, H.C. (1934) 'An analysis of two hundred quarrels of preschool children', *Child Development* 5: 139–57.

Deal, J.E. and Wampler, K.S. (1986) 'Dating violence: the primacy of previous experience', *Journal of Personal and Social Relationships* 3: 457–71.

Delamont, S. and Hamilton, D. (1984) 'Revisiting classroom research: a continuing cautionary tale', in S. Delamont (ed.) *Readings on Interaction in the Classroom*, London and New York: Methuen.

Dlugokinski, E. (1985) 'Victims of auto accidents: the quiet victims', *American Psychologist* 40: 116–17.

Drinkwater, J. (1982) 'Violence in psychiatric hospitals', in M.P. Feldman (ed.) *Developments in the Study of Criminal Behavior, Vol 2: Violence*, Chichester: Wiley.

Edmunds, G. and Kendrick, D.C. (1980) *The Measurement of Human Aggressiveness*, Chichester: Ellis Horwood.

Fishman, D.B. and Neigher, W.D. (1982) 'American psychology in the eighties: who will buy?', *American Psychologist* 37: 533–46.

Frodi, A., Macaulay, J., and Thome, P.R. (1977) 'Are women always less aggressive than men? A review of the experimental literature', *Psychological Bulletin* 84: 634–60.

Gardner, J. and Gray, M. (1982) 'Violence towards children', in M.P. Feldman (ed.) *Developments in the Study of Criminal Behaviour Vol. 2: Violence*, Chichester: Wiley.

Gates, G.S. (1926) 'An observational study of anger', *Journal of Experimental Psychology* 9: 325–36.

Geist, V. (1978) 'On weapons, combat and ecology', in L. Krames, P. Pliner, and T. Alloway (eds) *Advances in the Study of Communication and Affect, Vol. 4. Aggression, Dominance and Individual Spacing*, New York: Plenum.

Gelles, R.J. (1987) *The Violent Home* (2nd edn), Beverly Hills and London: Sage.

Goldstein, J.H. (1975) *Aggression and Crimes of Violence*, New York: Oxford University Press.

Goodenough, F.L. (1931) *Anger in Young Children*, Minneapolis: University of Minnesota Press.

Graebelein, J. (1981) 'Naturalistic versus experimental approaches to aggression', *Aggressive Behavior* 7: 325–39.

Grant, E.C. (1968) 'An ethological description of non-verbal behaviour during interviews', *British Journal of Medical Psychology* 41: 177–84.

Hall, G.S. (1899) 'A study of anger', *American Journal of Psychology* 10: 516–91.

Hinde, R.A., Easton, D.F., and Meller, R.E. (1984) 'Teacher questionnaire compared with observational data on effects of sex and sibling status on preschool behaviour', *Journal of Child Psychology and Psychiatry* 25: 285–303.

Huntingford, F.A. and Turner, A.K. (1987) *Animal Conflict*,

London: Chapman & Hall.

Jersild, A.T. and Markey, F.V. (1935) 'Conflicts between preschool children', *Child Development Monographs* 21.

Johnson, R.N. (1972) *Aggression in Man and Animals*, Philadelphia: Saunders.

Kaplan, R.M. (1984) 'The measurement of human aggression', in R.M. Kaplan, V.J. Konecni, and R.W. Novaco (eds) *Aggression in Children and Youth*, The Hague: Nijhoff.

Konecni, V.J. (1984) 'Methodological issues in human aggression research', in R.M. Kaplan, V.J. Konecni, and R.W. Novaco (eds) *Aggression in Children and Youth*, The Hague: Nijhoff.

Maccoby, E.E. and Jacklin, C.N. (1974) *The Psychology of Sex Differences*, Stanford, California: Stanford University Press.

Marler, P. (1976) 'On animal aggression: the roles of strangeness and familiarity', *American Psychologist* 31: 239–46.

Marris, P. (1958) *Widows and their Families*, London: Routledge & Kegan Paul.

Marsh, P. (1982) 'Rhetorics of violence', in P. Marsh and A. Campbell (eds) *Aggression and Violence*, Oxford: Blackwell, pp. 102–17.

Marsh, P., Rosser, E., and Harre, R. (1978) *The Rules of Disorder*, London: Routledge and Kegan Paul.

Meltzer, H. (1933) 'Students' adjustments in anger', *Journal of Social Psychology* 4: 285–309.

Milgram, S. (1974) *Obedience to Authority: An Experimental View*, New York: Harper and Row.

Minchin, L. (1982) 'Violence between couples', in M.P. Feldman (ed.) *Developments in the Study of Criminal Behavior, Vol. 2: Violence*, Chichester: Wiley.

Parkes, C.M. (1986) *Bereavement: Studies of Grief in Adult Life* (2nd edn), London: Tavistock.

Richardson, R.F. (1918) *The Psychology and Pedagogy of Anger*, Baltimore (Md.): Warwick & York.

Roper, R. and Hinde, R.A. (1978) 'Social behaviour in a play group: consistency and complexity', *Child Development* 49: 570–9.

Roy, M. (1977) 'A survey of 150 cases', in M. Roy (ed.) *Battered Women: A Psychosociological Study of Domestic Violence*, New York: Van Nostrand.

Sluckin, A. (1981) *Growing Up in the Playground*, London: Routledge and Kegan Paul.

Smith, P.K. and Connolly, K.J. (1980) *The Ecology of Preschool Behaviour*, Cambridge: Cambridge University Press.

Steinmetz, S.K. (1977) 'Wifebeating, husbandbeating: a comparison of the use of physical violence between spouses to resolve marital fights', in M. Roy (ed.) *Battered Women: A Psychosociological Study of Domestic Violence*, New York: Van Nostrand.

Weiss, R.S. (1976) 'The emotional impact of marital separation', *Journal of Social Issues* 32: 135–45.

White, J.W. (1983) 'Sex and gender issues in aggression research', in R.G. Green and E.I. Donnerstein (eds) *Aggression: Theoretical and Empirical Reviews. Volume 2: Issues in Research*, New York: Academic Press.

Whiting, B. and Edwards, C.P. (1973) 'Cross-cultural analysis of sex differences in the behaviour of children aged 3 through 11', *Journal of Social Psychology* 91: 171–88.

Chapter 3

LABORATORY EXPERIMENTS IN THE STUDY OF AGGRESSION

LEONARD BERKOWITZ

INTRODUCTION

To begin with, they seem reluctant to consider either aggression or violence as social phenomena. Perhaps because their conclusions are based on the aggregation of experiments in which the behaviour of subjects is always measured individually, they seem unable to even consider those social or group aspects of aggression which we all know to be relevant. Secondly, they very seldom locate their discussion of aggression and violence in the real world of perceived and actual inequalities, environmental stress and political conflict. Thus, they seem reluctant to come to terms with real-life instances of aggression and violence . . . it seems to me that the restrictiveness of the experimental psychologists is not confined only to their subject matter, for I would argue that their excessive reliance on the positivist approach blinds them to even considering whether or not psychology can be legitimately explored using methods other than those derived from the experimental methodology of the natural sciences.

(Siann 1985: 165–6)

Here, in this paragraph, taken from a recent survey of different theoretical approaches to the study of aggression, we have some of the common criticisms of laboratory research in general and of laboratory studies of aggression in particular: experiments do not adequately represent the rich complexity of human behaviour. These investigations are far too limited in scope (in part, according to a number of critics, because they are focused on

42

the actions of individuals). They fail to consider many of the important determinants of human aggression in the natural world, and do not show the many different ways in which human aggression is manifested outside the laboratory.

Even stronger criticisms have been voiced. Some have questioned whether the behaviour taken as indicative of aggression in the laboratory has anything to do with the 'real' aggression exhibited in social settings. Others have gone even further and have insisted that the experimental situation is so far removed from the social contexts in which aggression actually occurs that the laboratory findings tell us little about the hostility, fights, and attacks displayed in the outside world. The senior editor of the current collection has put this argument in these terms:

> to seek to understand a specific form of aggression such as child abuse or violence by children at school through a laboratory model would be to divest it of its specific context and meaning. Real-life acts of violence are embedded in a web of social structures, relationships, and interactions that provide them with a setting which needs to be considered in understanding their meaning.
>
> (Archer, Chapter 2 of this volume, p. 28)

Needless to say, I do not agree with these criticisms of laboratory experimentation, and indeed, suggest that the charges reflect a fundamental misunderstanding of this mode of investigation – a misunderstanding shared by many advocates as well as opponents of this type of research. In a sense, the critics think of experiments far too broadly, while many laboratory researchers share in this misconception and claim too much for their approach. The present chapter will argue that laboratory experiments have a number of decided advantages over other modes of research, and consequently, have contributed in important ways to our understanding of human aggression. On the other side, however, they also have some decided limitations and should not be used in an attempt to answer certain kinds of questions.

A brief digression is warranted here. The last-mentioned observation, that laboratory experiments cannot serve all purposes, gives us a reply to one of the charges levelled against experimentalists in the paragraph quoted at the very start of this chapter. Siann criticized them for failing to pay attention to non-experimental research methods. She is right in a way: even a casual examination of the journal articles and books on aggression written by laboratory researchers in recent years will show that they focus overwhelmingly on experimental findings. However, this narrowness is more of a reflection of the writers' somewhat limited interests and scholarship then of a widespread belief that correlation and/or naturalistic observations cannot tell us anything worthwhile about human aggression.

I will return to this matter briefly later when I discuss what experiments cannot do. First, however, let us examine the more common criticisms of laboratory research, including the accusations just mentioned.

ECOLOGICAL VALIDITY AND EXTERNAL VALIDITY

Can experimental findings be generalized?

Probably the most frequent criticism of laboratory experiments has to do with their supposed artificiality. The university laboratory in which most experiments are conducted obviously has little similarity to the home, pub, city street, or other naturalistic settings in which aggression usually occurs, and the laboratory measures of aggression rarely resemble the actual behaviour people display when they assault others or defend themselves from attacks. In many experiments, as an illustration, the subjects are asked to punish a fellow student by administering aversive stimuli to him or her (often electric shocks or blasts of loud noise), typically either when that person has made a mistake on an assigned task – as in the Buss (1961) paradigm – or in judgement of her/his performance – as in many of my own experiments (cf. Berkowitz 1974a) – and the intensity and/or number of these stimuli delivered is taken as the index of the subjects' aggressiveness. Critics have disputed the construct validity of these measures. 'Who gives electric shocks in real life?', they essentially ask. The laboratory actions have little similarity to the aggression shown in the outside world, and therefore, they maintain, cannot tell us much about 'real' aggression.

I have discussed this claim in some detail elsewhere (Berkowitz and Donnerstein 1982), and will here take up only some of the main points in my answer. First, to put the criticism in a broader context, we should note that the critics are calling for ecological validity. Following Egon Brunswik (1955), who originated this term, and Campbell and Stanley (1963), they basically argue that we can generalize from the laboratory setting to the outside world only to the degree that the immediate (proximal) and somewhat further removed (distal) cues in the experiment are representative of the proximal and distal cues in the natural situations of interest to us. Thus, the argument holds, the experimental setting has to resemble these 'real-world' situations in important respects. Ecological validity makes for external validity – our ability to extend the laboratory findings to other settings in the outside world.

Are naturalistic studies typically more generalizable?

Going on from here, many of these critics insist that laboratory experiments are inherently low in external validity. These studies, and not only those dealing with aggression, are said to be too unrealistic, too lacking in ecological validity, to permit generalizations to natural situations. Field research is what is wanted, they maintain, rather than laboratory experiments.

While this reasoning might seem persuasive at first, we actually cannot conclude that the results of field studies conducted in naturalistic settings are necessarily more generalizable to yet other situations than are the findings of laboratory experiments. Dipboye and Flanagan (1979, cited in Berkowitz and Donnerstein 1982: 249) made just this point after examining almost 200 laboratory experiments and 300 field studies in industrial-organizational psychology. As they commented later (Dipboye and Flanagan 1980, cited in Berkowitz and Donnerstein 1982: 249), 'Too often the assumption is made that because a study was conducted in a field setting, it is inherently more externally valid than a laboratory study', but this need not be so. Some 'real-world' situations may be very special so that the results obtained in them stem from unique circumstances. Or more generally, the factors operating in these settings may have little to do with the factors governing behaviour in the other situations of interest to us.

Psychological realism and the imparting of meaning

We have now come to the heart of the issue. What are the important determinants of behaviour? In accord with Bruns-
wikian–Campbell and Stanley reasoning, it is usually assumed
that even relatively superficial aspects of the research setting can
influence the subjects' actions, and thus, the representativeness of
the subject population, and setting characteristics supposedly
determines the extent to which the investigation's findings be
generalized. The present chapter questions this widespread
assumption. Bass and Firestone (1980, cited in Berkowitz and
Donnerstein 1982: 249) put my argument in these terms: The
psychological attributes of the research may affect the generalizability of the results far more than the study's objective features,
such as the demographic characteristics of the sample or the
physical nature of the situation the subjects are in. These
attributes can include the participants' definition of their task and
their interpretations and judgements.

The important distinction between mundane and experimental
realism drawn by Carlsmith *et al.* (1976) is relevant here. Mundane realism exists where the experimental setting and procedure
resembles events that occur in the 'real world', that is, when there
is the superficial appearance of reality. Those who criticize
laboratory experiments for not being realistic are essentially calling for mundane realism. However, experimental realism is far
more important than this surface similarity. When this latter state
exists, the research participants are thoroughly taken up by what
is happening before them and become involved in the situation.

Caught up by the psychological reality of the laboratory events,
the subjects are especially likely to interpret what is taking place
much as they might interpret other, conceptually similar occurrences in the outside world. As Berkowitz and Donnerstein (1982)
emphasized, this common meaning can tie the laboratory to more
naturalistic settings. Indeed, we held that

> the meaning the subjects assign to the situation they are in
> and the behavior they are carrying out plays a greater part
> in determining the generalizability of an experiment's
> outcome than does the sample's demographic
> representativeness or the setting's surface realism.
>
> (ibid.: 249)

In a sense, Bandura's now classical experiments demonstrating modelling influences on children's aggression (for example, Bandura *et al.* 1961) subscribed to this desire for mundane realism. The youngsters were allowed to punch and kick the plastic bobo doll because the investigators wanted laboratory behaviours that looked like realistic aggression. What is troublesome about this type of measure, of course, if that we cannot be sure just how the subjects in these investigations understood their actions. Were they only playing or did they think of themselves as hurting someone or something? In the former case we can say the children were not really being aggressive even though their behaviour resembled naturalistic aggression. Underlying meaning is more important than surface appearance. By the same token, even the widely used Buss 'aggression machine' procedure is equivocal in its original form. In many of the early studies employing this paradigm, the subjects conceivably might have thought the electric shocks they administered were actually helping their target perform better on the assigned task. We can have a greater confidence that the shock scores actually reflect aggression if the subjects think they are hurting rather than helping the other person.

It is this meaning that the subjects impart to their behaviour that determines the laboratory measure's external validity. Whether they are punishing someone else with electric shocks, unpleasant blasts of noise, or unfavourable evaluations, they realize that they are deliberately injuring this individual. Interpreting their responses in this manner, they might well act toward the target person much as they act toward other possible victims in the outside world. Evidence in fact indicates that this is often the case. As Berkowitz and Donnerstein (1982: 253–4) have reported, a number of studies have shown that the participants' laboratory aggressiveness tends to parallel the aggressiveness they exhibit in other situations. Thus, for example, in an experiment conducted by Leyens (cited in ibid.: 254), schoolchildren were frustrated by a peer working as their partner on an assigned task and then were given an opportunity to deliver aversive stimuli to their partner in response to that child's performance. They were informed that their high-level responses would prevent their partner from doing what he had wanted (i.e. these responses would hurt the other child in a way). Those

47

youngsters who had been rated by their classmates as most aggressive in their everyday contacts were generally the most intense in their aggressive reactions with the laboratory apparatus.[1]

Taking all of the evidence together, Berkowitz and Donnerstein (1982: 254) concluded:

> Not only do we regard the laboratory responses as 'aggression' but, we believe, so do most of the subjects. Although the responses they make in the experiment certainly do not physically resemble the attacks they display in their daily lives, all of these actions appear to have much the same meaning to the participants: they know they are intentionally hurting someone else. This common meaning relates the laboratory behavior to the conduct shown in more naturalistic settings.

All of this is not to say that even highly involved laboratory subjects will necessarily interpret the experimental happenings just the way they understand any other particular social occasion. They may see authority figures in one situation but not the other and believe one setting is far more permissive than the other. The research conditions, whether in the laboratory or outside, may not have the same meaning as the conditions existing in a given situation. We therefore have to agree with Dipboye and Flanagan (1980, cited in ibid.: 249), who concluded, 'There are limits on the generalizability of all findings, which can be revealed only through systematic testing with different subjects, settings, and responses.' Basically, it is an empirical matter whether research findings can be generalized to other people at other times and places.

THE EXPERIMENT'S NARROW FOCUS

Studying behaviour out of context

So far I have suggested that virtually every investigator of human behaviour, whether experimentalist or naturalistic observer, essentially recognizes the overriding importance of the meaning that people impart to their actions and the situation before them. The researchers are apt to differ, however, in what they regard as the major determinant of this meaning. Critics such as the writer quoted at the beginning of this chapter (Siann 1985) and the senior editor of this volume basically argue that the meaning of what takes place grows out of the total context in which the happening occurs. We supposedly cannot adequately understand most acts of violence – husbands striking their wives, mothers abusing their children, a drunk punching a stranger who had offended him in a bar, a mugging on a dark street corner, or what have you – unless we consider not only the time and place but also the historical and cultural background of the people involved. As Archer in Chapter 2 put this view in his comment, reported earlier, 'Real-life acts of violence are embedded in a web of social structures, relationships, and interactions that provide them with a setting which needs to be considered in understanding their meaning.' Here is the clear difference of opinion: where I and other experimentalists maintain that we can gain an adequate understanding of 'real-life acts of violence' by abstracting out certain limited features of the behaviour and the surrounding situation and investigating their effects, this emphasis on the natural context holds that the experimentalists' understanding of the violence will inevitably be seriously incomplete.

To answer this objection we have to consider what the researcher's purpose is and what level of understanding is regarded as 'adequate' or only 'incomplete'. Kruglanski (1975) addressed these matters when he noted that many criticisms of laboratory experiments fail to distinguish between two very different types of psychological research: (a) particularistic enquiries, in which attention is focused mainly on specific instances and the intended generalizations are restricted in scope; and (b) universalistic (or theoretically oriented) studies, in which the investigator tentatively claims a universal scope of generality for the findings over a wide variety of theoretically irrelevant conditions.[2] According to Kruglanski, the representativeness of the subjects, their behaviours, and the characteristics of the research setting is not especially important in this latter type of investigation. The hypothesis tested in such an experiment, he said,

concerns the causal relations among general constructs . . .
of which the specific manipulations and measures constitute
arbitrary operational definitions, and the subject sample is
an arbitrary group from the general universe (e.g., the
class of all humans) to which the hypothesis is assumed to
apply.

(ibid.: 105)

We can have greater confidence in the validity of the causal
relationships that are uncovered when the relationships are
'replicated with alternative operational definitions of the same
constructs and with other samples' (ibid.). In any given experiment, however, we want to know if the experimental situation
'captures the intended essence of the theoretical variables'
(ibid.: 306).

This reasoning carries an important implication that should
be made explicit. The experimentalists' working assumption is
that the causal relationships they will uncover in their research
will also hold on other occasions with other participants in other
circumstances unless there is good reason to expect otherwise.
Those who stress the overriding importance of the study's
immediate context are essentially unwilling to make such an
assumption. Moreover, since the study is concerned with the
causal relationships among theoretical variables, the surrounding context is of decidedly secondary importance unless there
is some theoretical reason to expect that aspects of the surrounding situation will interact with the variables of major interest
to the researchers.

An example: a possible influence on child abuse

The issues just summarized can be highlighted by an experiment I conducted with Ann Frodi (Berkowitz and Frodi 1979).
In his discussion of the differences between experiments and
naturalistic field studies in Chapter 2, Archer said that child
abuse was one kind of aggression that could not be removed
from its social context. Investigating this phenomenon 'through
a laboratory model would be to divest it of its specific context
and meaning' (p. 28). In my view the Berkowitz–Frodi experiment demonstrates how laboratory research can improve our

understanding of child abuse in general even though this behaviour is taken from its ordinary context.

Much of my research over the years, both in the laboratory (for example, Berkowitz 1974a, b) and outside (Berkowitz 1978), has been concerned with factors influencing impulsive aggression. I have suggested that people who are set to be aggressive for one reason or another are apt to strike out at an available target more strongly than they consciously intend if they encounter stimuli in the situation that are associated either with (a) prior reinforcements for aggression, or (b) aversive events. Thus, in the latter case, not only do decidedly unpleasant occurrences instigate aggressive inclinations (Berkowitz 1984), but people who happen to be linked in our minds with some negative state of affairs might also draw impulsive aggressive reactions from us if we are not fully aware of what we are doing.

The Berkowitz–Frodi experiment tested whether this general principle could be extended to handicapped children. We reasoned that persons who are afflicted in some way are associated with pain and suffering (psychological if not physical) in the minds of those who encounter them. As a consequence, we can say, the unfortunate individuals are basically aversive stimuli for others. People who are not handicapped might sympathise with those who are, but at the same time, they could also feel some distaste or even hostility for them. Studies of people's reactions to handicapped or disfigured individuals have provided evidence consistent with this analysis. A number of investigations have shown how afflicted or crippled persons are often aversive to those they happen to encounter so that they evoke ambivalence and even dislike from these others (cf. Berkowitz and Frodi 1979: 421; also cf. Kleck *et al.* 1966). More pertinent to my present point, research into the factors affecting child abuse indicate that physically unattractive youngsters are more likely to be battered by their adult caretakers than are children of normal appearance (Parke and Collmer 1975). In many of these cases the unfortunate handicapped or disfigured or unattractive individuals could have involuntarily drawn aggressive reactions from others around them who were otherwise disposed to be aggressive for some reason.

To test their reasoning Berkowitz and Frodi (1979) carried

out two experiments in which undergraduate university women were led to believe they were engaged in a study of parent–child interactions. After the subjects were deliberately provoked by the experimenter's confederate, they watched a brief encounter between the experimenter and a ten-year-old child over a television monitor and were then required to discipline the youngster with a blast of noise when the child made a mistake on an assigned learning task. In both experiments the participants actually saw a previously videotaped interaction between the experimenter and the child which was designed to show them that the ten-year-old was either handicapped in some way or was relatively normal, and administered their 'discipline' while they were engaged in another assignment so that they were not fully attentive to how they were responding to the youngster.

Although both studies supported our analysis, the second experiment was somewhat more elaborate than the first and will be summarized here. In this investigation, as they watched the experimenter instruct the child at the start of the session, half of the (previously insulted) subjects saw that the young boy they supposedly were to supervise was unattractive in appearance, whereas for the other women he was much more attractive-looking. Furthermore, cross-cutting this variation, in half of the cases the child was a stutterer but spoke normally in the remaining instances. The youngster could therefore be afflicted in one or both of two different ways: by being unattractive-looking and/or by not speaking normally. We assumed that both characteristics were aversive to the subjects and would involuntarily evoke aggressive reactions from the provoked but distracted women.

The results confirmed this expectation. Over all of the trials in which the child supposedly made a mistake, the unattractive-appearing boy was punished more severely than the normal-looking youngster and the most intense punishment of all was given to the doubly afflicted child who was both unattractive and a stutterer. Ready to be aggressive and not fully aware of what they were doing, the women were impulsively harshest to the boy having both unpleasant qualities.

This research tested a general theoretical principle: persons having unpleasant characteristics are apt to draw aggressive reactions from those who are disposed to be aggressive for some reason and do not restrain themselves. However, it seems to me that in supporting this analysis the investigations add to our understanding of the factors that can influence child abuse. It is true that the studies were conducted in a laboratory setting isolated from the social conditions that ordinarily play a major role in child abuse. The subjects had not suffered from prolonged periods of domestic and economic stress and were not being nagged or harassed by a troublesome child. Nor did the youngster in the studies represent a parent's dashed hopes for a loving, idyllic child. Moreover, the rules of the experimental situation allowed the participants to treat the youngster relatively harshly. However, it could also be that the provocation to which the subjects were exposed at the start of the experimental session was a conceptual sample of many of the provocations and frustrations that people experience in society, that the permissiveness of the experimental situation was somewhat parallel to those occasions in the home when restraints against aggression are weak, and that the intense punishment delivered by the participants was analogous to the severe punishment a harassed parent might give a disturbing child. The experiments did not deal with all the complex meanings that a handicapped child might have for a parent, and they do not tell us in general how powerful an effect a child's appearance might have on adults. What they do demonstrate is that a child's unattractive physical characteristics can sometimes prompt involuntary aggressive reactions.[3]

What experiments can and cannot do

The central point to my argument is that experimental research is not necessarily best served by an overriding concern with the natural context within which the behaviour of interest to us ordinarily occurs and the representativeness of the subject and setting characteristics. As Postman (1955, cited in Berkowitz and Donnerstein 1982: 247) has pointed out, such a concern must 'necessarily entail the abandonment of classical notions of [experimental] control; we must take the interaction among variables as we find it'. This means we can only make statements about correlations between proximal or distal stimuli, on the one hand, and the person's responses on the other, on the basis of such designs, and cannot draw any definite conclusions from this research about the causal relationships.

This statement is obvious, of course, and is repeatedly emphasized in research methodology courses. Nevertheless, since it is also an exceedingly important point that seems to be forgotten, or at least slighted, by critics of laboratory experimentation, it is worth citing two instances in which laboratory studies demonstrated causal relationships that could only be guessed at in naturalistic observations. One of these, dealing with the effects of a child's physical unattractiveness, has already been mentioned. I have noted that representative designs (Brunswik's term for research designs in which the matters of interest are allowed to vary freely as they do in nature) can tell us that a child's physical characteristics are correlated with child abuse (Parke and Collmer 1975). However, by their very nature these designs cannot ascertain with an adequate level of assurance whether these qualities are capable of evoking (causing) abuse. Clearly, any number of other factors associated with the child's characteristics might be responsible for the adult's mistreatment of the youngster. Only a well-designed experiment that controls many of these possibly significant factors has the degree of internal validity that enables us to assign a relatively high probability value to the causal relationships that are uncovered.

Yet another example can be found in studies of the effects of the mere presence of weapons. There is a considerable controversy in the United States as to what part is played by the ready availability of guns in the rate of violent crimes in that country. Although social scientists are by no means in complete agreement on this matter (cf. Lester 1984), some evidence suggests that firearms contribute substantially to homicides. As a sample of this evidence, an investigation of the homicide rate in Detroit from 1963 to 1971 found that the rate of these killings was associated with gun availability as measured by the number of firearm registrations and permits to buy guns issued each year (Fisher 1976, cited in ibid.: 6). Going further, Zimring (1968, 1977, cited in ibid.: 8) has argued that a reduced availability of guns would reduce the number of murders committed. Many homicides are not the result of a deliberate and intentional attempt to kill the victim, he noted. They are usually the outcome of some altercation in which a firearm was nearby and was used.

However plausible Zimring's theory is to many of us, the research on which he based his argument is only correlational and does not rule out the possible role of other factors. Thus, many of the people who own guns might have somewhat violent personalities so that they are readily inflamed by disputes with others. Their aggressive disposition could be responsible for the homicides and not the weapons themselves. However, a series of experimental studies initiated by Berkowitz and LePage (1967) has demonstrated that the mere presence of guns can stimulate people to be more aggressive than they otherwise would have been. In a variety of natural as well as 'artificial' settings outside as well as inside university laboratories, and including subjects who did not realize they were participating in an experiment, the sight of a gun often induced stronger aggressive reactions than otherwise would have occurred (cf. Turner *et al.* 1977). It is now also clear that these findings are not due simply to the participants' compliance to the researchers' supposed 'demands' (cf. Berkowitz and Donnerstein 1982: 254–5).

This research again illustrates the advantages of laboratory experimentation. At the risk of being unduly repetitious, I can point out that here too the study was carried out to test a causal hypothesis (and might also note that this hypothesis was derived from a theoretical analysis of impulsive aggression). In devising this test we assumed that the basic principles governing the subjects' laboratory behaviour would also operate with other people in other circumstance, and this assumption seems warranted. Even though the initial experiment was conducted in a laboratory setting isolated from the natural context within which aggression ordinarily takes place and employed a highly artificial measure of aggression (the delivery of electric shocks), its results have been replicated with far more realistic measures in natural situations.

I should clarify my position regarding this 'weapons effect'. As I have repeatedly emphasized in discussing this phenomenon, my formulation does not hold – nor do experimentalists generally believe – that people are only automatons who respond in a totally nonthoughtful manner to the crucial stimulus. Along with the overwhelming majority of laboratory-oriented psychologists, I contend that the stimulus's meaning – in the present case, the weapon's meaning – is a primary determinant of how the participants will respond to it, although they are also affected to some extent by the meaning of the setting they are in. Thus, although our laboratory subjects knew they were in a relatively permissive experiment, they were apparently carried away by the study's experimental realism and responded to the highly salient weapons lying on the table before them. However, it was the objects' meaning for them that was presumably most important. If they thought of these objects as *aggressive* in nature, as being used to hurt someone, other ideas and motor reactions associated with aggression were activated in them which heightened the punishment they delivered to the available target. This would not have happened if the guns had not had this aggressive meaning and if the participants had believed they would get into trouble in some way by displaying aggression (cf. Turner *et al*. 1977).

We obviously cannot guarantee that everyone will interpret the experimental stimuli in the same way at all times and in every situation. They may understand the stimuli in the same manner or they may not. Some persons may think of guns as aggressive objects whereas others may interpret them as horrible and dangerous and may therefore react very differently. Thus, to quote Berkowitz and Donnerstein (1982: 255),

> we are not insisting that the laboratory findings are necessarily generalizable to the world outside. No blanket statement can be made one way or another about experiments as a whole. Just as it is incorrect to say laboratory behavior will not arise in other settings that are physically very different, so it is equally wrong to hold that the subjects' laboratory reactions will definitely occur on more naturalistic occasions. Appropriate questioning is vital to ensure that the participants have interpreted the experimental treatments in the desired way.

These latter provisos highlight yet another important consideration. Experimentalists ordinarily assume that their findings might well generalize to other people in other situations but they certainly do not deny the possibility of limiting conditions. Indeed, in being at least somewhat theoretically oriented, most experimentalists seek to uncover the psychological processes involved in the causal relationships of interest to them. In this endeavour they typically hold that the governing processes will operate under some conditions but not on other occasions, and often design their experiments to see if these situational variations do exist. Naturalistic observations that do not control possibly extraneous influences are generally not as good in investigating these causal processes.

The experiment's lack of representativeness does pose some problems, of course. Since the study's subjects, measures, and setting do not accurately mirror the people, behaviour, and situations in the broader populations that may be of interest to us, the former sample cannot be used to make estimates about the likelihood of events in that larger population. The above-mentioned research into the weapons effect does not indicate how many people in the 'real world' will become more aggressive in the presence of firearms and how substantial this influence will be. Some laboratory researchers seem to have forgotten this simple point and have made unwarranted claims on the basis of laboratory results. To take just one example, several experiments have tried to determine whether frustrations were more or less powerful than insults in generating aggressive reactions, and have compared the aggressive behaviour exhibited by thwarted subjects with the behaviour displayed by other participants who had been deliberately provoked (cf. Baron 1977). In these instances the investigators essentially sought to make unjustified magnitude estimates on the basis of their results: since the frustrations and insults employed in the experiments were not necessarily representative of the frustrations and insults occurring in daily life and the settings' permissiveness did not necessarily parallel the degree of permissiveness existing in many social situations, we cannot say from the experiments how potent frustrations and insults might be in life generally.

CONCLUSIONS

In this chapter I have only dealt with the two most common

criticisms of laboratory experimentation – the laboratory's 'artificiality' and thus supposed lack of external validity, and the study's isolation from the natural context – and have not discussed other objections that have also been raised (cf. Kruglanski (1975) and Berkowitz and Donnerstein (1982) for a wider-ranging consideration of many of the issues involved in this research approach). For that matter, I have also said little about some of the advantages of laboratory experiments other than their relatively precise tests of causal hypotheses.

As just one example of these other advantages, laboratory experiments are an exceedingly efficient mode of research that can provide fairly quick benefits for the effort required in carrying them out. Where the findings of correlational naturalistic field studies can often be explained in a great many different ways, well-designed experiments typically permit a smaller range of possibilities, partly because of the experimental controls but also because the research questions are usually more narrowly and more precisely focused. Thus, they give relatively clear-cut answers to the causal questions asked by the investigators. As a consequence of this relative efficiency, experimental research can yield much faster progress than naturalistic observations in our understanding of those social phenomena that are susceptible to experimental investigation.

In my view, we can see this fairly rapid progress particularly well in the research into the effects of mass-media depictions of violence. Society has long been concerned about the possible harm that might be done to children and even adults by the frequent and graphic portrayals of violence in newspapers, films and television, and national commissions in the United States have inquired into these possible consequences at least since the 1930s. From my perspective social science has learned more about the impact of media portrayals of violence from laboratory experiments in the past two or three decades than from the scores of correlational field studies that have been carried out since the 1930s. Experiments have demonstrated how people can get ideas from what they see on the screen or printed page and also what processes affect the likelihood that these thoughts will be translated into open behaviour (cf. Berkowitz 1984). Where the controversy remains in this particular research area is on matters that are not easily investigated experimentally, notably the long-term effects of frequent exposure to media violence. By contrast, laboratory experiments have clearly identified many of the conditions governing the short-term influence that can be more readily studied by this approach.

The research into media effects also provides another lesson that applies to the role of experiments generally, whether in the study of aggression or in other areas. Laboratory experiments have a definite place in the behavioural sciences, and can contribute in important ways to our understanding of human social behaviour, primarily because of their 'artificiality' – their high degree of control over extraneous influences. However, this particular virtue also limits the functions that experiments can serve. A truly comprehensive science of human behaviour must encompass both correlational studies in natural settings and experiments in the field and laboratory.

NOTES

1 There obviously are some studies in which laboratory measures of aggression were not correlated with indices of real-life aggressiveness. In at least some of these instances the laboratory subjects might not have believed that they were intentionally hurting the target person when they delivered noxious stimulation to that individual so that, in these cases, the laboratory behaviour did not have the same meaning as the actions in more naturalistic settings. In any event, it is a serious mistake to contend that the external validity of the laboratory measures is best determined by ascertaining whether more studies obtain the desired findings than do not: the investigations' outcomes can be influenced by how well designed they are, whether their conceptions of aggression are the same, and so on.

2 Archer (Chapter 2) had essentially recognized this difference in pointing out that the laboratory approach 'is limited to answering certain types of general questions about aggression', (p. 28) whereas, he claimed, 'more specific questions concerning areas of social concern cannot be tackled in this way' (pp. 28–9). We can say that these latter, 'more specific' questions are the focus of particularistic research essentially concentrating on very specific situations, while universalistic investigations pursue what Archer termed 'general' questions.

3 For the benefit of the casual reader, let me repeat that this research is not attempting to 'explain' all child abuse. There is no claim that our experimental setting is representative of many of those natural situations in which child abuse occurs or that

LEONARD BERKOWITZ

the causal relationship being examined can account for most instances of child abuse. We only sought to determine if the child-victim's personal characteristics could influence the harshness of the discipline given the youngster when the disciplinarian was not fully aware of what he or she was doing.

REFERENCES

Bandura, A., Ross, D., and Ross, S.A. (1961) 'Transmission of aggression through imitation of aggressive models', *Journal of Abnormal and Social Psychology* 63: 575–82.
Baron, A. (1977) *Human Aggression*, New York: Wiley.
Berkowitz, L. (1974a) 'Some determinants of impulsive aggression: the role of mediated associations with reinforcements for aggression', *Psychological Review* 81: 165–76.
────── (1974b) 'External determinants of impulsive aggression', in J. De Wit and W.W. Hartup (eds) *Determinants and Origins of Aggressive Behavior*, The Hague: Mouton.
────── (1978) 'Is criminal violence normative behavior? Hostile and instrumental aggression in violent incidents', *Journal of Research in Crime and Delinquency* 15: 148–61.
────── (1984) 'Some effects of thoughts on anti- and prosocial influences of media events: a cognitive-neoassociation analysis', *Psychological Bulletin* 95: 410–26.
Berkowitz, L. and Donnerstein, E. (1982) 'External validity is more than skin deep: some answers to criticisms of laboratory experiments', *American Psychologist* 37: 245–57.
Berkowitz, L. and Frodi, A. (1979) 'Reactions to a child's mistakes as affected by her/his looks and speech', *Social Psychology Quarterly*, 42: 420–5.
Berkowitz, L. and LePage, A. (1967) 'Weapons as aggression-eliciting stimuli', *Journal of Personality and Social Psychology* 7: 202–7.
Brunswik, E. (1955) 'Representative design and probablistic theory in a functional psychology', *Psychological Review* 62: 193–217.
Buss, A.H. (1961) *The Psychology of Aggression*, New York: Wiley.
Campbell, D.T. and Stanley, J.C. (1963) *Experimental and Quasi-experimental Designs for Research*, Chicago: Rand-McNally.
Carlsmith, J.M., Ellsworth, P.C., and Aronson, E. (1976) *Methods of Research in Social Psychology*, Reading, Mass.: Addison-Wesley.
Kleck, R., Ono, H., and Hastorf, A. (1966) 'The effects of physical deviance upon face-to-face interaction', *Human Relations* 19: 425–36.
Kruglanski, A.W. (1975) 'The human subject in the psychology experiment: fact and artifact', in L. Berkowitz (ed.) *Advances in Experimental Social Psychology, Vol. 8*, New York: Academic Press.
Lester, D. (1984) *Gun Control: Issues and Answers*, Springfield, Ill.:

Charles C. Thomas.

Parke, R.D. and Collmer, C.W. (1975) 'Child abuse: an interdisciplinary analysis', in E.M. Hetherington (ed.) *Review of Child Development Research, Vol. 5*, Chicago: University of Chicago Press.

Siann, G. (1985) *Accounting for Aggression: Perspectives on Aggression and Violence*, London: Allen & Unwin.

Turner, C.W., Simons, L.S., Berkowitz, L., and Frodi, A. (1977) 'The stimulating and inhibiting effects of weapons on aggressive behavior', *Aggressive Behavior* 3: 355–78.

Part Two

NATURALISTIC METHODS: SPECIFIC EXAMPLES

Chapter 4

ETHOLOGICAL APPROACHES TO THE STUDY OF AGGRESSION IN CHILDREN

PETER K. SMITH

INTRODUCTION

In this chapter I shall take the 'ethological approach' to refer to studies which satisfy at least two out of three criteria: first, they primarily rely on direct, nonparticipant observation of behaviour; second, such data is gathered in natural settings; and third, there is an interest in the functional and the comparative evolutionary significance of the behaviour. These criteria are those which are usually implied when the 'ethological approach' is referred to, and they do delineate a certain kind of methodology and a certain set of studies.

'Direct' observation means that no intervening procedure (of written or verbal enquiry about feelings, attitudes, or behaviour, such as tests or interviews) stands between the observer and the observed, and that records are compiled immediately, not retrospectively; 'nonparticipant' means that the observer stands apart from the persons being observed, interacting minimally if at all. Ethology normally refers to the study of behaviour in nonhuman species: when we are studying aggressive behaviour in, say, herring gulls, or macaques, direct nonparticipant observation in natural settings is an obvious methodology to adopt. We cannot be participant observers, or interview our subjects. We can of course experiment with animals, and many researchers might combine observation in natural settings with experimental approaches and still call themselves 'ethologists'. Tinbergen, for example, used many experimental manipulations in his pioneering ethological text, *The Study of Instinct* (1951), and studied the reactions of animals to test objects and stimuli. Thus, to some extent, equating 'ethological' purely with study in natural settings is misplaced. However, direct observation in natural settings does have a special place in the study of animal behaviour for another reason: many zoologists, from Lorenz and Tinbergen onwards, have felt that unobtrusive recording of what went on in the animal's natural environment was an essential first step if we wanted to get a clear idea of the animal's behavioural repertoire, and if we wanted to have any reasonable chance of understanding the functional significance of such behaviour. Whereas ethologists have been as much interested as psychologists in understanding the causation and development of behaviour, it has been a more distinctive concern of ethologists to understand the adaptive value of behaviour for the individual, and the evolutionary history of how natural selection has favoured this mode of behavioural adaptation.

A number of researchers, often called 'human ethologists', have felt that similar arguments, techniques, and interests could be applied to the study of human behaviour. The first two criteria I have referred to – direct, nonparticipant observation, and in natural settings – have tended to be the most characteristic of this approach. Clearly there are problems. Can observation really be unobtrusive? What is a 'natural setting' for the human species anyway? Nevertheless, the 'ethological approach' to human behaviour has had a distinctive impact, and the area of aggressive behaviour is a notable example of this. Most such research has been carried out with children. This is probably because it has been felt that it is difficult or impossible to interview them (this applies especially to very young children); because they are relatively easy to observe unobtrusively; and because researchers have felt reasonably comfortable considering a playgroup or school playground as a 'natural setting', at least in comparison with the setting of a typical psychological laboratory.

Nonparticipant observational studies of children have in fact occurred in two main phases this century. The first was in the 1930s, largely uninfluenced by animal research, and the second was in the 1970s, heavily influenced by animal ethology. I shall start with a brief review of some of the 1930s work, then discuss the origins of the 1970s phase in more detail, considering such issues as definitions and typologies of aggression, aggression and dominance, environmental influences on aggression, and the distinction between 'real' fighting and 'play' fighting. Finally, the merits and limitations of the 'ethological approach' will be assessed.

THE 1930S PHASE OF
OBSERVATIONAL STUDIES

Prior to the 1920s, child psychology consisted mainly of indirect observations, based on diary or interview reports. As an example, Burk's (1897) account of teasing and bullying is based on a questionnaire asking for accounts of this type of behaviour. Respondents furnished examples such as 'girl (7) often passed a house where five boys regularly threw stones at her', or 'Dora (3) bullied Mamie (4) into giving up everything, toys, sweetmeats, cakes, etc. Mamie is afraid to tell, as I have heard Dora say to her: "If you tell my mamma, Mamie Reed, I will cut your curls off and then you'll die".' Burk classified such reports into a number of different categories of teasing and bullying. Nevertheless, such indirect observation is often lacking in precision, and is subject to memory selection and distortion.

More systematic programmes of research began to be carried out in the late 1920s, with the foundation in North America of institutes or research stations of child development or child welfare in such centres as Columbia, Iowa, Minnesota, Yale, Berkeley, Oakland, Toronto, and elsewhere (see Senn 1975). Amongst the techniques employed, that of 'time sampling' came to have a prominent place. As stated by Goodenough (1928: 230–1),

a method has been developed . . . which in certain respects is free from both the subjective elements that constitute the chief objections to the use of rating scales and similar devices and from the artificial aspects of the laboratory experiment . . . Briefly stated, this consists simply in the observation of the everyday behavior of an individual or a group of individuals for definite short periods of time and the recording of the occurrence or non-occurrence of certain specified and objectively defined forms of behavior

67

during each of these periods . . . It is a direct method. The individual is measured in terms of actual samples of his everyday behavior as displayed under ordinary conditions . . . Measurements can be taken without interfering with or interrupting the usual activities of the subject.

The time sampling method came to be quite widely used through the 1930s and early 1940s. With this went the aim of observing unobtrusively in 'ordinary conditions' – in practice, often the nursery school or playgroup, one or more of which had usually been established at the child development institutes and welfare stations where most of these studies were carried out. Many studies provided information on aggressive behaviour in children. Much of this was basic data on what causes 'quarrels' and how they are settled; individual, age, and sex differences; effects of the nursery environment; and the measurement of dominance or 'ascendancy'. I will discuss four of these studies in some detail in order to give the flavour of both the methodology of these studies, and the kinds of data available from them.

Dawe's study of quarrels in preschool children

Dawe (1934) reported observations of forty children aged between 2 and 4 years in the nursery school at the Institute of Child Welfare, University of Minnesota, made in 1931 and 1932. She used an event sampling procedure during morning free-play periods, recording details of any struggle or quarrel which was noticed. Altogether 200 quarrels were recorded. Observer reliability, and split-half reliability of the data on individual differences, were reported. The following represent the kinds of results in the published paper.

Quarrels occurred on average at the rate of 3.4 per hour. They lasted on average about 24 seconds, with only 13/200 lasting a minute or over. Indoor quarrels were a bit shorter when a teacher interfered. An average of 2.22 children were involved in each quarrel, with the largest number involved being five.

The children observed averaged about twelve quarrels each,

with a range from 300 to thirty-nine. Quarrels were more frequent in boys than girls, and declined with age. Frequency of quarreling was not related to frequency of attendance, or IQ, but was less in children of lower social class. The more quarrelsome children did not seem to have particular 'enemies', but quarrelled with many other children.

Quarrels were classified as starting over possessions, physical violence, interference with activity, or social adjustment (i.e. sanctions or social rules). The majority were quarrels over possessions, though this percentage decreased with age. Pushing, striking, and pulling occurred frequently at all ages, while kicking, pinching, stamping, and throwing things were less frequent. Crying became less frequent with age but other forms of vocal activity during the quarrel were more likely with older children.

About two-thirds of the quarrels were settled by the children themselves. In 47 per cent the child yielded to force, in 10 per cent the child yielded voluntarily, in 6 per cent there was a compromise. Generally, younger children yielded to older children.

Jersild and Markey's study of conflicts between preschool children

Jersild and Markey (1935), based at Teachers College, Columbia University, carried out an intensive study of conflicts in children at three nursery schools. A total of fifty-four children were each observed for ten 15-minute focal samples (focusing on one child at a time) over a five-month period. Inter-observer agreements and split-half reliabilities were reported. Forty-two items of conflict behaviour were defined and used. Two examples are *snatches*: takes or grabs toys or objects held, used, or occupied by another child; uses, tugs at, or pushes material away with hands or feet: all contacts with material which, if completed, would deprive the other child of the use and possession of material; and *unfavourable remark about person*: 'you're no good at it'; 'you don't do it right'; 'I don't like you.' In addition, Jersild and Markey recorded who was the aggressor and who the victim, what the outcome of the struggle was, and the role of the teacher.

69

A total of 1,595 conflicts were recorded. There was found to be some decline with age, and overall, boys took part in more conflicts than girls in two of the three nurseries. Correlations with IQ, height, weight, and racial group are reported. The three nurseries differed considerably in rates of conflict, but no simple interpretation of this was possible due to the many confounding factors: age, racial composition, play space available, attitudes of teachers. A follow-up was made of twenty-four of the original children, after about nine months had elapsed. Again ten 15-minute focal samples were obtained. The rate of conflicts increased: this was contrary to the earlier age difference based on cross-sectional data, suggesting that nursery experience rather than age might be the explanation. Conflicts had also become more verbal. Individual differences between children in types and frequencies of conflict tended to be maintained. A further follow-up was made of twelve children, into kindergarten. An increase in conflicts was observed in those children who experienced a relaxation of teacher constraints on moving from the nursery to kindergarten environment.

Appel's study on adult procedures in dealing with aggression in nursery school

Appel (1942) made observations in fourteen different nursery schools. Six enrolled children of high socio-economic status, eight children of low socio-economic status. Records were made by event sampling (it is not stated for how long), and a total of 641 episodes were recorded. Eight categories of aggressive acts were described, and inter-observer agreements reported. Frequencies of aggression in the various categories, and age differences, were first described. Appel then delineated fifteen kinds of adult response to children's aggression. Five are 'ending techniques': diverting; separating or removing; restraining; arbitrary decision; enforcing a rule. Ten are 'teaching techniques': explaining property rights; urging self-defence; suggesting a solution; suggesting children find solution; interpreting; encouraging friendly acts; making light of troubles or hurts; requiring good manners; disapproval; retaliation. In the different nursery schools, between 22 and 58 per cent of aggressive incidents elicited adult intervention of one of these types.

Table 4.1 Effectiveness of different techniques of adult intervention in ending conflicts in nursery school (from Appel, 1943)

	% *effectiveness*
Diverting (to new activity)	93
Separating (children) or removing (item)	85
Interpreting (wishes and feelings of one child to another)	71
Explaining property rights	69
Suggesting a solution	66
(Making) arbitrary decision	65
(Expressing) arbitrary disapproval	40
Suggesting children find solution	33

An evaluation of the effectiveness of these different techniques was made, by deciding in each case whether the conflict continued or ended after the adult intervention. A complete table of results was not presented, but the results quoted in the article are shown in Table 4.1. Some techniques were clearly much more effective than others at ending the immediate conflict. Least effective was suggesting to the children that they find a solution themselves. Of course, longer-term effects of different techniques might conceivably lead to a different preference ranking. Appel herself concluded that 'teachers should not intervene too readily in children's conflicts. Children will teach each other a great deal. Too much interference prevents self-reliance.'

Hanfmann's study of social structure and dominance in a kindergarten

Hanfmann (1935) investigated the dominance relationships within a kindergarten group of ten 5-year-old boys. The method of paired comparisons was used: each child was paired with each other child for at least one play session. The sessions lasted between fifteen and thirty minutes and the children had coloured blocks to play with. Two observers 'recorded everything both children did and said'. On this basis an estimate was made immediately afterwards of which child was more dominant, in the sense of controlling both his own play and that of his

Figure 4.1 The dominance hierarchy reported by Hanfmann (1935)

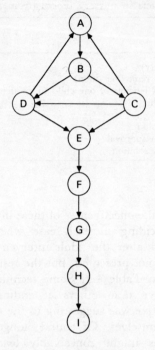

Source: Adapted from Hanfmann (1935).
Note the intransitive relationships between A,B,D, and A,B,C.

companion. Coding agreement was not reported. The results of this ranking process are summarized in Figure 4.1. Hanfmann found a linear rank order amongst the lowest five children, but a more complex, non-linear pattern in the top five. Children C and D were both adept at play with the blocks: C was especially good at construction, and D at the social skills of co-operative play. Both were dominated by B, who forcefully grabbed all the blocks for himself, and whom Hanfmann compares to a little gangster. B is in turn dominated by A, who simply threw blocks around and destroyed the play. Yet the activities and social skills of C and D were sufficiently interesting to A that he modified his destructive tendencies with them, and is scored as being dominated by them.

THE 1970s PHASE OF
OBSERVATIONAL STUDIES

Although a small number of observational studies continued to be published through the 1950s and early 1960s, by and large direct observation in natural settings does not seem to have been considered highly in this period. More constrained investigations in laboratories, often experimental in nature, were seen as the preferred method, in psychology in general and in the study of children's aggression in particular. This is the era of assessing aggression in doll play, punching of bobo dolls, and pressing buttons supposedly to deliver punishment to another child (see Chapter 2 this volume).

By the mid-1970s, however, direct observation had made a comeback (see, for example, the exchange of views in the *BPS Bulletin* between Cooper *et al*. 1974, Hutt 1974, and Richer 1974). The impetus for this first came from ethology. Ethological methodology had been developed through the preceding decades, initially at least largely independent from psychological research on animal behaviour. Lorenz and Tinbergen, the two great pioneers of modern ethology, both advocated the application of ethology to the study of human behaviour. By the late 1960s examples of such application were appearing in both Britain and Germany.

In Britain, Blurton Jones (having completed a PhD with Tinbergen) started studying the social behaviour of children in nursery school. His first publication in this area (Blurton Jones 1967) was published in a book entitled *Primate Ethology*. Most of the aggressive behaviour which he observed occurred in the context of property fights. The commonest action was a beating movement – an overarm blow with the palm side of the tightly clenched fist. Other behaviour seen in aggression and submission was described in some detail. Blurton Jones drew a quantitative distinction between aggressive behaviour (consisting of beat, low frown, and fixate) and rough-and-tumble (consisting of run, jumps, open beat, and wrestle). Rough-and-tumble looked superficially like aggression, but could be distinguished by the details of the movement patterns, its context, and the effects it had. Subsequently (Blurton Jones 1972) he confirmed these findings in another sample of children, and suggested that aggressive behaviour could be partially separated into take–tug–grab situations (simply taking of objects) which might not have aggressive intent (although they might evoke aggression), and the fixate, frowns, hit, push, behaviours he had described earlier.

Another pioneer of the application of ethological methods to humans was Hutt. The 1970 volume by Hutt and Hutt, *Direct Observation and Measurement of Behavior*, helped to revive interest in observational methodology generally, as well as arguing the benefits of drawing on the work of the animal ethologists. McGrew (1972) and Hutt published work on the behaviour patterns seen in aggression, the existence of a dominance hierarchy in preschool children, and the influence of the physical environment, especially density, on social and aggressive behaviour.

These and other researchers in Britain formed a lively nucleus of 'human ethologists' who formed links with researchers in Germany (for example, Eibl-Eibesfeldt 1967) and soon with researchers in the USA. International human ethology workshop meetings were initiated, the first being organized by Charlesworth and Hartup in Minneapolis (1972), followed by meetings at Percha (W. Germany) and London (1973), London (1974), and Sheffield (1975).

By the mid-1970s, human ethology was being strongly influenced by the theoretical ideas of sociobiology, brought to the attention of the general scientific community by Wilson (1975). This brought about some rethinking and regrouping in the human ethology movement. The international workshops did not resume until 1982 (in Atlanta) and 1986 (Tutzing), and the journal which started in 1979 was titled *Ethology and Sociobiology*. This movement now combines 'ethological' work, still much of it observational research on children, with 'sociobiological' work, much of it based on anthropological research, and examining the adaptive value, or fitness, of human behaviour in different cultural contexts. The links between the two strands do exist, in terms of an overall interest in the functional aspects of behaviour and its evolutionary context; but in practice they are rather tenuous.

Over the same period of the last decade, however, observational techniques have returned to the mainstream of use in psychology generally, and child development in particular. Large numbers of articles on parent–child and peer relationship, in premier journals such as *Child Development* or *Developmental Psychology*, use observational methodology in natural settings such as the home, day-care centre, preschool, or school. Whether these are considered as 'ethological' really centres on whether one thinks that an explicit functional and evolutionary perspective is a necessary and distinctive ingredient of the latter.

Both the human ethological and more general child developmental research areas have seen a great deal of research on aggression in children. The area of developmental research generally (not specifically observational) is well reviewed by Parke and Slaby (1983). In the remainder of this chapter I will highlight certain areas where research in the human ethological tradition has advanced over the last decade. The areas considered are the types of aggressive behaviour; the distinction between aggression, and rough-and-tumble play; environmental effects on aggression; and the characterization of dominance relationships. I shall conclude by considering the strengths and weaknesses of this work, compared with other methodological approaches.

Types and typologies of aggressive behaviour

Many researchers have used 'aggressive behaviour' as an umbrella term to cover an area of study, and have defined it broadly in terms of intentional behaviour which causes distress or harm to another person. However, it has also often been pointed out that there are many types of aggressive behaviour, and that it may be important to distinguish them. Indeed, it is often argued that a distinctive advantage of an observational approach is that it enables valid distinctions to be made between different types of aggression (for example, Attili 1985).

There are a number of ways in which distinctions can be drawn. These include verbal and nonverbal aggression (based on the presence or absence of verbal threats or insults); instrumental or hostile aggression (based on whether the distress or harm is inferred to be the primary intent of the act: see Chapter 1 this volume); and individual or group aggression (depending on whether more than one child attacks another).

75

The distinction based on intent was elaborated by Manning *et al.* (1978). They proposed a three-way classification of hostile incidents, based on observations of children in nursery school. They defined 'specific hostility' as that which occurs in a specific situation which annoys or frustrates the aggressor. Hostility is used as a tool enabling the aggressor to get his/her own way or assert his/her opinion: the victim is often incidental. They distinguished six sub-categories of this: property or territorial disputes; exclusion of another child from a group or game; ordering about; precedence; organization-ordering; and judgement. (The last two of these are similar to what some authors – for example, Szegal 1985 – call 'prosocial aggression'.)

In contrast, 'harassment' appears unprovoked (at least in the immediate situation) and is directed at a person. The aggressor gains nothing tangible from the act; the reward appears to be the victim's reaction. They distinguished three sub-categories of this: physical harassment; teasing; and threat. Finally, 'games hostility' is seen as rough, intimidating or restrictive activities which occur in a rough-and-tumble or fantasy game: for example very rough variants of rough-and-tumble, or bullying, intimidating, or imprisoning against the victim's will in a fantasy game.

Attili and Hinde (1986) built on this threefold distinction and included a fourth, defensive or reactive hostility, provoked by the action of others (see Chapter 5 this volume). This might, however, link to specific hostility where the dispute is over objects or space, or to harassment if the response to provocation is particularly strong.

Some construct validity for these distinctions has been found by a number of researchers: for example, boys seem to score higher in harassment but not in specific hostility (Manning *et al.* 1978; Smith and Connolly 1980). Provoked aggression (for example, defensive hostility) is correlated with popularity in school children, whereas unprovoked aggression (for example, harassment) is correlated with sociometric rejection (Lesser 1959). Different kinds of aggression may show a characteristic ontogenetic sequence of appearance in the first few years of life (Szegal 1985).

These distinctions are ultimately based on inferences of the

Figure 4.2 Postulated relationships between motivational factors and observed behaviours

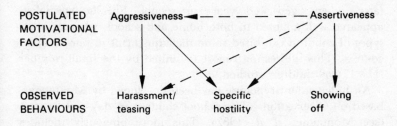

POSTULATED MOTIVATIONAL FACTORS — Aggressiveness ◄ — — — — — — Assertiveness

OBSERVED BEHAVIOURS — Harassment/teasing — Specific hostility — Showing off

Source: Adapted from Hinde (1985).
The doted lines are possible additions or variants to the model.

intent of the actors, though the observer uses aspects such as the context of the incident, its temporal structure, and the facial expressions and vocalizations of the participants as the observable cues for such inferences. Nevertheless, the full complexity of how such inferences are based on observable phenomena has not been spelt out. Thus, these distinctions are somewhat different from those of Blurton Jones, for example, which are apparently based just on the occurrence of actions defined in physical rather than motivational terms.

Hinde (1985) and Attili and Hinde (1986) have taken the issue of intent a step further. They have postulated two distinct motivational factors. Aggressiveness is seen as a general propensity towards violence. Assertiveness is seen as a motivation to elevate one's position or push oneself forward, whether in general terms or in relation to particular objects or goals (as in acquisitiveness with regard to specific objects or situations). These motivations are postulated to underlie observer behaviour in some systematic way, as for example in Figure 4.2. Note that in this figure showing-off behaviour (to be discussed later) is an example of an assertive but not an aggressive behaviour.

Another related development has been the attempt to categorize children into certain types, according to their characteristic patterns of aggression. Manning *et al.* (1978) distinguished specific specialists, harassment specialists, games specialists, and also teaser-specifics (who showed a considerable amount of both specific hostility and harassment). These types of children, determined at nursery school, were linked to family communication patterns, and to social adjustment both at nursery and later, when aged 7–8 years at school. Specific specialists appeared well adapted in both home and school, whereas other types of children exhibited some maladjustment in one or other context. This interesting report is limited by the small number (N = 17) of children studied.

An independent typology has been developed by Montagner, based on observations of preschool children in day-care centres (see Montagner *et al.* 1982). This more obviously includes elements of dominance than does that of Manning. Montagner's six types of children are as follows: leaders (who frequently compete, impose themselves on others, and show appeasement); dominated with leader mechanisms (who compete less often); dominant-aggressive (who frequently compete and impose themselves on others, but do not frequently show appeasement); dominated-aggressive (who compete less often); dominant-fearful (who do not impose themselves and are often targets of aggression by others); and dominant-isolated (who seldom interact with other children). These types were related to family profiles, and also to biological rhythms based on measurements of corticosteroid excretion in urine samples.

Discussion of possible links between the typologies of Manning and Montagner can be found in Sluckin (1981) and Attili and Hinde (1986).

Aggression and rough-and-tumble play

A particularly important outcome of the ethological approach to aggression has been the distinction made between aggressive behaviour and rough-and-tumble play. Blurton Jones (1967) took the term 'rough-and-tumble' from Harlow's descriptions of play in rhesus monkeys. Blurton Jones first explicitly described the behaviours involved in rough-and-tumble, and showed that it occurred in separate behaviour sequences from aggression in his observations of preschool children. However, the general types of 'fighting play' had been described at least as far back as Groos (1901).

Subsequent research on rough-and-tumble has confirmed that

it can be distinguished from aggressive behaviour in terms of the specific acts and postures present (for example, open rather than closed beat; play face rather than frown and fixate), and the context (for example, participants tend to stay together rather than separate) (Smith and Lewis 1985). In addition, children who are often seen behaving aggressively are not necessarily often seen engaged in rough-and-tumble (Blurton Jones 1972). Through the preschool and middle school years, sociometric assessments show that children tend to like their rough-and-tumble play partners (Smith and Lewis 1985; Humphreys and Smith 1987).

Nevertheless, the distinction has not always been observed in more traditional psychological research. As Blurton Jones (1972) pointed out, studies of the imitation of aggression in children (for example, Bandura *et al.* 1961; Nelson *et al.* 1969) confounded the two. Measures such as punching a doll could be (and as illustrations in Bandura's article showed, sometimes were) associated with rough-and-tumble indicators such as a play face, while measures such as gun play or fantasy aggression clearly implicated rough-and-tumble. Thus, one cannot conclude from these studies that watching aggression makes children more aggressive. Even more recent studies, such as Huston-Stein *et al.* (1981) and Potts *et al.* (1986) include hitting an inflated clown or bobo doll as aggressive, and are thus perpetuating this confound.

These studies on aggression, imitation, and the mass media are not the only examples. In a study of the effects of density on aggression, Loo (1972) did not distinguish rough-and-tumble. Her finding that reduced space led to reduced aggression in boys (but not girls) is probably artifactual because of this confound (it was not confirmed by the research of Smith and Connolly 1980 – see next section). In a study of children's social networks, Ladd (1983) defined 'rough-and-tumble' as 'unorganised agonistic activity with others, for example, fights or mock-fights, wrestling, pushing/shoving'. Again, this means that his substantive finding, that 'rough-and-tumble' is higher in sociometrically rejected than in popular or average children, may be due to (unprovoked?) aggression rather than rough-and-tumble play *per se*.

Up to around 9 or 10 years of age, the consensus of evidence is that rough-and-tumble and aggression are clearly distinct. There is no excuse for continuing to confound them in observational studies. Their relationship around adolescence requires further research. Neill (1976), based on observations of boys at one school, argued that by 12–13 years some substantial proportion of rough-and-tumble episodes involved aggressive elements or became aggressive in intent. This was not specifically confirmed by Humphreys and Smith (1987) in a study of 7–11 year olds, but by 11 years it was found that rough-and-tumble partners were chosen on a basis of strength and dominance ranking, as well as liking (see also Humphreys and Smith 1984; Neill 1985).

Environmental effects on aggression

Two main research fronts have used observational methods to look at the impact of environmental factors on aggressive behaviour. One has examined the incidence of aggression in relation to specific reinforcement contingencies or responses of others in the immediate environment. The other has considered the wider impact of the child's environment, in relation to ecological factors such as spatial or resource densities, or nursery curricula (which might of course be mediated through reinforcement contingencies, as well as other aspects such as the likelihood of competition for resources).

An excellent example of the former type of study is a report by Fagot et al. (1985). They observed thirty-four infants, mean age 13 months, in playgroups. They defined two types of 'assertive act': hit, push, shove; and grab or take object or try to take object (these being very similar to the two types of aggression described by Blurton Jones 1972). The same children were observed again some 9–11 months later, as toddlers.

No sex differences were observed in the infants' behaviour, for either type of assertive act. Nor did peers respond differentially to boys' and girls' aggression. However, teachers responded to 41 per cent of the boys' assertive acts, but only 10 per cent of the girls'; teachers' reactions tended to be about equally positive, or negative. In the toddlers, boys were now found to be more assertive than girls, specifically for 'grab or take object'; this was largely because the level in girls had declined over the period. However, the sex inequality in teacher response had disappeared.

Fagot et al. (1985) interpreted their results as follows: in infancy, it is difficult to interpret the meaning of acts (for example, is a push meant aggressively or not?). Thus, teachers or caregivers will tend to fall back on stereotyped beliefs to guide their behaviour. Since it is a stereotyped belief that boys will become aggressive, whereas girls will not, boys' assertive acts are given more attention generally (some of this is positive, as in Appel's study described earlier), while those of girls are ignored. Thus, boys come to feel that assertive acts can be efficacious, i.e. bring about a change in the situation, more than girls do. By the time they are toddlers, acts are less ambiguous in meaning. Caregivers now respond to children as individuals, rather than being guided by stereotypes. However, the prior reinforcement history (as well as continuing stereotyped responses of adults who do not yet know particular children well as individuals) continues the sex difference, which then perpetuates the stereotype. This interpretation is not, of course, the only one possible from the data, nor does it exclude any possible influence of biological factors; but it does fit in with findings from many other studies of a similar type.

An example of a study of the second kind outlined above is the programme of research reported by Smith and Connolly (1980). They carried out a series of systematic environmental variations on two preschool playgroups, and made observations of the children's behavior, including categories of aggressive and submissive behaviour, and (separately) rough-and-tumble play.

One study was on the effects of a 'free-play' nursery regime, compared with a 'structured activities' nursery regime. One playgroup in each condition was observed over an eight-month period. In the analysis of this study, the aggression types of Manning *et al.* (1978) were used. It was found that initially, frequencies of aggression did not differ between the two groups. Frequencies did not change significantly in the children experiencing the free play regime, but they increased steadily for the children in the structured activities regime (for all categories of aggression), especially when the children were allowed back into free play in a final baseline assessment period. The authors concluded (similarly to Jersild and Markey, and Appel, as discussed earlier) that the decreased peer interaction which characterized the structured activities condition might have decreased the ability of the children to manage their own conflict situations without escalation.

Other studies by Smith and Connolly (1980) examined the effects of numbers of children, spatial density, and resource density. Within a range of 10–30 children in the group, numbers of children did not affect the incidence of aggression, provided that space and resources were varied commensurately. Variations in spatial density within a range of 75–25 sq.ft./child did not affect aggression; but a further reduction to 15 sq.ft/child did increase aggression, suggesting a threshold effect, and leading to a recommendation that 25 sq.ft/child should be a minimum provision in preschool facilities (as is often the case – though see Fagot 1977 for a contrasting view). Finally, providing more toys per child did systematically reduce the frequency of aggression between children, though it did also reduce the frequency of sharing and of children being together in large subgroups, due to the greater dispersal of the children amongst the available items of toys and equipment.

Dominance relationships

For some decades, dominance has been used as a concept in the study of animal social groups. If one animal is dominant over another one, it usually has priority of access to resources over the other, often without overt fighting and with little more than a ritualized signal; though who wins fights has also been taken as a measure of dominance. Stable dominance relationships in a social group can sometimes be described in terms of a dominance hierarchy. The usefulness of the concept has been challenged in ethology, but it does often predict other aspects of behaviour. Several researchers in the ethological tradition have examined groups of children or adolescents to see if dominance has the same salience or predictive characteristics that have been found in groups of primates and other species. While some of the research has involved asking children for their rankings of peers for 'toughness' or 'dominance', or 'strength', much of it has relied on direct observation of which individuals win conflicts in (usually) dyadic encounters. An edited volume by Omark *et al.* (1980) is a sourcebook for a great deal of this research.

Although Blurton Jones (1967) initially doubted whether a

linear dominance hierarchy would be useful in describing the social behaviour or organization of children as young as preschool age, subsequent researchers have clearly shown its value. McGrew (1972), for example, found a nearly linear hierarchy of dominance, based on naturalistic observation of wins and losses during conflict over the possession of preferred objects. The most systematic programme of research in this area has been that of Strayer and his associates.

Strayer and Strayer (1976), observing eighteen children in a preschool, separated out three kinds of measures: first, threat-gesture (comprising intention hit, intention kick, intention bite, and face/body posture); second, physical attack (comprising bite, chase, hit, kick, push–pull and wrestle); and third, object/position struggles (with or without physical contact). They also classified responses to these as submission, object/position loss, help seeking, counterattack, and no response. They then examined the usefulness of a dominance hierarchy based on the three mean measures of initiated behaviour, when the response was either submission or object/position loss, i.e. where there was a clear winner or loser.

Observations were made using a matrix-completion method, to try and fill as many dyadic cells of the matrix as possible. An example of a dyadic dominance matrix is shown in Figure 4.3. The order of children maximizes the number of entries above the diagonal of the matrix: thus, the most dominant children are at the top of the list on the left-hand vertical. The numbers represent incidents with a clear win by the child higher in dominance (above diagonal) or lower in dominance (below diagonal). Strayer and Strayer used two statistics, linearity and rigidity to assess how descriptively useful the concept of a hierarchy was. Percentage linearity was defined as 100 × (Total Dyads – Relational Reversals)/Total Dyads, while percentage rigidity is defined as 100 × (Total Episodes – Episodes Reversals)/Total Episodes. Here, the term Relational Reversals refers to dyads whose individual relative position goes against the overall hierarchy (in Figure 4.3 there are two such dyads: Ch–If and Se–Sd; there are also four relational ties). The term Episodic Reversals refers to all episodes below the diagonal. In Figure 4.3, the linearity is 98 per cent, and the rigidity is 95 per cent. This figure excludes results from 'object/position struggles',

Figure 4.3 A matrix showing dyadic dominance relationships in a preschool group

TARGETS

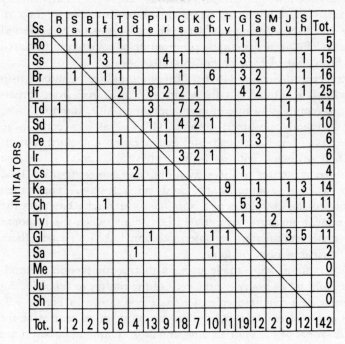

INITIATORS

Ss	Ro	Ss	Br	Lf	Td	Sd	Pe	Ir	Cs	Ka	Ch	Ty	Gl	Sa	Me	Ju	Sh	Tot.
Ro		1	1	1									1	1				5
Ss			1	3	1			4	1			1	3				1	15
Br	1			1	1				1		6		3	2			1	16
If					2	1	8	2	2	1			4	2		2	1	25
Td	1						3		7	2						1		14
Sd							1	1	4	2	1					1		10
Pe					1			1					1	3				6
Ir									3	2	1							6
Cs					2		1						1					4
Ka												9		1		1	3	14
Ch				1									5	3		1	1	11
Ty													1		2			3
Gl							1				1	1				3	5	11
Sa					1						1							2
Me																		0
Ju																		0
Sh																		0
Tot.	1	2	2	5	6	4	13	9	18	7	10	11	19	12	2	9	12	142

Source: Adapted from Strayer and Strayer (1976).

since this data showed slightly lower linearity and rigidity than did the other two measures used. These general findings have been confirmed in other preschools (Strayer 1980).

A related concept to that of social dominance, has been that of 'attention structure'. This refers to the amount of visual attention (looking) directed to individuals by others in the group. A collection of both primate and human studies on this is in a volume edited by Chance and Larsen (1976). Several studies have examined the relationships between dominance and attention structure in preschool groups. The correlations are generally high, but not so substantial that the two constructs can be considered as interchangeable.

One example of such a study is that by LaFreniere and Charlesworth (1983), on a class of twenty 4- and 5-year olds. Dominance was calculated in a similar manner to Strayer and Strayer (1976), while attention was based on observations of looking behaviour. In addition, affiliation was assessed by observations of interactive play with other children. Besides confirming a highly linear and rigid hierarchy in their group, LaFreniere and Charlesworth found that it was reasonably stable over a nine-month period of observations, as was the attention structure. Dominance and attention ranks correlated within the range $r = 0.60$ to 0.68 over the period. The correlations of dominance with affiliation, and also with sociometric popularity, were smaller and non-significant; however, attention structure did correlate with these latter measures. Thus, it seems that attention structure may be picking up both aspects of dominance (children monitoring what highly dominant children are up to) and of affiliation (children watching their friends, or children with whom they were playing).

Related to attention structure is the phenomenon of 'showing-off' behaviour, discussed by Hold-Cavell (1985). The most frequent items of showing-off observed in a group of twenty-five kindergarten children were: attracting attention verbally (for example, calling someone); intensity of voice or noise (for example, singing loudly); aggrandizement of body size (for example, climbing on a chair); obvious body movement (for example, jumping around in the room); and seeking attention with an object (for example, wearing unusual headgear). Both showing-off behaviour, and also threat displays, were found to correlate significantly with attention structure and with physical aggression. Looking also at the temporal patterns of these behaviours over a school year, Hold-Cavell suggest that both showing-off and threat display may serve as strategies for getting high regard in the group.

Most, but not all, of the observational work on dominance and attention has been carried out with preschool children. Ginsburg and Miller (1981), for example, observed fights between 9–11 year olds in a school playground. They were particularly interested in children who intervened as third parties in dyadic fights. Such interventions often terminated the initial fight, though usually with some aggression being redirected to the child who intervened. The latter did not usually get help from the child on whose behalf intervention took place (who usually stood back and watched); but it did seem that these children who intervened were high up in the dominance and attention structures in the group.

Studies of dominance have also been made in adolescents by Savin-Williams (1976, 1980). These were based on observations of small groups of adolescents (boys and girls) at short summer camps. These children did not know each other previously, but stable, ordered dominance hierarchies emerged within a few days. 'Verbal ridicule' was the most frequently observed index of dominance at this age.

The research inspired by the concept of dominance has been quite vigorous and fruitful. However, a few reservations may be noted to apply here, as in the animal literature. Some aspects of dominance may be context-specific – that is, A might dominate B in one context (for example in the school classroom) but not another (for example, school playground). In addition, a linear hierarchy may be too simple to describe three-party or multi-party relationships. Hanfmann's earlier study brought out these points to some extent. Finally, it is clear that there are many other aspects to relationships, apart from dominance: one that ethologists have paid much attention to is affiliation or friendship.

DISCUSSION

This final section attempts to summarize some of the pros and cons of the various methodological aspects which are often associated with the 'ethological approach': direct nonparticipant observation; study in natural settings; and explicit adherence to a functional and comparative/evolutionary perspective.

Direct nonparticipant observation

As compared with interview, questionnaire, or rating scales, direct observation has the advantage that the investigator can record what 'really' happens, rather than what someone says happens, or has an impression of happening. In this sense, direct observation appears to yield more valid data, or at least data whose validity we can be more confident of, than other methods of data-gathering. In particular, interview or question-naire may draw out socially desirable responses.

It is of course true that the act of observing may itself induce socially desirable behaviour to be produced for the observer, or socially undesirable behaviour to be inhibited. This can be partly overcome by making concealed observations (for exam-ple, Ginsburg and Miller 1981), or by making observations over such extensive periods that habituation to the observer occurs, and/or the observations cover most of the time in the setting under consideration (for example, Smith and Connolly 1980). Nevertheless, certain phenomena, such as bullying in secondary schools, may remain more tractable to interview or rating studies than to direct observation (for example, Olweus 1978). It is also true that what people say happens may be as interesting as what 'really' happens (see the following chapters). In fact, many of the studies cited have combined observational data with other kinds of data such as sociometric data based on interview. Few current researchers would want to argue that direct observation is the only useful way of getting data (though many might wish to advocate it as the most useful way, for certain purposes).

Another advantage of direct observation is that, following a period of relatively unstructured watching, the investigator may come up with behavioural categories or distinctions which were not previously conceived but which turn out to be useful or have some construct validity. The examples of aggressive types (for example, Manning *et al.* 1978) and of rough-and-tumble play (for example, Blurton Jones 1967) support this consideration. This line of argument has traditionally been advanced by etho-logists, and it characterizes the 1970s phase of observational research more than that of the 1930s.

Both these phases of observational research dealt with the methodology of time sampling, and both concentrated on social behaviour in young children. The 1930s work has been rather neglected, and more recent publications have sometimes gone over ground trodden fifty years previously. However, the older

body of work has clear limitations in terms of available technology, statistical sophistication, and theoretical insights. The
relationships and differences between the two are discussed
further by Smith and Connolly (1972) and Fassnacht (1982).

Natural settings

Studies in both the 1930s and 1970s phases have generally been
carried out in natural settings such as day-care centres,
playgroups, schools, or homes. This has been seen as an advantage in terms of the ecological validity of the study, and hence
the confidence with which results can be taken to be representative of real life, compared with, say, studies carried out in
contrived or laboratory situations. A contrived situation has
some clear disadvantages. By simplifying the environment,
certain forms of behaviour are excluded and certain hypotheses
just will not be generated or tested from the resulting data.
Thus, for example, effects of third party interventions in fights
just cannot be assessed if you watch dyads in a laboratory (cf.
Ginsburg and Miller 1981). In addition, contrived situations
may introduce unwanted behaviour, such as responses to a
novel situation, or behaviour directed to the experimenter.
Hence, unwanted hypotheses (such as experimenter effects or
response to novelty) may confound the clear testing of the
hypotheses supposedly under study.

The use of natural settings does not necessarily exclude some
experimental control: for example, Smith and Connolly (1980)
carried out experimental manipulations of the environment of
their playgroups in a reasonably ecologically valid way. In
addition, few researchers would disagree that some more
contrived studies can supplement those in natural settings.
Hanfmann (1935), for example, contrived her dyadic pairings to
examine dominance: this allowed rapid 'matrix completion' for
her relevant data set. It reduced validity *vis-à-vis* the occurrence
of dominance in the total peer group, but may have some
usefulness provided that information on dominance in the more
natural social group is also obtained.

At a deeper level of meaning, no setting is totally 'natural' for
humans in the way that certain settings can be seen as 'natural'
for particular nonhuman species in terms of what ecological

niche that species' behaviour is adapted to. As cultural animals, we have changed our environment too much: even the home of a nuclear family, or the large peer groups of a school, can be argued to be somewhat 'unnatural' in these terms. Thus, it would be wrong to be too dogmatic about the naturalness of settings in studying human behaviour. The basic points at issue are to which range of settings the investigator wishes to be able to generalize results, and how important and feasible it is, at the current level of knowledge, to include or exclude certain hypotheses from testing.

The functional and comparative/evolutionary significance of behaviour

This aspect was almost entirely absent in the 1930s phase of research. In the 1970s phase, however, a number of researchers have been inspired by comparative work, especially methodologies and concepts used in the study of nonhuman primates. Examples include nonverbal communication signals for threat and appeasement; rough-and-tumble play; attention structure and dominance hierarchies. There has been some interest in at least considering the function of behaviour. Sociobiological theorizing has had an input in this, encouraging a shift from thinking about functional significance of behaviour for the group to its significance for the individual. It has also encouraged interest in more specific hypotheses, such as the extent of reciprocation for aid-giving behaviour.

The functional and evolutionary aspect has probably been strongest in the research on dominance relationships and attention structure. Distinctively, it leads to questions as to why individuals should seek high regard or high dominance rank, and hence encourages a longer time perspective. In addition, it lays emphasis on alternative 'strategies' which individuals may pursue towards the same functional ends. This may have interesting implications for the traditional developmental distinctions between 'normal' and 'maladaptive' behaviour (cf. Manning *et al.* 1978). As yet, however, the functional and evolutionary perspective has had relatively little impact on the observational research with children. Functional questions are notoriously difficult to address, and perhaps especially for children since function is ultimately referred to adult survival and reproductive success (for example, Neill 1985). Children remain amongst the easiest population to observe in natural settings.

SUMMARY

The 1930s period of research laid out a lot of groundwork in observational methodology and basic data on social behaviour, including aggression in young children. Much of this groundwork has been retrodden in the 1970s by human ethologists and by observational research in child development. However the later phase of research has carried forward more sophisticated methodological techniques (for example, use of tape recorders, video replay), statistical and analytic techniques (for example, analysis of multivariate data; sequence analysis; dominance matrices), and theoretical interpretations (for example, reinforcement theory; cognitive-development theory; human sociobiology).

None of the three criteria which characterize the 'ethological approach' would be defended as the 'only way forward' by many researchers in the area. They can often be usefully combined with other approaches, and on occasions may just be unsuitable or inappropriate. However, all three have important advantages to them in the study of aggression and dominance. In particular, despite the comeback which direct, nonparticipant observation in natural settings has made, many researchers (the present author included) still see it as relatively undervalued in the whole body of behavioural research on aggression.

REFERENCES

Appel, M.H. (1942) 'Aggressive behavior of nursery school children and adult procedures in dealing with such behavior', *Journal of Experimental Education* 11: 185–99.
Attili, G. (1985) 'Aggression in young children – introduction: some methodological issues related to the nature of aggression', *Aggressive Behavior* 11: 279–81.
Attili, G. and Hinde, R.A. (1986) 'Categories of aggression and their motivational heterogeneity', *Ethology and Sociobiology* 7: 17–27.

Bandura, A., Ross, D., and Ross, S.A. (1961) 'Transmission of aggression through imitation of aggressive models', *Journal of Abnormal and Social Psychology* 63: 575–82.
Blurton Jones, N. (1967) 'An ethological study of some aspects of social behaviour of children in nursery school', in D. Morris (ed.) *Primate Ethology*, London: Weidenfeld & Nicolson, pp. 347–68.
—————— (1972) 'Categories of child–child interaction', in N. Blurton Jones (ed.) *Ethological Studies of Child Development*, Cambridge: Cambridge University Press, pp. 97–127.
Burk, F.L. (1897) 'Teasing and bullying', *Pedagogical Seminary* 4: 336–71.
Chance, M.R.A. and Larsen, R.R. (eds) (1976) *The Social Structure of Attention*, London: Wiley.
Cooper, E.S., Costello, A.J., Douglas, J.W.B., Ingleby, J.D., and Turner, R.K. (1974) 'Direct observation?', *Bulletin of the British Psychological Society* 27: 3–7.
Dawe, H.C. (1934) 'An analysis of two hundred quarrels of preschool children', *Child Development* 5: 139–57.
Eibl-Eibesfeldt, I. (1967) 'Concepts of ethology and their significance in the study of human behavior', in H.W. Stevenson, E.H. Hess, and H.L. Rheingold (eds) *Early Behavior: Comparative and Developmental Approaches*, New York: Wiley.
Fagot, B.I. (1977) 'Variations in density: effect on task and social behaviors of preschool children', *Developmental Psychology* 13: 166–7.
Fagot, B.I., Hagan, R., Leinbach, M.D., and Krosberg, S. (1985) 'Differential reactions to assertive and communicative acts of toddler boys and girls', *Child Development* 56: 1499–505.
Fassnacht, G. (1982) *Theory and Practice of Observing Behaviour*, London: Academic Press.
Ginsburg, H.J. and Miller, S.M. (1981) 'Altruism in children: a naturalistic study of reciprocation and an examination of the relationship between social dominance and aid-giving behavior', *Ethology and Sociobiology* 2: 75–83.
Goodenough, F.L. (1928) 'Measuring behavior traits by means of repeated short samples', *Journal of Juvenile Research* 12: 230–5.
Groos, K. (1901) *The Play of Man*, London: W. Heinemann.
Hanfmann, E. (1935) 'Social structure of a group of kindergarten children', *American Journal of Orthopsychiatry* 5: 407–10.
Hinde, R.A. (1985) 'Categories of behavior and ontogeny of aggression', *Aggressive Behavior* 11: 333–5.
Hold-Cavell, B.C.L. (1985) 'Showing-off and aggression in young children', *Aggressive Behavior* 11: 303–14.
Humphreys, A.P. and Smith, P.K. (1984) 'Rough-and-tumble in preschool and playground', in P.K. Smith (ed.) *Play in Animals and Humans*, Oxford: Basil Blackwell, pp. 241–66.
—————— (1987) 'Rough and tumble, friendship, and dominance in

schoolchildren: evidence for continuity and change with age',
Child Development 58: 201–12.

Huston-Stein, A., Fox, S., Greer, D., Watkins, B.A., and
Whitaker, J. (1981) 'The effects of TV action and violence on
children's social behaviour', *Journal of Genetic Psychology* 138:
183–91.

Hutt, C. (1974) 'Critique of 'Direct observation' by Cooper *et al.*',
Bulletin of the British Psychological Society 27: 503–4.

Hutt, S.J. and Hutt, C. (1970) *Direct Observation and Measurement of
Behavior*, Illinois: C.C. Thomas.

Jersild, A.T. and Markey, F.V. (1935) 'Conflicts between preschool
children', *Child Development Monographs, Teachers College, Columbia
University* 21.

Ladd, G.W. (1983) 'Social networks of popular, average and
rejected children in school settings', *Merrill-Palmer Quarterly* 29:
283–307.

LaFreniere, P. and Charlesworth, W.R. (1983) 'Dominance,
attention, and affiliation in a preschool group: a nine-month
longitudinal study', *Ethology and Sociobiology* 4: 55–67.

Lesser, G.S. (1959) 'The relationship between various forms of
aggression and popularity among lower-class children', *Journal of
Educational Psychology* 50: 20–5.

Loo, C.M. (1972) 'The effects of spatial density on the social
behavior of children', *Journal of Applied Social Psychology* 2: 372–81.

McGrew, W.C. (1972) *An Ethological Study of Children's Behaviour*,
London: Academic Press.

Manning, M., Heron, J., and Marshall, T. (1978) 'Styles of
hostility and social interactions at nursery, at school, and at
home. An extended study of children', in L.A. Hersov, M.
Berger, and D. Shaffer (eds) *Aggression and Anti-Social Behaviour in
Childhood and Adolescence*, Oxford: Pergamon Press, pp. 29–58.

Montagner, H., Restoin, A., and Henry, J.C. (1982) 'Biological
defense rhythms, stress, and communication in children', in
W.W. Hartup (ed.) *Review of Child Development Research, Volume 6*,
Chicago and London: University of Chicago Press, pp. 291–319.

Neill, S.R. St. J. (1976) 'Aggressive and non-aggressive fighting in
twelve-to-thirteen year old pre-adolescent boys', *Journal of Child
Psychology and Psychiatry* 17: 213–20.

—— (1985) 'Rough-and-tumble and aggression in school
children: serious play?', *Animal Behaviour* 33: 1380–2.

Nelson, J.D., Gelfand, D.M., and Hartmann, D.P. (1969)
'Children's aggression following competition and exposure to an
aggressive model', *Child Development* 40: 1085–99.

Olweus, D. (1978) *Aggression in the Schools: Bullies and Whipping Boys*,
New York: Wiley.

Omark, D.R., Strayer, F.F., and Freedman, D.G. (1980) *Dominance
Relations: An Ethological View of Human Conflict and Social Interaction*,
New York; Garland STPM Press.

Parke, R.D. and Slaby, R.G. (1983) 'The development of aggression', in P. Mussen (ed.) *Handbook of Child Psychology, 4th edn, Vol. IV*, New York: Wiley.

Potts, R., Huston, A.C., and Wright, J.C. (1986) 'The effects of television form and violent content on boys' attention and social behavior', *Journal of Experimental Child Psychology* 41: 1–17.

Richer, J. (1974) 'Direct observation: a reply to Cooper *et al.*', *Bulletin of the British Psychological Society* 27: 500–2.

Savin-Williams, R.C. (1976) 'An ethological study of dominance formation and maintenance in a group of human adolescents', *Child Development* 47: 972–9.

——— (1980) 'Social interactions of adolescent females in natural groups', in H.C. Foot, A.J. Chapman, and J.R. Smith (eds) *Friendship and Social Relations in Children*, Chichester: Wiley, pp. 343–64.

Senn, M.J.E. (1975) 'Insights on the child development movement in the United States', *Monographs of the Society for Research in Child Development* 40 (3–4).

Sluckin, A. (1981) *Growing Up in the Playground: The Social Development of Children*, London: Routledge & Kegan Paul.

Smith, P.K. and Connolly, K. (1972) 'Patterns of play and social interaction in pre-school children', in N. Blurton Jones (ed.) *Ethological Studies of Child Behaviour*, Cambridge: Cambridge University Press, pp. 65–95.

——— (1980) *The Ecology of Preschool Behaviour*, Cambridge: Cambridge University Press.

Smith, P.K. and Lewis, K. (1985) 'Rough-and-tumble play, fighting and chasing in nursery school children', *Ethology and Sociobiology* 6: 175–81.

Strayer, F.F. (1980) 'Child etholody and the study of preschool social relations', in H.C. Foot, A.J. Chapman, and J.R. Smith (eds) *Friendship and Social Relations in Children*, Chichester: Wiley, pp. 235–65.

Strayer, F.F. and Strayer, J. (1976) 'An ethological analysis of social agonism and dominance relations among preschool children', *Child Development* 47: 980–9.

Szegal, B. (1985) 'Stages in the development of aggressive behavior in early childhood', *Aggressive Behavior* 11: 315–21.

Tinbergen, N. (1951) *The Study of Instinct*, London: Oxford University Press.

Wilson, E.O. (1975) *Sociobiology: The New Synthesis*, Harvard, Mass.: Belknap Press.

Chapter 5

EXPERIMENTAL ANIMAL MODELS OF AGGRESSION: WHAT DO THEY SAY ABOUT HUMAN BEHAVIOUR?

D. CAROLINE BLANCHARD
AND ROBERT J. BLANCHARD

INTRODUCTION

The creation of relatively simple, relatively controlled, situations and events to serve as models for more complex or less easily manipulated phenomena has come to be a more deliberate aspect of scientific research in recent years. This emphasis becomes especially important when research is explicitly aimed toward understanding important 'real world' phenomena such as aggression.

When a model is used, it is obvious that the quality of the resulting conclusions will depend on the fit between this model and the phenomenon that is to be explained, and here may be found a common problem: scientists are taught to simplify concepts as much as possible, and sometimes the call to simplify is honoured much more than the accompanying qualification. In a model, simplicity has no virtue unless it is combined with an adequate relationship to the criterion phenomenon. If an experimental model is chosen on the basis of apparent resemblances to only one or two aspects of a complex human phenomenon, without any systematic effort to determine if this resemblance is valid and functional, then the use of this model may provide only an illusion of information; a counterproductive situation in which research grinds away, without any real hope of advancing knowledge.

We would like to suggest a two-part strategy for dealing with this dilemma in psychological research. The first component of this strategy is to work, as far as possible, through biological models. These have the advantages of forcing the researcher to examine behaviour in the context in which it has evolved and naturally occurs, and of encouraging a great deal of description and low-level analysis (for example, sequential and dyadic analysis) prior to a leap into theory. The second component of this strategy is to analyse the human phenomenon systematically in terms of detailed, point-to-point correspondence with this biological model, attempting to determine if there is enough agreement to make the model useful.

This strategy will be exemplified by research using a model of aggression developed in this and other laboratories over the past decade or so, outlining the animal model itself and attempting to relate this model to some important aspects of human aggression as these are described in existing literature.

THE ANIMAL MODEL

When mixed-sex groups of laboratory rats are maintained together in large enclosures, the males of the group soon begin to show consistent patterns of fighting, with one animal coming more and more clearly to dominate the others. This dominant or alpha male will also take the most active role in attacking any male intruder into the established colony (Blanchard, Takahashi, and Blanchard 1977). When conditions of life for the colony are extremely close to those which obtain for most wild rats in their natural habitat, for example when the large enclosure has a deep soil substrate into which the animals can burrow, these aggressive patterns occur very quickly indeed, even for socially naïve rats. Within an hour after being placed into such an enclosure, both burrowing and fighting are seen.

These naïve animals are given free access to food and water; they are not crowded (the new enclosure gives them considerably more room per animal than a typical rat cage with a single inhabitant), nor pained or frustrated in any other obvious way. Yet they not only fight, but also show a very consistent and complex pattern of actions during these fights. Fighting, to much the same degree as burrowing, appears to represent a species-typical, pre-programmed response pattern in the rat, to situations of biological significance in the history of the species (Adams 1979; Blanchard and Blanchard 1984). Like other complex species-typical behaviour patterns, fighting varies considerably with the adequacy of the eliciting stimuli and situation: when laboratory conditions are made more normal for rats through the provision of such features as conspecific females and the burrowing substrate, conspecific fighting becomes much more intense (Blanchard *et al.* 1985).

In fact, two very different patterns of fighting emerge in such situations, a pattern typical of the rat who is dominant and in his territory, and a pattern typical of less-dominant colony members when they are attacked, or, even more clearly, of a stranger introduced into an established colony and there attacked by the dominant or alpha colony male. This latter pattern, defence, may also be elicited and investigated in situations involving confrontation by a predator, or environmental hazards. Defence is thus a more general pattern than offence, occurring in a variety of situations. Defence has been responsible for much of the confusion in animal aggression research: despite the fact that it is different in terms of situation, aim, and behaviour from the pattern shown by the attacking alpha, components of it have historically been taken for aggression (Hutchinson 1983; Blanchard and Blanchard 1984).

Defence and defensive attack

Defensive behaviour occurs to threatening – that is, fear-eliciting – stimuli, with a very close relationship between specific features of the threat stimulus and situation, and the specific defensive behaviour (Russell 1979).

One important function of defence, in addition to its role in conspecific encounters, is as an antipredator pattern (Archer 1979). In fact, the reactions of a wild rat to an approaching predator have been used to demonstrate the basic elements of the self-defence pattern (Blanchard, Flannelly and Blanchard 1986). As described in Figure 5.1, wild rat defensive behaviours are under the joint control of the predator and the environment in which the predator is encountered.

When flight or avoidance is possible it is the dominant response (left side of the figure). The intensity (rapidity) of

Figure 5.1 Graph depicting intensity of defensive behaviour as a function of distance from the predator

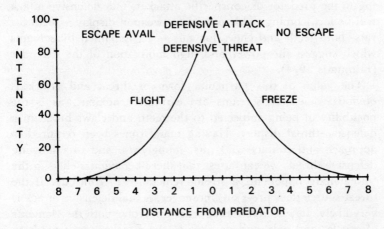

flight varies directly as a function of the distance between the predator and the subject (defensive distance). As the predator comes close to contact, prey flight abruptly gives way to defensive vocalization, and jump attacks and bites at the predator's head. When escape is not possible (right side of the figure), the subject freezes while oriented toward the predator. Increases in muscle tension as indexed by the amplitude of the startle response to sudden stimuli accompany decreasing defensive distance. As the predator approaches within a metre defensive vocalization and threat, then jump attack and biting, occur.

In mammals such as the rat, little of this is disorganized or random even when a naïve subject is used (cf. Curti 1935). The specific adaptiveness of each such reaction in the context in which it normally occurs suggests an evolutionary basis for not only individual behaviour, but also for the stimulus–response relationships involved in the defence pattern. Thus, rats freeze under circumstances in which freezing is likely to be the most successful behaviour in avoiding further attack. Similarly, flight occurs only when the threat stimulus comes too close, and is sufficiently discriminable as to make avoidance profitable. The riskiest defence – defensive attack – will occur only when freezing and flight are no longer useful, at near-contact defensive distances. Defensive attack is normally preceded by ample warning to the predator or conspecific attacker, that defensive attack will be forthcoming. This consists of weapon display – teeth for rats, both teeth and claws for cats – accompanied by screams which suggest the power and high motivation of the defender (Edmunds 1974).

The value of this particular form of threat and attack is obvious: defensive screams are extremely noxious, as is the possibility of being subjected to the teeth and claws bared in a defensive threat display. Having many times been required to approach and contact wild rats, mongooses, and cats showing defensive threat, we can attest that these behaviours elicit in the 'threatening opponent' a strong reluctance to continue. If the threat source does press on, moreover, actual defensive attack is very likely. Its effectiveness appears to involve both the elements of startle, and pain and damage to the attacker, as it tends to consist of very sudden jumps or lunges toward the attacker, and to be aimed at especially vulnerable sites such as face and eyes (Blanchard *et al.* 1978).

Substantial components of this defence system are 'built in' for lower animals (Russell 1979). Indeed, they would probably not survive long enough to learn it, if such learning were necessary. Although practice does improve the form and precision of each behaviour which is a component of the defence pattern, and individual experience may alter the relationship between threat stimuli and these responses, both the responses and their relationships to specific features of threatening stimulus and situation appear to represent basic neural preprogramming.

Human defence/defensive attack patterns

Human defence, including defensive attack, is still a rather primitive system. If something unexpected occurs – a loud noise or sudden movement – people tend to respond immediately with a precisely patterned defensive sequence which is very similar to that of lower mammals: they stop what they are doing (again showing a startle to sudden onset stimuli), orient toward the stimulus, and try to identify its potentiality for actual danger. This happens very quickly, in a reflex-like sequence in which action precedes any voluntary or consciously intentioned behaviour. A poorly localizable or identifiable threat source, such as a sound in the night, may elicit an active immobility so profound that the frightened person can hardly speak or even breathe, i.e. freezing. However, if the danger source has been localized and an avenue for flight or concealment is possible, the person will probably try to flee or hide. As the danger comes closer, facial and bodily signs of fear become obvious (Ekman *et al.* 1972), including a 'rictus of fear' in which the lips are drawn back to expose the teeth while the hands are often drawn up and forward, presenting the 'claws' (well, fingernails, anyway) to their attacker (Darwin 1872). Screaming is more likely as the threat comes closer, although, depending on the circumstances and the individual, freezing may be so profound that vocalization is impossible. Actual contact, particularly painful contact, with the threat source is also likely to elicit thrashing, biting, scratching, and other potentially damaging activities by the terrified person.

Thus, people share, in a relatively unchanged fashion, the primitive defence system seen in other mammals: actual defensive attack is one component of this. However, while many other elements of defence are quite common, it is rather difficult to find pure examples of defensive attack in people. The situations necessary to produce defensive attack are both very specific, and sufficiently unpleasant that human societies have worked hard to eliminate them from the experience of most individuals. Defensive attack almost never occurs unless something or someone is attacking the person, and is right there on top of him or her. Escape is impossible, and for whatever reason those penultimate human defences of begging for mercy, agreeing to whatever the attacker wants, and so on, will clearly not work. Even then, if there is some existing relationship which implies that the attacker will stop short of grievous bodily harm, the victim may submit rather than fighting back, a response which might intensify the attack. When relatively pure examples of defensive attack do occur, it is usually in the context of a very lop-sided agonistic encounter, the attack of an adult on a child, a man on a woman, an animal or a gang on an individual: the capacity for defensive attack is present in varying degrees in each person, though most of us are lucky enough to avoid the types of threat and pain which make it occur.

Animal models and human defence-related behaviours

The defence pattern, including defensive attack, is quite easy to produce in laboratory animals. In fact, many of the traditional tests of 'aggression' such as reflexive fighting and the tube-tail shock test (Blanchard *et al.* 1978; Brain 1981) appear largely to reflect defensive attack. However, several problems have interfered with successful attempts to forge links between information gathered on defence in lower animals, and related human phenomena. Firstly, despite a brief flurry of interest in defence some two decades ago which focused on the interaction of elicited defensive responses and the acquisition of experimenter-selected criterion measures, this interesting and important area of animal behaviour has been largely ignored. In particular, few studies have attempted to deal with the linkage between specific defensive behaviours and features of the eliciting stimuli and situation, or to investigate possible differential reactions of varying components of the defence pattern to important independent variables. As one example of the latter, recent work from this laboratory suggests that varying doses of alcohol (Blanchard, Flannelly and Blanchard 1986) may have different effects on several components of the defence pattern, as do both classic and nontraditional anxiolytics (Blanchard, Blanchard, Flannelly and Hori 1986).

On the human level, moreover, many of the problems which may be assumed to be related to the defence pattern are relatively specific (Marks 1969, 1987). Pathologies of defensiveness may involve extreme degrees of specific components, such as freezing in catatonia or greatly exaggerated fear to specific stimuli (often in the absence of any precipitating traumatic events: Carr 1979), as with phobias, or heightened defensive attack in the 'dyscontrol' syndromes and (perhaps) paranoia. In fact, the parallels between animal models of defence and human fear/anxiety reactions may be at least as precise as those for aggression (Blanchard and Blanchard 1988), but that is another story. These correspondences suggest that the potential value of animal models of defence and defensive attack in understanding a range of human neurotic and perhaps psychotic conditions may be enormous; but these models are presently underinvestigated, imperfectly understood, and sufficiently complex and precise that much of their value is lost when they are simplified.

An additional problem is that domesticated animals generally, and laboratory rats in particular, have been stringently selected for many generations for a lack of defensiveness, especially defensive attack, to human contact and to new stimuli (Robinson 1984). This situation has promoted the use of painful stimuli to elicit fear, which confounds fearfulness with reactivity to pain. The use of domesticated animals to study defensiveness has an even more problematic aspect: shifts within the defence pattern (from active defences such as defensive attack, and even flight, to freezing; Blanchard, Flannelly and Blanchard 1986) do occur with domestication. This suggests that studies of independent-variable effects on the defence pattern, using such subjects, may produce results that are systematically different to those which would be obtained with 'natural' animals. In the context of systematic selection against active defence, people appear to be more 'natural' than do laboratory rats. The solution to this problem, we feel, is to use wild-trapped animals, or at least early-generation offspring of wild-trapped animals, for the study of defence, until sufficient information is obtained as to clarify the circumstances in which the use of laboratory animals is scientifically productive and efficient.

OFFENSIVE ATTACK

In partial contrast to the defence/defensive attack system, offensive attack appears to have changed considerably in the transition from lower to higher mammals. More specifically, some particular aspects of it have changed, while others are more conservative.

Situational elicitors of offence in lower mammals

Most instances of offensive aggression in lower animals involve disputes over two types of items (Wilson 1975). The first are resource disputes. If, for example, a desirable food item is thrown into a group of chimpanzees or bears or dogs, then fights may result. Just to be precise, it might be noted that in such cases there often is no fighting, and either the first animal to get to the food, or the most dominant animal of a well-established group, may get the food item without an actual fight. However – especially if the item is scarce and highly desirable, and the animals are hungry – fights are not uncommon.

The second occasion for intraspecies fighting involves dominance. Although such fighting does not depend on the presence of specific disputable resources, dominance does indirectly influence access to resources, and fighting which facilitates the establishment of dominance may be temporally or spatially related to the presence of such resources: for example, male mountain sheep or elephant seals tend to live peacefully until the onset of the breeding season, when they fight for the control of an area in which they have access to breeding females.

Resource-based and dominance-based disputes tend to overlap and merge in complex ways, varying with different environments, degrees of coloniality of the species, and other features of individual and group ecology (Wilson 1975; Archer 1988). A few laboratory studies of the relationship between dominance patterns established in the absence of specific, scarce, resources, and those seen in resource fights suggest that dominance in one context does not automatically result in enhanced access to all resources (Baenninger 1970; Flannelly and Blanchard 1981). However, these studies typically involve very low degrees of deprivation of the disputed resource, and the results may not reflect the more extreme conditions in nature in which enhanced access by dominant animals might be most adaptive. The most reasonable summary statement of the immediate occasion for offensive aggression in infra-human animals is probably that both resource and dominance factors are usually involved, in some varying mix. Both factors also involve a challenge from a conspecific, which is likely to serve as an immediate elicitor of offence in most mammalian species regardless of the resource/dominance focus of any actual dispute (Blanchard and Blanchard 1984).

Response correlates of offensive attack: behaviour,
motivations, goals, and reinforcers

The specific behaviour involved in offence varies somewhat from species to species, and has been described in detail elsewhere (Blanchard, Blanchard, Takahashi and Kelley 1977; Adams 1979; Blanchard and Blanchard 1984) so they need not be repeated here. However, the basic structure of offence for most mammalian species seems clear. The actual offensive attack pattern involves two components: first, gaining access to target sites on the body of an opponent, and second, delivering a bite or blow. The first component includes activities such as chasing, as well as specific manoeuvres designed to make the desired target site available (most animals do appear to have some preference for specific sites, this preference in some cases so strong as to determine the form of the attack). The form of the second component depends, of course, on available weaponry such as teeth, claws, sharp hooves, and the like: thus, although there is great variation in the specific behaviour by which damage is inflicted on a conspecific, it in each case involves the application of some set of weapons to the body of the opponent.

The actions of seeking access to specific targets and systematically attacking these suggest a strong motivational, goal-directed aspect to offensive attack. We have elsewhere (Blanchard and Blanchard 1984) suggested that this motivation, which is directed toward attack on an opponent in disputes over resources or dominance, may form a primitive functional analogue to human anger.

In fact, some highly aggressive animals actively seek out opponents to attack (Blanchard *et al.* 1985), suggesting that aggressiveness may reflect an ongoing motivational feature of the individual, rather than an action pattern arising only from specific types of resource/dominance dispute situations. In addition, aggressive animals appear to be reinforce by opportunities to attack, injure, chase away, or dominate a conspecific (Scott and Fredericson 1951; Potegal 1979). Offensive attack thus involves a specifiable set of reinforcements (in addition to gain of disputed resources), plus characteristic motivations and behaviour patterns.

The decision to fight: an emotional calculus

Although the benefits of successful fighting are considerable, there is a negative side as well. Fighting can result in injury, reproductive incapacity, or even death. Additionally, since offensive attack is based on potential gain – of resources, status, or both – a 'decision' to fight should reflect the chances of success. A defeated animal not only runs a risk of injury, it also fails to achieve its resource/status goal, wasting time, energy, and other chances for gain in the process. In evolutionary terms, this means that the successful individuals will be those with techniques which enable them to avoid agonistic situations involving serious possibility of defeat or injury, while leaving them to continue in more promising situations.

The process by which the diverse factors influencing the decision to fight are evaluated constitutes an affective cost–benefit analysis. We have elsewhere (Blanchard and Blanchard 1984) suggested that this analysis compares the relative values of offence-promoting emotional/motivational states (a primitive analogue of human anger) and fear. While each of these emotions is based in considerable degree upon the specifics of the situation, they are certainly more than short-latency, short-lived reflexive reactions to simple stimuli. Thus, for example, a resident's offence towards an intruder may be more enhanced by a recent 'incomplete victory' – removal of a prior intruder after only two minutes of fighting – than by fights resulting in clear victory (Leshner and Nock 1976), a finding which suggests that some of the reinforcement value of victory involves a reduction in anger. In similar fashion, offence is markedly reduced through prior manipulations (exposure to a cat) which increase fear (Blanchard, Kleinschmidt, Flannelly, and Blanchard 1984). Thus, the affective cost–benefit analysis appears to involve recent experience, in addition to prior learning and biological factors leading to individual differences.

The cost–benefit analysis leading to offensive attack is thus quite complex, certainly more complex than the analysis leading to defence. The offence cost–benefit analysis includes evaluation of several types of information, including the challenging or non-challenging behaviour or status of the opponent (which impacts anger), and the relative potential of the opponent's size, strength, and weapons (which impact fear). When opponents are very familiar with each other these evaluations may be brief. However, for strangers, or closely matched familiar individuals, or for situations involving ambiguity, considerable time may be devoted to the process of information-gathering and affective analysis.

This is an active, interactive, process. Evaluation of the behaviour and characteristics of the opponent in terms of resource or dominance challenge can be an especially subtle cognitive/affective event. While the process is by no means fully understood, such factors as the presence of the disputed resource, the specific behaviours of the putative challenger, and the characteristics of the challenger with reference to that specific resource all appear to be involved. As one example of the last consideration, male rats show much less offence to sexually immature or castrated (Barfield 1984) intruders than intact adult males. This apparently relates to the function of resident offence in protecting sexual perogatives (Flannelly and Lore 1977).

The fear side of this analysis may involve even more active forms of behaviour, which permit direct comparison of relevant features such as size (compared through juxtapositions of body organs or voice pitch) and strength (wrestling, pushing, shoving, or butting matches provide information). These mutually informative activities are frequently interpreted as displays, a concept allied to the view that infrahuman animals settle disputes without injury, through use of such displays and signals. At least for the species which we have personally studied, a more prosaic view of these activities seems sufficient: if the relevant comparisons suggest a high probability of defeat for one of the opponents, then this animal will usually cease to dispute. While members of most mammalian species are both willing and competent to inflict injury or death on a conspecific, it would be insanely maladaptive for every conspecific dispute to proceed directly to injury and death, regardless of the importance of the disputed item, or the disproportionality in size or ability of the participants.

A final characteristic of the affective cost–benefit analysis is that it takes time. Latency to offensive attack characteristically varies with the situation, the experience of the subject and so on, with longer latencies typical of situations in which there is some degree of fear, uncertainty, or novelty (Flannelly *et al.* 1984). This latency to attack may serve as a clue to the processes impacted by independent variable manipulations: low doses of ethanol often decrease attack latencies, producing higher levels of attack but only in the initial moments of an encounter (Blanchard, Flannelly, Hori, Blanchard and Hall 1987; Blanchard, Hori, Blanchard and Hall 1987). This pattern suggests that ethanol somehow short-circuits the normal affective cost–benefit analysis, though it is not clear whether information-processing or affect is more directly involved.

While the affective cost–benefit analysis concept is clearly related to game-theory models of fighting such as those developed by Maynard-Smith and his co-workers (cf. Maynard Smith and Price 1973), those models tend to focus on the overall adaptive qualities of different fighting strategies, while the affective cost–benefit analysis approach describes factors within conspecific interactions which determine relative attack-defence tendencies and behaviours. While the two approaches are to a considerable degree complementary, (Blanchard, Blanchard and Flannelly 1984), the specific focus of affective cost–benefit analyses on emotional and physiological mechanisms underlying conspecific interactions, and the empirical and experimental emphasis of the ethoexperimental model by which it is studied, make this situation especially suitable for the investigation of independent-variable effects on various aspects of conspecific aggressive and defensive behaviour.

Individual differences in offensive attack

In contrast to defensive attack, which tends to be quite stable within a given species and strain, individuals of the same sex and species may vary tremendously in terms of offensive attack tendencies. Some male rats, for example, consistently show no offence (Blanchard, Flannelly, Hori, Blanchard and Hall 1987), while others show high magnitude offensive behaviour with the same experience. The consistency of this individual variation has been documented for rats for spans stretching from early adulthood to old age and death (Blanchard, Takahashi and Blanchard 1977; Blanchard, Flannelly and Blanchard, in press).

This suggestion of stable individual differences in aggressiveness of infrahuman animals brings up the important topic of organismic, as opposed to either stimulus or response, correlates of offence. The factors responsible for these differences are not well understood. There appears to be a substantial genetic component to such variability, at least in rodents (Maxon *et al.* 1979), and in view of the growing body of work indicating that a number of neurochemical (Miczek *et al.* 1984) and hormonal (Barfield 1984; Brain 1984) systems influence the magnitude of offensive attack, it seems reasonable to believe that these may in part serve as mediating mechanisms for this genetic influence. However, experience can strongly influence offensive tendencies, so much so that early learning may be able to produce long-term changes in offence and dominance relationships (Nikoletseas and Lore 1981). In fact, individual differences in aggressive tendencies are probably best viewed as the result of an interaction between genetic and experiential factors resulting in stable characteristics of individual organisms.

HUMAN AGGRESSION

The animal model of aggression sketched above specifies the causes of offence, the form of offence and its allied motivations, goals, and reinforcement, the affective cost–benefit analysis leading to offensive attack, and some possible factors involved in individual variation in offence. How do these aspects of the model apply to human aggression? What are the differences between people and subhuman mammals which might be expected to alter these different aspects of aggression? Is there sufficient correspondence between the specifics of the animal model, and human aggressive behaviour, as to warrant the continued use of the first to suggest factors for study in the second?

There are several respects in which people differ substantially and systematically from lower mammals, that might be expected to have an impact on human aggression. The first aspect of human difference is an indisputable increase in cognitive ability, intimately tied to a uniquely developed mechanism for conceptualizing and communicating abstractions – human language. A second important consideration involves social structure: people are not only colonial, in the sense that they live in groups, but are also occupation and role-specialized to a degree unique among mammals. Moreover, these specializations are overwhelmingly based on learning. Such considerations suggest that, other factors notwithstanding, people should be capable of high levels of offence-promoting motivations and emotions in dominance dispute situations (as do other highly socialized species), and that human language should contain a number of terms abstracting, conceptualizing, and indeed reifying factors relating to aggression.

The causes of human aggression

Resource disputes

In many people, the resource dispute continues as a major source of offensive, angry aggression. The people who are most likely to show this in a relatively primitive and unchanged form are small children. One of the surest ways to make a small child angry is to take away a desired toy or other possession away. If the taker-away – the resource disputer, as it were – is another child, then a fight is not unlikely. When such fights do occur, they tend to be bound by the same sorts of inhibitory factors as occur in subhuman mammals: for example, an attack is more likely when the attacker is on his or her own home ground, when the other child is one whom the attacker does not fear, when the attacker has had previous success in reclaiming disputed resources through fighting, and so forth.

Up to a certain age, property disputes may be the most common cause of aggression: a group of college students, asked to provide retrospective descriptions of disputes with their siblings while they were in junior high school, provided data indicating that over 60 per cent of these involved access to, use of, or ownership of, property (Felson 1983).

As children grow up, however, fights over specific objects decrease somewhat (Hall *et al.* 1982), probably because codes relating to ownership and use of property becomes so clearly specified for most items and situations that misunderstandings and disagreements are less frequent. As they grow older, children generally learn what items belong to, or may be used by, themselves and which do not. Anyone violating these dicta may find him- or herself disputing, not only with the other putative owner, but with a range of authority figures, from parents to law-enforcement and judicial agencies. Thus, the apparently ubiquitous mammalian tendency to show some aggressive impulses in resource dispute situations is countered in human societies by cultural mechanisms centering around laws of ownership and property use.

A 'rights' model

The other side of the 'resource or dominance' system which serves as the immediate cause of offensive aggression in animals is also very greatly magnified in importance and complexity in human societies. Just as animal 'resources' have become human 'property', dominance relationships have been transformed into an elaborate system of rights and obligations which apply to almost every area of human life. In place of the old divisions of 'dominant' or 'subordinate', the list of human legal and social relationships, together with the rights and duties which these entail, is almost endless.

The term 'human rights' tends to suggest some fairly high-level abstractions - 'life, liberty and the pursuit of happiness', and so on. These elegant abstractions are, in fact, one end of the continuum, the intellectual and highly conceptualized end. At the opposite pole lies a much more primitive action concept which may be seen in the disputes of small children, as well as animals. This action concept involves a premiss that actions allowed in the past should be allowed in the future, that what one has consistently gotten away with becomes a 'right'. In addition, opportunistic animals that they, and we, are, children attempt to push the limits of what is allowed, easily assimilating new rights and giving up old rights only with great difficulty.

Sources of 'rights' schemas

While the behaviours of nonhuman mammals and preverbal children suggest some biological basis for the *motivation* to acquire and exercise 'rights', most of the specific content of an individual's conceptions of his or her own rights stems from experience. An example might be beneficial here. Between the ages of about one and four months, babies spend much time manipulating their own limbs, kicking out their legs and moving their arms, and observing the results. They appear, in fact, to be learning that they can move their own body parts through this voluntary effort. Babies reared in most western cultures, where infants' movements are less restricted, object strenuously to being tightly confined after they are several months of age. However, babies who have been consistently swaddled or enclosed in a backboard or other movement-limiting device from birth do not object to being confined, either originally or at the same ages where unrestricted infants do protest. While such infants clearly cannot verbalize any conception of their 'rights' to move their bodies at will, the unrestricted infant shows facial and body movements expressive of anger when this is denied, while the customarily swaddled infant does not.

In addition to direct experience, rights and obligations are taught through all the components of social learning. Books, television and films, conversations with family and friends, formal training in church and at school, all these add to a complex, but in most cases relatively consistent, view of what constitutes individual rights and obligations in human relationships. This system, piecemeal and often poorly verbalized as it is, is a major factor in many human behaviour patterns. It provides, for example, the basis for self-reinforcement for one's own good behaviours and shame or guilt when the person's actions violate his or her own strictures. Moreover, these same rules are applied – no doubt even more stringently – to the behaviours of others: violations by another party of one's own personal views of 'how things should be' are a major cause of anger (Averill 1982), even in the absence of specific hurt to the angry individual.

It should be emphasized again that one does not need to be a philosopher in order to be angry. For most people this value system is largely unexamined, and perhaps even unconscious. To a very considerable degree people tend to foreshorten the different analyses involved in conscious, cognitive evaluation of a situation in terms of their personal value systems, relying more on perceptions of the other individual's intent, as expressed through gestures or words. If confronted with someone who is acting furtively, people become suspicious;

sadness tends to elicit sympathy; both explicit and implicit challenges or insults are capable of eliciting anger, just as conspecific challenge elicits offence. It may easily be seen, however, that the underlying trigger for this anger is cognitive: an explanation which provides a satisfactory justification for the apparently challenging or insulting action will usually defuse anger.

Response correlates of offensive attack in people: behaviour, motivations, goals, and reinforcers

The actual behaviour patterns involved in human offensive attack have been given surprisingly little study. The facial expressions associated with anger have been investigated, with results suggesting a substantial agreement for persons of different cultural backgrounds (Izard 1972), and even for blind infants who could not possibly have learned these expressions on the basis of observation (Eibl-Eibesfeldt 1979). In terms of the actual attack, slaps and overarm or closed-fist blows tend to be associated with offence (Scott 1984), while screams, and biting and clawing are more typical of defensive attack (Blanchard and Blanchard 1984): human attack, however, so often involves the use of weapons and actions based on specialized 'marital arts' training that these differences are much less apparent than in animals.

The goals, motivations, and reinforcements in human offensive attack appear to be straightforwardly related to those of the animal model: one 'practical' or 'rational' set of motivations, goal, and reinforcements stems directly from the immediate cause of the attack, and involves the remedying of this cause. Thus, in a property dispute the goal (and, if achieved, the reinforcement for attack) is to gain access to, control of, or possession of, the disputed property. When a 'rights' dispute is involved, the goal is to assert one's right *vis-à-vis* the other, and the achievement of this goal is also reinforcing. Moreover, in most serious disputes, there is a parallel and sometimes even more powerful goal of hurting the other person. For some individuals and situations, this goal becomes virtually the sole emotional/motivational force of the dispute, and it is undoubtedly reinforcing; for highly aggressive children, stimuli

111

suggesting hurt or harm to another child (as a consequence of the subject's actions) lead to higher levels of such behaviour (Dubanoski and Tokioka 1981). Furthermore, these disparate goals of aggression can and do of course coexist: we have previously (Blanchard and Blanchard 1984) reported the self-analysis of an habitual wife abuser who explained that his abuse of his wife always occurred in the context of a quarrel or dispute. In this situation, wife-beating ended any quarrel in favour of the husband's viewpoint, and, second, he enjoyed hurting her when he was angry with her. The motivational, goal, or reinforcement value of harm to someone who has previously been successful at challenging one's rights has by no means gone unnoticed in human history: the sweetness of revenge is a theme which has been echoed in many cultures and languages.

Affective cost–benefit analyses in human aggression

Although there have been few studies directed specifically toward affective cost–benefit analyses in human aggression, recent work on anger has provided a number of intriguing items of information with reference to this process. One common finding is that angry people engage in a great deal of 'non aggressive' verbal behaviour such as talking the incident over with the opponent (Averill 1982), or searching for an explanation for the problem (Davitz 1952). This persistent association of anger with speech was also noted by Richardson (1918): 'Anger rarely, if ever, occurs without its vocal expression in some manner, if not by direct vocalization either by inner speech or voco-motor imagery' (quoted in Averill 1982).

The association of words, silent as well as spoken, with anger suggests that the angry person is almost inevitably engaged in some sort of analysis. There appears to be no parallel to this inwardly directed dialogue in other strong emotions such as fear or sexual arousal, and indeed there may be no externally directed words either. The anger analysis is, in fact, intrinsic to the emotion: Novaco's (1986) treatment of anger suggests that 'cognitive "mediation" should be understood as an automatic and intrinsic part of the perceptual process'. A corresponding association of cognitive processes and overt attack may be seen in the finding that child-abusing mothers make systematically different attributions of their children's behaviour than do normal mothers, seeing transgression or failure as a stable, internal characteristic (Larrance and Twentyman 1983). This characteristic human activity of angry dialogue and its common outcome of attribution of blame appears to correspond to one component of the affective cost–benefit analysis seen in lower mammals. This is the component involved in evaluation of the challenge represented by a conspecific, in which both the behaviour and relevant status characteristics (cf. sex, age, familiar, unfamiliar) of the opponent are assessed in relationship to either resource or dominance disputes. Again in parallel with the animal model, this process may be especially lengthy when people are confronted by ambiguous challenges or insults: the typical response is a highly motivated attempt to determine the opponent's intent, the possible degree of justification for his actions, and the degree of challenge to status or resources posed by this individual's actions. In responses to a questionnaire (Blanchard and Blanchard 1984) designed to tap differences between offensive and defensive aggression in people, subjects reported that their most likely response in an offence-eliciting scenario, was to 'demand an explanation' from the opponent. They also reported high levels of motivation to attack the instigator which were, however, inhibited by fear of the physical or social consequences of the attack. In the same study, but with a defence scenario, it was notable that defensive attack propensities did not suffer from such an inhibition.

When overt offensive attack is a real possibility, then the size, strength, and skill comparisons which occur in subhuman mammals as the inhibitory component of the affective cost–benefit analysis are also a prominent feature of human fighting. We remain deeply impressed by the only personally witnessed, spontaneous, 'real world' fight we have seen since becoming interested in aggression: two young men, obviously strangers to each other, collided in a doorway of a public bar. After (and while) words were exchanged, they postured, moved their upper bodies for maximum effect, pushed up sleeves to display biceps, and generally exchanged information relative to their fighting abilities, for some twenty-five minutes before actually exchanging the first blow. Numerous retrospective reports of physical fights suggest that such strength/skill revealing actions are common and typical of offensive fights among human males.

That fear does interact with offence-directed motivations to influence overt attack is unquestionable. One additional aspect of this influence may be seen in the relationship between punishment of attack, and future attack behaviour, a relationship which has, in one form or another, engendered a massive and often confusing literature. A recent review of this area (Blanchard and Blanchard 1986) suggests that when punishment is contingent on attack it is indeed inhibitory, and that even noncontingent fear may inhibit offence. This relationship appears to be as effective in people (cf. Donnerstein *et al.* 1975) as in lower mammals (Blanchard, Kleinschmidt, Flannelly and Blanchard 1984), and we have suggested (Blanchard and Blanchard 1984, 1986) that the patterns of punishment for aggression typical of different child-rearing systems may be a major factor in cultural differences in overt aggression.

A final aspect of the cost–benefit analysis for humans, as for animals, is the latency to attack, once an attack-provoking situation has arisen. Formal studies of overt human behaviour in 'real life settings' are virtually non-existent, but it is notable that latency to press a button ostensibly delivering shock to another person does increase as the shock levels set are increased (Jeavons and Taylor 1985), suggesting extended analysis in cases where higher magnitude attack is contemplated. It is also notable in this context that alcohol intake tends to decrease the latency to attack in humans (ibid.) as well as in rats (Blanchard, Hori, Flannelly and Blanchard 1987), indicating a very close and specific correspondence between measures taken in the animal model, and human behaviour.

Organismic correlates of offence: consistent individual differences in human aggression

As in other mammalian species, humans show long-term individual variations in aggressiveness. This has been documented consistently in studies spanning intervals from months to decades, often beginning in early childhood (for an excellent recent summary, see Olweus 1984a). This consistency does not, of course, necessarily reflect biological factors alone: almost any of the factors responsible for aggressive tendencies at a specific point in time may be involved in consistency of aggressive behaviour over time.

However, at least some of these factors do appear to be biological. In teenage boys, angry reactivity to an insult appears to be substantially correlated with testosterone levels (Olweus 1984b). Virkkunen and his colleagues have also found a number of biological factors, including low serum cholesterol (Virkkunen 1983; Virkkunen and Penttinen 1984) and low 5-hydroxyindoleacetic acid (Linnoila *et al.* 1983) associated with habitual violence, or with specific forms of violence.

The experiential factors associated with individual differences in aggression are perhaps the most interesting for students of human behaviour, and certainly offer the most scope for attempts to prevent individuals from developing abnormally high tendencies toward aggression or violence. These experiential factors include parental permissiveness for aggression, the quality of the emotional relationship between child and parents, parents' use of power assertive methods (Olweus 1984a, b) and levels of exposure to violent media (Eron and Huesman 1984).

What can an animal model say about such factors? In some cases, perhaps very little. We certainly do not, for example, expect to find modelling – and especially media-exposure – effects in lower mammals comparable to those in humans. On the other hand, we see no reason to doubt the usefulness of rodent models in clarifying the role of punishment variables such as contingency, celerity, and certainty, in the control of overt offensive aggression. While it is predictable that experiential factors in individual differences in aggression may permit fewer or less precise generalizations between lower mammals and humans than do some other aspects of the animal model, this is basically an empirical question, more in need of research than of discussion.

The usefulness of animal models for the study of human aggression

As the present discussion has indicated, there are a number of important aspects of aggression for which substantial parallels between animal models and human behavior can be discerned.

115

These include stimulus ('causes'), organismic (individual differences; biological factors; previous experience) and response (behavioural, motivational, goal, and reinforcement) aspects of the offence syndrome. The present chapter is hardly a comprehensive account of the existing literature in this area, being instead a schematic approach designed to illustrate correspondences in an important array of aggression phenomena. Even in this sketchy outline (and bearing in mind that relatively few attempts have been made to collect data on this relationship), these animal models have given results which appear to provide surprisingly precise parallels with a number of aspects of human aggressive behaviour.

This situation provides several spurs to future aggression research. First, the animal model itself is validated by the parallel with human findings, indicating a continuing value of this model in work designed to delineate a structure and function for mammalian aggression in general. This validation serves as an important impetus to further work with the rat model, work which will undoubtedly benefit from the higher degrees of control and wider range of experimental procedures possible with rodent subjects in comparison to human or even higher primate research.

Second, the specific dynamic relationships outlined in the animal model suggest a number of new directions for human aggression research. In fact, these models present a system which, in terms of completeness, closure, and recognition of diverse excitatory and inhibitory factors, provides a closer parallel to ordinary human experience of aggression than does the human aggression literature. Although human aggression research has enlarged its scope somewhat in recent years, this literature still tends to be fragmented, and rather simplistic, often relying on specific and sometimes poorly justified individual tasks, with little feel for aggression as a functional, dynamic system. Data from the animal model forces a focus on the larger issues in aggression, suggesting a number of studies that should be undertaken in order to provide a basic description of the major situational and behavioural aspects of human offensive and defensive attack. The animal work may thus serve an heuristic, hypothesis-generating function with reference to human work.

Finally, correspondences between the animal model and human aggression suggest that animal tests of the behavioural effects of specific independent variables may be in large part generalizable to human behaviour. Hormonal and especially pharmacological factors in aggression constitute one important set of independent variables which are already being investigated using this model or variants thereof. Pharmacological effects on various aspects of defence appear to be another, emerging focus. Experiential factors in aggression are perhaps a less systematic focus: however, the present analysis suggests that this model may be very appropriate for such studies, with the possible exception of work on factors involving long parent–child interaction, or imitation, neither of which is a strong feature of rodent behaviour.

We do not know where the parallels between animal and human aggression will break down, but we see no reason to believe that these models are anywhere near the end of their usefulness. Moreover, as they continue to work, they should provide encouragement for the development and use of natural, complete, dynamic animal models for other aspects of behaviour. Animal behavioural research is presently in a period of underfunding and neglect. Some of the reasons for this are economic and political; but scientists themselves have also not provided sufficient advocacy for what they are doing, perhaps because of inadequate belief in the value of the animal models they use, which can easily be extended to a more general scepticism concerning the validity of all animal models. Our own experience over a decade or more of work suggests that at least some animal models can be very valuable indeed, and that recognition of the deep parallels between some aspects of animal and human behaviour can provide an effective antidote to the scepticism of scientists and non-scientists alike.

REFERENCES

Adams, D.B. (1979) 'Brain mechanisms for offense, defense, and submission', *The Behavioral and Brain Sciences* 2: 201–41.
Archer, J. (1979) 'Behavioral aspects of fear', in W. Sluckin (ed.) *Fear in Animals and Man*, New York: Van Nostrand Reinhold.
——— (1988) *The Behavioural Biology of Aggression*, Cambridge: Cambridge University Press.

Averill, James R. (1982) *Anger and Aggression, An Essay on Emotion*, New York: Springer-Verlag.

Baenninger, L.P. (1970) 'Social dominance orders in the rat: 'spontaneous', food and water competition', *Journal of Comparative and Physiological Psychology* 71: 202–9.

Barfield, R.J. (1984) 'Reproductive hormones and aggressive behavior', in K.J. Flannelly, R.J. Blanchard, and D.C. Blanchard (eds) *Biological Perspectives on Aggression*, New York: Alan R. Liss.

Blanchard, D.C. and Blanchard, R.J. (1984) 'Affect and aggression: an animal model applied to human behaviour', in R. J. Blanchard and D.C. Blanchard (eds) *Advances in the Study of Aggression, Vol. 1*, Orlando: Academic Press.

—— (1986) 'Punishment and aggression: a critical reexamination', in R. J. Blanchard and D.C. Blanchard (eds) *Advances in the Study of Aggression, Vol. 2*, Orlando: Academic Press.

—— (1988) 'Ethoexperimental approaches to the biology of emotion', in *Annual Review of Psychology, Vol. 39*, Palo Alto: Annual Reviews.

Blanchard, D.C., Blanchard, R.J., and Flannelly, K.J. (1984) 'Cost–benefit analysis: an emotional calculus', *The Behavioral and Brain Sciences* 7: 103–4.

—— (1985) 'Social stress, mortality and aggression in colonies and burrowing habitats', *Behavioural Processes* 11: 209–15.

Blanchard, R.J., Blanchard, D.C., and Takahashi, L.K. (1978) 'Pain and aggression in the rat', *Behavioral Biology* 23: 291–305.

Blanchard, R.J., Flannelly, K.J. and Blanchard, D.C. (1986) 'Defensive behaviors of laboratory and wild *Rattus norvegicus*', *Journal of Comparative Psychology* 100: 101–7.

—— (in press) 'Life span studies of dominance and aggression in established colonies of laboratory rats', *Physiology and Behavior*.

Blanchard, R.J., Takahashi, L.K., and Blanchard, D.C. (1977) 'The development of intruder attack in colonies of laboratory rats', *Animal Learning and Behavior* 5: 365–9.

Blanchard, R.J., Blanchard, D.C., Flannelly, K.J., and Hori, K. (1986) 'Ethanol changes patterns of defensive behavior in wild rats', *Physiology and Behavior* 38: 645–50.

Blanchard, R.J., Blanchard, D.C., Takahashi, T., and Kelley, M.J. (1977) 'Attack and defensive behaviour in the albino rat', *Animal Behaviour* 25: 622–34.

Blanchard, R.J., Hori, K,. Blanchard, D.C., and Hall, J. (1987) 'Ethanol effects on aggression of rats selected for different levels of aggressiveness', *Pharmacology, Biochemistry and Behavior* 27: 641–4.

Blanchard, R.J., Hori, K., Flannelly, K., and Blanchard, D.C. (1987) 'The effects of ethanol on the offense and defensive behaviors of male and female rats during group formation',

Pharmacology, Biochemistry and Behavior 26: 61–4.

Blanchard, R.J., Kleinschmidt, C.K., Flannelly, K.J., and Blanchard, D.C. (1984) 'Fear and aggression in the rat', *Aggressive Behavior* 10: 309–15.

Blanchard, R.J., Flannelly, K., Hori, K., Blanchard, D.C., and Hall, J. (1987) 'Ethanol effects on female aggression vary with opponent size and time within session', *Pharmacology, Biochemistry and Behavior* 27: 645–8.

Blanchard, D.C., Hori, K., Rodgers, R.J., Hendrie, C.A., and Blanchard, R.J. (in press) 'Differential effects of $5HT_{1A}$ agonists and benzodiazepines on defensive patterns in wild *Rattus rattus*', in P. Bevan, B. Olivier, and T. Archer (eds) *Behavioral Pharmacology of 5 H–T*, New York: LEA.

Brain, P.F. (1981) 'Differentiating types of attack and defense in rodents', in P.F. Brain and D. Benton (eds) *Multidisciplinary Approaches to Aggression Research*, Amsterdam: Elsevier/North-Holland Biomedical Press.

——— (1984) 'Biological explanations of human aggression and the resulting therapies offered by such approaches: a critical evaluation', in R.J. Blanchard and D.C. Blanchard (eds) *Advances in the Study of Aggression, Vol. I*, New York: Academic Press.

Carr, A.T. (1979) 'The psychopathology of fear', in W. Sluckin (ed.) *Fear in Animals and Man*, New York: Van Nostrand Reinhold, pp. 199–234.

Curti, M.W. (1935) 'Native fear responses of white rats in the presence of cats', *Psychological Monographs* 46: 78–98.

Darwin, C. (1872) *Expression of the Emotions*, London: John Murray.

Davitz, J.R. (1952) 'The effects of previous training on postfrustration behavior', *Journal of Abnormal and Social Psychology* 47: 309–15.

Donnerstein, E., Donnerstein, M., and Evans, R. (1975) 'Erotic stimuli and aggression: facilitation or inhibition', *Journal of Personality and Social Psychology* 32: 237–44.

Dubanoski, R.A. and Tokioka, A.B. (1981) 'The effects of verbal pain stimuli on the behavior of children', *Social Behavior and Personality* 9: 159–62.

Edmunds, M. (1974) *Defence in Animals*, Harlow, Essex: Longmans.

Eibl-Eibesfeldt, I. (1979) 'Human ethology: concepts and implications for the sciences of man', *The Behavioral and Brain Sciences* 2: 1–57.

Ekman, P., Friesen, W.V., and Ellsworth, P. (1972) *Emotions in the Human Face*, New York: Pergamon.

Eron, L.D. and Huesman, L.R. (1984) 'The relation of prosocial behavior to the development of aggression and psychopathology', *Aggressive Behavior* 10: 201–12.

Felson, R.B. (1983) 'Aggression and violence between siblings', *Social Psychology Quarterly* 47: 271–85.

Flannelly, K.J. and Blanchard, R.J. (1981) 'Dominance: cause or

119

description of social relationships', *The Behavioral and Brain Sciences* 4: 438–40.

Flannelly, K.J. and Lore, R. (1977) 'Observations of the subterranean activity of domesticated and wild rats (*Rattus norvegicus*): a descriptive study', *Psychological Records* 27: 315–29.

Flannelly, K.J., Flannelly, L., and Blanchard, R.J. (1984) 'Adult experience and the expression of aggression', in K.J. Flannelly, R.J. Blanchard, and D.C. Blanchard (eds) *Biological Perspectives on Aggression*, New York: Alan R. Liss.

Grant, E.C. (1963) 'An analysis of the social behavior of the male laboratory rat', *Behaviour* 21: 260–81.

Hall, E., Lamb, M.E., and Perlmutter, M. (1982) *Child Psychology Today*, New York: Random House.

Hutchinson, R.R. (1983) 'The pain–aggression relationship and its expression in naturalistic settings', *Aggressive Behavior* 9: 229–42.

Izard, C.E. (1972) *Patterns of Emotions: A New Analysis of Anxiety and Depression*, New York: Academic Press.

Jeavons, C. and Taylor, S. (1985) 'The control of alcohol-related aggression', *Aggressive Behavior* 11: 93–101.

Larrance, D.T. and Twentyman, C.T. (1983) 'Maternal attributions and child abuse', *Journal of Abnormal Psychology*, 92: 449–57.

Leshner, A.I. and Nock, B.L. (1976) 'The effects of experience on agonistic responding: an expectancy theory interpretation', *Behavioral Biology* 17: 561–6.

Linnoila, M., Virkkunen, M., Scheinin, M., Nuutila, A., Rimon, R., and Goodwin, F.K. (1983) 'Low cerebrospinal fluid 5-hydroxyindoleacetic acid concentration differentiates impulsive from nonimpulsive violent behavior', *Life Sciences* 33: 2609–14.

Marks, I.M. (1969) *Fears and Phobias*, London: William Heinemann Medical Books.

—— (1987) *Fears, Phobias and Rituals*, Oxford: Oxford University Press.

Maxon, S.C., Platt, T., Shrenker, P., and Trattner, A. (1979) 'Interaction of Y-chromosomal and autosomal gene(s) in the development of intermale aggression in mice', *Behavior Genetics* 9: 219–25.

Maynard-Smith, J. and Price, G.R. (1973) 'The logic of animal conflict', *Nature* 246: 15–18.

Miczek, K.A., Kruk, M.R., and Olivier, B. (1984) *Ethopharmocological Aggression Research*, New York: Alan R. Liss.

Nikoletseas, M. and Lore, R. (1981) 'Aggression in domesticated rats reared in a burrow-digging environment', *Aggressive Behavior* 7: 245–52.

Novaco, R.W. (1986) 'Anger as a clinical and social problem', in R.J. Blanchard and D.C. Blanchard (eds) *Advances in the Study of Aggression, Vol. 2*, Orlando: Academic Press.

Olweus, D. (1984a) 'Development of stable aggressive reaction patterns in males', in R.J. Blanchard and D.C. Blanchard (eds)

Advances in the Study of Aggression, Vol. 1, Orlando: Academic Press.

────── (1984b) 'Stability in aggressive and withdrawn, inhibited behavior patterns', in R.M. Kaplan, V.J. Konecni, and R.W. Novaco (eds) *Aggression in Children and Youth*, The Hague: Nijhoff.

Potegal, M. (1979) 'The reinforcing value of several types of aggressive behavior: a review', *Aggressive Behavior* 5: 353–73.

Robinson, R. (1984) 'Norway rat', in I.L. Mason (ed.) *Evolution of Domesticated Animals*, London and New York: Longman.

Russell, P.A. (1979) 'Fear evoking stimuli', in W. Sluckin (ed.) *Fear in Animals and Man*, New York: Van Nostrand Reinhold.

Scott, J.P. and Fredericson, E. (1951) 'The causes of fighting in mice and rats', *Physiological Zoology* 26: 273–309.

────── (1984) 'Advances in aggression research: the future', in R.J. Blanchard and D.C. Blanchard (eds) *Advances in the Study of Aggression, Vol. 1*, Orlando: Academic Press.

Virkkunen, M. (1983) 'Serum cholesterol levels in homicidal offenders', *Neuropsychobiology* 10: 65–9.

Virkkunen, M. and Penttinen, H. (1984) 'Serum cholesterol in aggressive conduct disorder: a preliminary study', *Biological Psychiatry* 19: 435–9.

Wilson, E.O. (1975) *Sociobiology*, Cambridge, Mass.: The Belknap Press of Harvard University Press.

Chapter 6

A SCHOOL FOR MEN: AN ETHNOGRAPHIC CASE STUDY OF ROUTINE VIOLENCE IN SCHOOLING

JOHN BEYNON

INTRODUCTION

The approach taken in this chapter is consistent with the argument that real life acts of violence must be understood in their context of social structures, relationships, and interactions. Most research on pupil violence is decontextualized from the school locale in which it occurs, whilst very little has been written to date on teacher violence. What follows is intended, in small measure, to rectify these shortcomings through a naturalistic examination of violence in Lower Secondary School [children aged 11–12]; the purposes it served to further both teacher and pupil tasks-at-hand; and the meanings it held for them. It must be made clear, however, that I did not enter Lower School to study violence *per se*. I undertook fieldwork on a wider project, namely the initial encounters between teachers and pupils at the start of the latter's secondary school careers and to observe staff induction strategies towards the new intake of 11–12 year olds; and to discover how, in turn, pupils reacted to the new regime and its varied academic and disciplinary demands (Beynon 1985a). In this chapter I argue the case for 'educational ethnography' in that I seek to show that both *actual* and *symbolic violence* in Lower Secondary School could only be understood through the meanings it held for teachers and pupils alike and its functions in the following: *temporal* (time of year demands); the *historical/institutional* (the 'secondary modern' origins of the dominant educational paradigm in Lower School, as propagated by the headmaster, Mr Changeable); the *pedagogical* (highly traditional, transmission teaching); and the *ecological* (the characteristics of site and area) *contexts* of Lower School. Routine violence was, indeed, one of the ways teachers and pupils coped with the process of establishment at the onset of the school year.

Lower School housed the 350 first-year boys of Victoria Road, a large 11–18, all-male comprehensive in Seatown, South Wales. During the period of initial encounters (here defined as the first eight weeks of the autumn term), institutional and teachers' personal demands are announced before becoming settled and taken-for-granted as part of the everyday, negotiated order.

To observe how teachers introduced their subjects and ground rules, and how pupils reacted and established themselves with staff and peers, I collected data through participant observation and followed up with formal and informal interviewing. I sat in the back of classrooms and accompanied one class, Form 1Y across the school day. As an outsider I had first to be accepted by teachers and ensure I was regarded by pupils as a trusted adult in whom they could confide, rather than just another authority figure (see Beynon 1983 for a discussion of the difficulties of the fieldwork process). A number of the fourteen Lower School staff I observed employed threats and physical coercion from the outset as part of the institutional 'welcome' (Goffman 1968). Boys were hit, pushed, and shaken, even by the apparently docile Mr Piano who, on discovering in the second week that I was a former teacher, commented, 'Well, well, fancy that! I can start thumping them now!', erroneously assuming that the experience had naturally led me to accept teacher violence as legitimate. This is surprising in that teachers have good reason to conceal violence: it can, at worst, lead to the courts, humiliation, and dismissal; at the least, to conflict with parents and the local authority. In Lower School, however, a hard core of male teachers regarded coercive measures as synonymous with good teaching itself and, therefore, a virtue to be upheld. They were mostly former 'secondary modern school teachers[1] who had lost out in career terms to the grammar school staff when Victoria Road comprehensive emerged out of an amalgamation a decade earlier. A high degree of uncompromising discipline was a mark of their identity as a group. Not all their colleagues agreed with them, but the rhetoric of tough, disciplinary schoolmastery, reminiscent of Grace's (1978) elementary teachers, predominated.[2] Therefore, shaking, pushing, and cuffing boys (which would have been deemed assaults outside in the street) were widely accepted as part of the Lower School landscape.

In observing such violence the researcher is invariably placed in an ethical dilemma: there were occasions when I clearly disapproved of what was happening and I felt like saying so, even intervening. That would have wrecked my stance as a fly-on-the-wall, 'neutral' observer and would probably have had no effect in preventing teacher or pupil violence in the long term. Most violence threatens personal rights, undermines social order, and is illegal. However, some violence is traditionally and commonsensically deemed acceptable between teachers and pupils. It takes the form of 'manhandling', a term particularly appropriate to Lower School in that it was male teachers who were the aggressors and women staff (with one exception) rarely threatened or hit boys. The manhandling increased the more accepted I became as a 'temporary' member of staff and, as the weeks passed, I inevitably moved from 'outsider' towards 'insider' status (Gold 1958). Violence towards pupils was clearly so deeply embedded in these teacher's practices of crowd control that no apology or explanation was ever offered. Rather, it was flaunted as necessary at this time to establish authority. From the earliest days of the fieldwork I became increasingly interested in the 'routine violence', its forms and occurrences; its meaning for both parties; and the functions it served as part of teacher–pupil induction and coping strategies, as well a its role in pupils' provocative 'sussing' of teachers. Routine, but often spectacular shows of violence appeared important at the start of the year as the moral climate of Lower School was being negotiated and was worthy of my closer attention.

Having established that regular, routine violence was significant at the start of the year to the establishment of the working and moral order of Lower School, I want briefly to say something about ethnography and its increasing application in recent times to the study of educational processes, given that this is an area with which some readers may not be familiar.

ETHNOGRAPHY AND EDUCATIONAL ETHNOGRAPHY

Early social investigators, as well as the great Chicago sociologists of the earlier part of the century, espoused naturalistic research methods, including the life history.[3] The advent of positivism narrowed research options and survey research increasingly came to be held and self-sufficient. Here was a paradigm characterized by quantification, with variables manipulated and measured; hypotheses confirmed, modified or falsified; appeals made through deduction to universal laws; and a strong emphasis upon both replicability and the generalization of findings. Its mode of experiment-based research modelled on the natural sciences established itself as the orthodoxy in the social sciences, although post-Second World War the spirit of George Herbert Mead's symbolic interactionism (1934) was kept alive by scholars such as Blumer (1969). From the mid-1960s naturalistic research was re-invigorated and placed on a firmer methodological basis by, amongst others, Goffman (1971), Lofland (1976), Denzin (1978), and Schatzman and Strauss (1973), who imported a range of relevant theoretical insights from symbolic interactionism, phenomenology, ethnomethodology, and sociolinguistics.[4] Indeed, nowhere is this renewed faith in naturalistic, qualitative research better illustrated than in Schutz's classic 1964 essay, 'The Stranger', which attacks positivism's causal science of human life, its standardized procedures, and rejects any simplistic stimulus–response model of human interaction. On the contrary, Schutz argues that attention must be paid to the natural state of settings and the interpretations and 'rationality' of the actors therein explored. Meanings are held to guide behaviour and shape people's actions. However, the same stimulus can mean different things to different people and even to the same person on different occasions. Individuals do not merely respond to, but interpret, circumstances, and the research enterprise must, as a consequence, focus on motives, beliefs, and attitudes, as well as behaviour, in real-life physical and temporal contexts,

JOHN BEYNON

not in artificial ones. Schutz maintains that social phenomena
are distinct from natural phenomena because human actions are
founded on values and interpretations. To capture these the
fieldworker must engage in prolonged fieldwork; explore the
implicit, taken-for-granted processes and assumptions underlying interaction in settings; and, if necessary, render the familiar
'anthropologically strange'. S/he must participate in the host
culture and, by retaining his/her objectivity, can generate
insights unavailable even to the actors trapped inside it.

The case for qualitative, naturalistic, ethnographic research is
that it alone, through the systematic deployment of multiple
data sources, can penetrate research settings and allow the
researcher to unravel the complexity of everyday social
processes, meanings, and interpretations. Moreover, it is good
at generating and substantiating hypotheses, thus opening up
the possibility of new theory emerging, 'grounded' (Glaser and
Strauss 1967) in high quality, first-hand data. It facilitates lines
of analyses unavailable to armchair theorists and often
challenges assumptions made about the activities and perspectives of members of a particular culture or institution.
Moreover, it can be used to test and correct the generalizations
of which macro theorists are sometimes guilty. It must be
stressed, however, that ethnography is not reducible to a set of
field research procedures drawn from social anthropology: it has
a well-developed theoretical basis.

Having stated its strengths, the case most frequently levelled
against ethnography is that it is little more than fleshed out,
academicized journalism and that its good points are more than
counterbalanced by the heavy time demands it makes on
researchers. Allied to this is the charge that it operates on the
level of description and that ethnographies are typically small-
scale, one-off, atheoretical little cameos which simplify in that
they are tied to observable forms and omit the unseen (macro)
currents operating externally on the setting and its members. As
a consequence, the argument goes, ethnography fails to produce
conceptual generalizations beyond the particular. The reply is
that this need not be so, and educational ethnographers, aware
of the charge, are increasingly introducing into their analyses
concepts which span micro and macro concerns (for example,
'coping strategy' as used in the work of Andy Hargreaves (1978,

Figure 6.1 Different kinds of theoretical approaches in ethnography

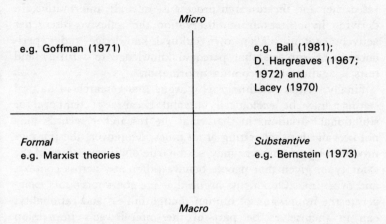

1979, 1980); Woods (1977, 1980a and b, 1983); Pollard (1980, 1982, 1984); and Beynon (1984, 1985a)). Furthermore, one could object that the macro and micro levels are not so readily separable as some critics assume but, in practice, interpenetrate one another. David Hargreaves (1978), for example, suggests that it is far more profitable to consider different kinds of theory, namely the 'micro formal'; 'micro substantive'; 'macro formal'; and 'macro substantive'. The formal is defined as abstract and theoretical, whereas the substantive refers to accounts and theories relating to the individual setting. Examples of the different kinds of theorizing are set out in Figure 6.1.

A second charge habitually voiced against ethnography concerns the 'contamination' of data by the fieldworker: moreover, in presenting a final report s/he has to prune and shape and thus creates, it is alleged, a highly selective and even idiosyncratic picture. A countercharge would be that all research involves selection and interpretation and that data untouched by the researcher-as-neutral-vessel is impossible: behind the planning and execution of all data collection is the researcher's guiding hand. Moreover, ethnographers hold that the reflexive researcher acknowledges from the outset that s/he is part of the setting and cannot avoid having an effect on it. Indeed, s/he consciously employs commonsense knowledge and openly exploits reactivity in that how people respond to both the researcher and the research process is, in itself, informative. In deriving hypotheses from observation the reflexive researcher actively exploits his/her own cultural knowledge and experiences: s/he subjects that personal knowledge to scrutiny and tests it against the incoming information.

Finally, critics of ethnography argue that research in natural settings may be ecologically invalid because of temporal or situational variations in that what the researcher records may not be valid for that setting at all times. Moreover, the findings produced by an observer may not be true of other settings of the same type, given that people behave differently across contexts and over time. Opponents argue that members' accounts exaggerate the impression of human thoughtfulness and rationality; can in themselves be part of the interviewee's impression management; and overemphasize the purposefulness of actions. Furthermore, what is actually going on need not be what participants say is taking place. Such criticisms, however, fail to acknowledge that ethnographers combine, verify, and cross-reference data sources, including participant observation, over a lengthy period in the field; the members' accounts, too, are taken and retaken over a lengthy period. The time-scale means that 'shopfronting' or the 'putting on a good face' factor, cannot be maintained and eventually crumbles: the setting and people's actions therein soon reflect the way things normally are, for no setting can maintain an elaborate pretence in the face of a persistent and perceptive observer.

The 'anthropology of schooling' was already a well-developed tradition in the United States[5] before it was placed on a firm footing in this country in the late 1960s by David Hargreaves (1967) and Colin Lacey (1970). In their studies of Lumley school and Hightown grammar respectively, neither sought to control variables, but focused through prolonged and intensive fieldwork on the internal processes of schooling. In doing so they were offering an alternative to the dominant paradigm of 'black box' research which dealt only in inputs and outputs rather than what actually went on inside schools. They rejected the 'political arithmetic' of educational inequality and focused, rather, on what schooling does; how it is done; to whom and, thereby, switched from a concern with product to one with process. That tradition has now been consolidated by a host of educational ethnographers over the past decade and a half, notably by Ball (1981); Delamont (1973, 1980, 1983); Hammersley and Atkinson (1983); Turner (1983); and Woods (1983), amongst others, all of whom have investigated members' cultural knowledge and patterns of interaction within schools and classrooms. Perhaps the best case for educational ethnography is still that provided by David Hargreaves in an article published in 1978, in which he argues that ethnography, with its underpinning of symbolic interactionism, has at least five functions which can be utilized in studying school processes:

(1) it offers an insight into actors' points of view and 'rationality' (the 'appreciative');
(2) it can help develop a conceptual language (the 'designatory');
(3) it charts actions, accounts, and processes (the 'reflective');
(4) it analyses changes and can warn against mistakes with reference to innovation (the 'immunological');
(5) it can correct macro or quantitative oversimplifications of settings or groups (the 'corrective').

I now turn my attention to the Lower School data on violence which I encountered at the start of the autumn term and discussed with teachers and boys. I begin with pupils' perceptions of teacher and peer violence and its role in 'sussing' and provisional typing (Beynon 1984), ending with an examination of the many 'myths of aggression' I recorded at this time.

PUPIL PERCEPTIONS OF
TEACHER VIOLENCE

Pupil perspectives of teacher violence fall into three categories, namely:

(a) aggression that was 'funny' as opposed to genuinely frightening or dangerous;
(b) 'real' violence; and
(c) violence on pupils which was deemed either 'deserved and fair' or 'undeserved and unfair'.

Funny violence

This often took the form of a pretend fight when teacher and pupils played at violence, or the physical education teacher's ritual slippering of offenders:

> When we arrived back in the yard, Mr Megaphone gathered 1Y around him whilst he dressed down Ginger for running on the road and racing across the junction without looking on the way back from Seaview Park. 'It's the dap for you, twit!' he said, 'and for any other idiots like you!' He then let the class into the changing rooms. Here he produced what he termed his 'size 11', ceremoniously bent Ginger over, and walloped him half a dozen times. Ginger hopped around smiling and rubbing his backside. 'Anyone else want a sore bum?' asked Mr Megaphone. There was a chorus of 'No thanks' and laughter. 'You'll listen to what I tell you next time', Mr Megaphone said to Ginger, 'or I'll really make it hurt!'

Alternatively, it could take the form of 'real' violence, but enjoyed from the standpoint of audience, not target. The following incident was talked about by pupils with relish for months afterwards because Mr Stern had come off worse in the encounter with the clowning Ginger:

> Mr Stern completely lost his temper with Ginger who was fooling and laughing idiotically behind his back as he stooped over a boy and marked his work. Mr Stern turned and lashed out with his fist. Ginger moved his head back and Mr Stern's knuckles came into contact with Ginger's front teeth. It seemed to have the same effect on Mr Stern as if Ginger had bitten him. Ginger was unhurt, but Mr Stern grabbed him and flung him out of the room shaking and whacking him around the head and shoulders as he did so. He was white-faced in fury and roared: 'Next time I hit you, idiot, close your mouth first!'

Violence was often enjoyed in retrospect when it was re-interpreted and embellished, as was this incident (see 'myths of aggression' later):

As Miss Floral was taking the afternoon register Ginger
was talking loudly and turning around to prod and push
the boy in the desk behind. Mr Changeable must have
spotted him through the glass panel in the classroom door
because it suddenly swung open and he strode in, walked
straight up to Ginger, smacked him across the head and
shoulder and pulled him out of his chair. 'Don't you
realise Miss Floral is marking a legal document, you
young ignoramus? Don't you?' he shouted. 'You will sit
quiet and behave yourself, do you understand? And that
goes for every single one of you!' With that he turned and
left, saying nothing to Miss Floral.

Months later Ginger was still recalling what had taken place
with considerable pleasure:

Ginger: I got clouted a first time an' all when I was talking
when Miss Floral was doing the register and Mr
Changeable came in behind me and then gave me a clout.
I was sitting down and he clocked me around the
shoulder.
J.B.: Did that worry you?
Ginger: No, 'cos it don't hurt because there's padding in
the shoulders in the blazer! [laughter]
King: And when I was in the yard in the first couple of
days, I was looking around and I got a clout. He chucked
me out of the barn [dinner hall], didn't he, Mike? I
laughed me head off at him. It didn't hurt . . ..
J.B.: Do you think a school can operate without physical
punishment?
Ginger: It wouldn't be any good without physical
punishment because you wouldn't be able to have a laugh
. . ..
King: No, you couldn't have a laugh.
Ginger: . . . you couldn't have a laugh watching other
people getting hit. That's the best fun in school.
King: . . . it wouldn't be a laugh unless the teachers hit
you, would it?

Funny violence was the boys' principal source of laughter,

enjoyment, and excitement in Lower School. It was repeatedly talked about by them as humour, as the following excerpts illustrate:

> You can't help laughing at it . . . it's just so funny it creases you up . . . it's really exciting and funny . . . it breaks up the day . . . it's a comedy . . . it's far better than Charlie's Angels . . . you come to school and you look forward to it happening . . . it's like a holiday camp . . ..

Although they subscribed to the view that physical punishment was necessary for school order (it was both proper and expected), they also argued that without it the daily experience of school would be less of a laugh, less enjoyable. What was intended as a deterrent to bad behaviour and mucking around was, paradoxically, transformed by pupils into 'a laugh'. They therefore created combative scenes and interludes of aggressive confrontation with teachers as a means of transforming the reality of school. This observation is supported by those writers who argue that for many pupils 'laughing' is the only satisfying part of school life and what makes it tolerable (for example, Walker *et al.* 1975; Walker and Goodson 1977; Woods 1983). Lower School boys spoke of 'laughing' and 'mucking' as the vehicles for redefining the school experience and creating a 'holiday camp atmosphere'.[6] Teacher violence was repeatedly appropriated and used by boys as they exploited and transformed teacher outbursts to turn the tables on their aggressors. Violence became the principle source of entertainment to neutralize the monotony, as well as being used by some to 'bodybuild'[7] – that is, impress peers through acts of cheeky bravado against staff. Indeed, the highest peer status was earned by standing up to teachers, exploiting their physical superiority through cockiness and defiances:

(I) As Mr Changeable lectured and 'drilled' the boys into straight lines in the yard at lunchtime today, King was seen to spit on the back of the boy in front of him. Mr Changeable went berserk and belted King so hard he nearly knocked him over. Absolute silence as he propelled King up to the front by the scruff of the neck. He allowed the others to 'lead on' into the 'barn' [lunch hall] and I left him lecturing King on hygiene and good manners. The amazing thing was how quickly King recovered his cockiness: he stands up to the teachers and doesn't appear to fear being hit, but trades off such assaults and is making his reputation that way.

(II) If a teacher starts throwing you around or belting you around the head an' that, like Mr Changeable does, well the thing is not to cry like a little girl or cower in the corner covering your head like some of them do! You stand up all cocky-like and laugh at 'em and give your mates a smile and things like that an' cheek 'em an' that! Like Mr Changeable goes to me, 'Did that hurt, King?' and I goes 'No!' all shouted out and he goes wild and goes 'Sir! Sir! You call me Sir!' and I just looks at him. If he hits me again this year I'm going to dead-leg him in the balls! [Laughter]

'Body building' (by grinning; waving at friends; retaliating with cheek and gestures; not showing hurt, pain, or contrition), was carried out with style and panache to make some teachers look silly, 'soft', and ineffectual. Many of them, on the other hand, admired boys who could take violence in this truculent manner: it was all part of Lower School's machismo culture as a 'school for men', a definition jointly created and supported by the activities of many teachers and many pupils. If boys engaged in 'bodybuilding' based on the ability to 'take violence', then a mirror image was found in the staffroom where some staff consciously publicized themselves through their ability to 'dish it out'. Here, for example, is what one of the rugby teachers said:

The young O'Brien is going the same way as the older one did. He was the only boy who the staff actually asked me to hurt. 'Get him on the rugby field' they said, 'really hurt him in a tackle!' So I did! He was like an angel after that. This kid looks to be the same – all mouth until he's sorted out. Just give me the word.

'Real' violence, or when the laughter stopped

'Real' violence was when a boy was either hurt; in danger of being hurt; or when events escalated beyond participants' control:

> *Bright*: Mr Megaphone, he just says, 'Right, next one to talk gets the dap', and he just bends you over and goes like that, whack! That's alright, but when teachers hit you around the head and throw you around the hall without warning, well that's all wrong . . ... Same with Peter Ross in our class, she [Mrs Bear] really lost her temper with him and caught him and sent him flying. She went too far, just lost all control over herself.
> *J.B.*: Was that funny?
> *Bright*: No, it wasn't. Not at all funny.

Real violence was most likely to erupt if pupils were foolhardy enough to stray into the teacher's personal domain:

> *Martin*: Sometimes when someone gets beaten up it isn't funny. Like in Geography Mr Scouse was saying how he had a nice car and a nice wife and a nice house an' that and when he said a nice wife somebody started to laugh and wolf-whistle. He thought it was Jason Slow – but it wasn't him – and he just went for him and grabbed him by the neck and lifted him about two feet off the ground. If the window had been open he'd have thrown him through – he was really that mad with him! That wasn't funny 'cos you could see Mr Scouse's expression, the expression on his face, that he was really mad, you know. I couldn't laugh then. If anyone had laughed he'd have gone really mad.

The boundary between funny and unamusing, real violence was being explored and settled at the time of the study, as boys defined the degree of teacher violence that was acceptable and also the style in which it was executed. The worst case of real violence I witnessed was when Michael Long (who had misbehaved throughout assembly, was kept behind, and then adopted a very provocative tone with the headmaster, Mr Changeable) was pushed backwards over a bench and fell awkwardly. He was clearly hurt and cried, much to the teacher's consternation. At a later date Long commented:

> He knew when he'd done wrong because he came to see me at break, then at the end of the afternoon, putting his arm around me and buttering me up. He'd nearly smashed me up and now he kept telling me it was my fault! The the next day he asked me if I'd said anything to my parents, but I hadn't. It would have been his word against mine. I thought he'd broken my back.

Fair and unfair violence

Boys held that teachers were duty-bound to use physical coercion in order to keep order and scorned 'soft' teachers:

> Teachers got a right to hit, mind you, because we're here to learn and they're here to teach us and they get paid for keeping us quiet and learning us and telling us what to do and not be noisy. I think that the only good teachers are the ones who smash you around because you'll learn in time 'cos the more they hit you, the more you'll learn to shut up.

They sanctioned 'fair' violence and held that 'good' teachers followed a protocol of warnings and avoided humiliating or hurting pupils. They use fair violence, which was held to be a central element in the teacher–pupil contract:

(I) A good teacher hits you sometimes when you deserve it, and a bad teacher just whacks you for no reason. Like some women.

(II) Mr Stern [a Maths master] was seen as a good teacher because, although 'hard', he warned pupils before punishing them. Ginger explained: 'I don't dislike Mr Stern even when he hits me 'cos he's a good teacher . . . he'll give you about three chances, about three, dun he, Dave?'

(III) I mess around and gets done a first time and then I starts talking and messing around and gets done a second time, and I ease up then, but you usually take it that a third time you have to go to Mr Changeable and get the cane, detention, or double detention, or the teacher wallops you. When they lose control, it happens all of a sudden, you can't control it.

(IV) *Ginger*: But she's got so much harder and she handles us real good, dun she, Dave?
King: She's got all hard, smacks you around and pulls you around by the hair. Whack! like that, right across the nut.

'Bad' teachers, on the other hand, 'picked on' or victimized pupils, either employing illegitimate violence that hurt or was dangerous (for example, heavy punching or vicious slapping across the head; the sudden hooking of chairs from under boys, and so on); or they set out to humiliate (for example, by making a pupil cry in front of the class):

Ginger: I haven't been made to cry once by the teachers – well only once. It was Mr Changeable, no, it was Mr Megaphone, PE, that was it. I want to forget about it.
King: Being made to cry is worst that can happen. I mean, if you don't cry it's just a laugh. But if you cry . . .
Ginger: Yes, they all made fun of me. They said 'A ya baby!' and all that. It's unfair to make you cry . . .
King: Phil Raymond was made to cry the other day, wun he! Mr New just tapped him on the head! Raymond said he cried because he'd had a bad day, but no-one believed him.

Indeed, the most humiliating thing that could happen to a boy was to be physically dominated, hurt, or 'showed up' by a woman teacher (Beynon 1985b). Finally, the two teacher-types boys disliked were either dangerously coercive 'sadists', or 'moody' ones, whose rapidly changing tempers meant they were hard to predict. Mr Changeable was the prime example of the former:

(I) Long was talking and laughing as boys filed out of the hall into classrooms after assembly. Mr Changeable rushed up, clouted him and threw him across the hall towards the office. Unfortunately he tripped over a gym mat [which was rolled and stored near Mr Changeable's room] and fell awkwardly. For a moment I thought he really was badly injured until he stood up holding his back sobbing. Mr Changeable put his arm round the boy's shoulders and was suddenly very solicitous. There must have been at least a hundred boys left in the hall and yet there was absolute silence.

(II) The form were queueing up outside the French room. There was a lot of movement between classes and boys were milling around. David King was using his weight to barge other boys out of his way. Suddenly Mr Changeable [the Head of the Lower School] shot across the hall . . . and manhandled King, then smacked him loudly over the head with a book. 'I've told you about barging before, boy' he shouted, 'Don't fool around with me! I'm more than a little tired of your ignorant behaviour, King!' There was absolute silence throughout the hall, boys quickly disappearing into their classes.

Mr Scouse, on the other hand, was 'moody':

You get to know what mood a teacher's in. Like Mr Scouse, you've got to know when he's in a laughing, mess-around mood and when he's in a nasty mood. Sometimes he'll have a laugh, other times he'll smash you around the room. It depends what he feels like.

I gathered ample evidence to illustrate how some Lower School boys purposely provoked teachers who were subsequently judged and provisionally typed on the basis of their reactions (whether 'hard', 'soft', 'moody', or 'sadist').[8] The nature of the teacher response provided pupils with valuable evidence far more trustworthy than the claims individuals made for themselves during early meetings. As one boy said, to know what a teacher was really like he had to 'put his fist where his mouth is!' What the pupils termed 'sussing' was composed of a wide variety of hypotheses – testing strategies by a network (what, in my study, I term a 'fraternity') of 1Y pupils as they negotiated with staff the working climates of classrooms. Through it was discovered what could only be found out in this way – namely, whether an agitated teacher, who had been placed in a difficult position, would employ violence to keep order; and, if so, whether it was 'soft', acceptable, or 'real' violence (Beynon 1984; Beynon and Atkinson 1984; Beynon 1985a):

(I) At first you don't know the teachers and you have to judge them by their reactions. Some give lines, some whack you or tell you off, and others throw you outside. You just got to see how they act. You got to suss them out – there's no other way.

(II) *King*: You go for a teacher's weak points, don't you?
Blond: Early in the morning or right at the end of the day, that's the time 'cos you know they're tired after a day's work.

(III) . . . in that first week we were messing around like anything and he took us back behind after a lesson and we knew that if he was soft that he would just tell us off, and if he was hard he'd hit us, and he hit us! He smacked Kingsy against the wall and kicked us both up the backside . . . that's how we found out about Mr New.

It was solicited teacher violence to establish the boundaries of tolerance; establish the ground rules for working relationships; and help crystallize identities. If it was to test teachers it was also a means for a boy to 'bodybuild' and adopt a high profile as an adventurous lad, as was pupil–pupil violence in the yard and the enviorns of Lower School. Violence of this sort was only understandable through the eyes of participants, taking into account the time of year and the urgency for boys to find out about teachers and establish, in this case, an oppositional pupil culture emanating from a small, tight group of 1Y 'muckers' (Beynon and Delamont 1984).

PUPIL VIOLENCE

Violence was not, of course, solely associated with teachers: in my time in Lower School I observed pupil violence in classrooms, corridors, playground, and outside school.[9] Definitions of acceptable and unacceptable pupil violence were being settled at the same time as those relating to teachers. Violence was observed being used to sort out a 'league table' of 'hard' and

138

'soft' pupils. Battles between boys were discussed and some-times resulted in the vanquished losing face and having to accept a changed reputation. An extensive typology, based on boys' physical prowess or lack of it, existed, with 'bullies' and 'bigheads' as the most feared and disliked, and 'hards' admired as playground brawlers.

> *Long*: Lawrence Klee could walk into any form in the school and smash up anyone who stood in his way. He could walk through all the desks and just push them out of the way with his legs. He's that hard I'd doubt anyone would stop him. What's he, thirteen stone?

There were widespread attacks on boys regarded as 'queers' or 'poofs', and the same effeminate boys were often also rejected by many teachers:

(I) You can't describe Mark Mallinder as normal. Look at the way he follows us [the staff] around. I told Bill [Mr Changeable] to give him a clip and send him out to play with the other kids, toughen him up a bit. 'I'm trying to build up Mark's confidence', that was his reply. He's spending more time on that one kid than all the others put together. (Mr Jovial)

(II) A group of boys was accused at break today of a 'poof-bashing exercise' in which Mark Mallinder was beaten up. He was badly roughed over, given a black eye and a cut lip. Mr Changeable was furious and could be heard shout-ing at them throughout the rest of the morning. They were caned and made to stand silently outside his office throughout the lunch break.

They faced, in effect, an onslaught from both peers and certain teachers and this was another aspect of the creation of a 'school for men'. Indeed, teachers generally were prepared to write off most pupil violence as normal, healthy, boyish exuberance, and horseplay. They distinguished between the acceptable 'boys standing up for themselves' and the 'hard knocks' brand of physicality (as, for example, in rugby) and the 'dirty stuff', namely, butting, gouging, kicking, and spitting, this being associated with soccer hooliganism. The need for and accept-ability of macho posturing and violence was conveyed to boys (and by boys) in the form of what I term 'myths of aggression', to which I now turn.

MYTHS OF AGGRESSION

One of the most noticeable features throughout my fieldwork was the extent to which both teachers and pupils talked about spectacular scenes of classroom violence:[10]

Long: Wilde had a fight with Mr Piano next door.
Green: Yes, they were in the hall, I heard that.
Long: He was in front of me and had a pile of pens and he was fooling and kept on taking these pens out and he came to his last pen and he [Mr Piano] came up and took 'em off Wilde and hit him across the head. He ran away to the other side of the class and Mr Piano was just pushing the tables away and when he got him Wilde just ran around to the other side of the room and he pushed him against the cupboard and he was on the floor fighting him. And Mr Changeable came in and he just took him out into the hall and he was just shaking him around and everything. Terrible!

These reports were, I concluded, not only part of impression management (both teachers and pupils used them), but also functioned to chart out an accepted code of practice (Wilde, it was felt, deserved what he got!). Violence, plus talk about violence, were mutually justifying. Furthermore these 'myths of aggression' fell into two broad categories: first- or second-hand accounts of *actual* confrontations; and stories which constituted a form of indirect, *symbolic* violence (in the absence of real violence) by pupils on teachers and teachers on teachers. These have been summarized in Table 6.1.

Taking symbolic violence first, in the examples below incidents are re-presented in such a manner that the actual loser becomes the winner. In one case a teacher just escapes a boy's revenge for a brutal assault, whilst in the second another appears as a coward unwilling and unable to counter a pupil's challenge:

Table 6.1 Myths of aggression

Nature of violence	Teacher on teacher	Pupil on pupil	Teacher on pupil	Pupil on teacher
Actual violence	None observed or recorded	✔	✔	None observed or recorded
		←————————→		
Symbolic violence	✔	Threats and aggressive postures: 'showing hard' by teachers and pupils		✔

(I) Mark Thompson was messing the music teacher and he was fooling around at the back of the room in the corner with Christopher O'Mally. They were just thumping each other and laughing. Mr Piano goes all mad and he was throwing Thompson around and then he banged their heads together and O'Mally breaks out crying. He shouldn't have done that so Thompson goes, to the teacher, 'If you don't fucking stop it I'll fucking bullshit your face', he goes. Well Mr Piano is mad and he hit Thompson and kicked him up the aisle and out of the room and smashed his head against the door frame on the way out, really bad! Well, Thompson went down to the drama room, put his bag in there, and he was punching the wall as hard as he could and then he went down to the cloakroom and then he, he had a drink of water to cool himself off, and then he brought out a knife and he said, 'I'm going to kill that sadist!' He went down through the yard and Mr Piano got into his car and drove off just in time. He saw Thompson coming and he knew he'd gone too far. All the kids were with Thompson, cheering him an' that. He would have used that knife, definite!

(II) When Mr Dancer first came here to teach French he went around all joking an' that, trying to be friendly. He used to say things like 'Hello horrible!' to kids and 'Watch it, tough guy!', funny things like that. Anyway, one day we were all pushing out of the door breaktime into the yard and he was trying to get in to the staffroom and he said to Vidal, 'Stop pushing, skinhead', or 'Watch it, skinhead!', something like that 'cos Vidal had had all his hair cut short and he had his City red and white scarf on over his blazer and his trousers tucked into his boots, all hard like. Anyway, Vidal didn't like it and he said to Mr Dancer, 'You'd better fucking watch it or I'll stick one on you!' and Mr Dancer he heard, but he was too scared to do anything about it.

J.B.: Are you sure he heard?

He definitely heard, I'm sure of it. He was just too scared to take Vidal on.

Similarly, I recorded a form of symbolic violence by teachers against colleagues who were unwilling to employ physical measures against pupils. They were frequently castigated and 'slagged off' behind their backs by the deputy head in the staff-room. I recorded many such attacks:

The rough demands are alright. We built the Empire with kids like them. A teacher in this school may look okay and sound great, but kids like that show his weaknesses. The test of a good teacher is whether he can deal with kids like that and remain on good terms with them. That's the real test, not being able to manage a crowd of nice, polite middle class kids – anyone can do that! A boy like King responds to a firm hand. The first time I met him he tried me out and got clobbered! From the very start he learned that I wasn't going to take any lip from him. After that we got on like a house on fire. I had to dish out a few gentle reminders now and then, but nothing serious. I had no trouble with him whatsoever. But some colleagues have no idea. They let him run rings around them, the women especially. Unless they can discipline kids, then they shouldn't be teaching. A test of who's a teacher and who's pretending is simple: put them in the hall alone with 350 first years, throw in a few kids like King and mad Freddie Wilde, and close the door! If you went in after half-an-hour with [names four staff] you'd still be able to hear a pin drop. If you left [names another four staff] in there then you'd have to scrape what was left of them off the wall and then you'd have to go out and find the kids!

A SCHOOL FOR MEN

Some of them like [names three staff] are totally dependent on Bill and myself. They can't do damn all for themselves and their classes sound more like football matches than anything else.

In the staffroom, teachers often told stories which showed approval of the 'manly' sort of boy:

(I) Darren Stephenson was a very powerful boy. He was one of the biggest kids in the school. He had the body of a man and when he turned nasty, watch out! He was a youth club boxer and he was in training. He carried an enormously heavy punch and all the kids knew it. Sometimes when I had to leave the room I'd say, 'Don't misbehave, because Darren is in charge. If I find some of you beaten up when I come back I won't blame Darren!' Of course I was never out of the place for long, but it always worked. There was never any trouble.

(II) He was the biggest, toughest, most foul-mouthed kid this school has ever known. I said to him, 'Talk to me like that and I'll sort you out here and now.' Well, he carried on, so I hit him! I hit him so hard I was off school for two days! I busted my hand on him I hit him so hard! But I had no trouble with him after that. He'd tested me and found he'd got nowhere but into hospital. A boy like that only understands this [shows a clenched fist], but you can work on a kid like that, make him work for you not against you.

(III) If there's anything nasty going on when I'm on duty then I step in – two or more on to one, that kind of thing. But if there's a good, clean scrap, and if no one's getting hurt, then I take my time. These boys have to settle things with their fists – it's the only language some of them understand.

Both teachers and pupils used cautionary tales to warn of the consequences of 'ignoring the rules' or 'not playing the game':

(I) If you swing on that rope the wrong way and it snaps and you go through the window, then you'll fall thirty feet into the yard and get a pile of stitches for being so clever! One

143

boy didn't listen to me one year. I went to visit him in hospital. He was covered from head to foot in plaster with two holes for his eyes and another hole so they could pour soup into his mouth! As far as I know he could be still there, or in a wheelchair somewhere.

(II) I heard about this kid last year who got beaten up in the yard because he was always telling on his mates. Barnsie they called him. Anyway, one lunch hour . . .. [He goes on to relate how the boy was set upon by his fellows and ended up in hospital].

The above, with their violent catalogue of fights, accidents, and brutal confrontations can best be regarded as 'myths' whereby what Measor and Woods (1983) term a 'cultural blueprint' detailing acceptable and unacceptable violence was disseminated. Their view is that during the status passage between schools myths serve a number of functions:

— they reflect in compressed form the principles by which reality should be interpreted;
— organize values and lay down conditions of cultural membership;
— communicate possibilities and help guide actions by offering practical solutions;
— draw attention to key situational features and operate symbolically in providing a social charter;
— encapsulate rules for behaviour and authenticate a set of beliefs and conventions about seeing and knowing in a given setting;
— convey a warning to stay clear of trouble and injury;
— present action dramatically, with the degree of accuracy less important than the general truths they contain;
— embody emotional and cognitive messages relating to behaviour and indicate the adjustments to be made in new surroundings.

CONCLUSION

I recorded on tape and in field notes numerous myths current in Lower School on the theme of the necessity of 'acceptable' teacher coercion; the consequences of violence escalating; the desirability of a machismo style for both the delivery and reception of violence, the aggrandisement of 'rough' kids by teachers; the rejection of 'soft' and 'abnormal' kids; the castigation of both female and 'soft' teachers; the rejection of 'bad', 'sadistic' and 'moody' teachers; the consequences of irresponsible behaviour; and revenge stories on all those who had ignored the official and unofficial rules governing violence. These teacher and pupil myths were mirror images and advocated that violence was not only acceptable, but necessary for the well-being of all in Lower School. Acceptable violence rendered life therein manageable and predictable. They vividly reflected and re-inforced the socio-economic, historical, cultural, and gender backdrop to the place; its staff; its first year cohort; and the geographical area.[11] Moreover, they expressed a great deal about the operating of mass public schooling at a time of falling rolls, low public expenditure, and depressed teacher morale, when there were few new appointments and little opportunity, stimuli, or encouragement for ageing (in this case, male) teachers to try new approaches or to retrain.

I have shown in this chapter how an ethnographic approach to routine violence in the temporal and spatial context of Lower School showed it to be central to the establishment strategies of both teachers and pupils as a working concensus was negotiated. It was the means by which both parties projected themselves, provisionally typed each other, and settled the social charter of Lower School at the start of the year as a 'school for men'. It was supported by symbolic violence in the form of myths of aggression which upheld the ideas of 'old fashioned schoolmastery', firm discipline, and appropriate 'manly' behaviour. Most violence in Lower School was premeditated and part of start-of-term impression management, yet 'real' (controlled or uncontrolled) violence, whether in classroom or playground, was condemned. Both parties drew on violence as an important strategic resource: it was the means by which pupils provoked and typed teachers, whilst some of the latter actively sought out and took every advantage of such opportunities to display their 'hardness'. Pupils, too, appropriated teacher violence to bolster their reputations through cocky resilience. Violence was double-edged in yet another sense in that what was meant as a deterrent was simultaneously a source

JOHN BEYNON

of 'laughs'. Such were the paradoxes that naturalistic enquiry revealed as the Lower School year got under way.

NOTES

1 For overseas readers who may not be familiar with the post-war history of British education, secondary modern schools had as their pupils those who had failed the Eleven-Plus Examination and had thereby been debarred from entering the grammar schools. Intended to provide a less academic, more practical, and overtly vocational curriculum for the 'less able', secondary moderns – in spite of some considerable achievements – won little public acclaim or status in comparison with the prestigious grammar schools. The advent of comprehensive schools in the late 1950s and 1960s was hailed by proponents as a means of abolishing both the Eleven-Plus and the chasm which had developed between education for the majority (in secondary modern schools) and education for the few (in the grammar schools), as well as the different philosophies which had come to characterize the two sectors.

2 I do not propose to dwell on the pedagogical and ecological contexts of Lower Secondary School except to say that in the overcrowded and confined space, teacher competence was related to the ability to keep classes silent and orderly. Ms Floral, for example, whose drama lessons were noisy and encouraged pupil involvement, was subjected to a great deal of critical pressure to conform by senior staff, especially Mr Changeable (see below), and to (a) keep her classes quiet, and (b) adopt a more conventional, teacher-controlled mode of instruction. Until she did this she was seen as lacking in both experience and expertise (Beynon, in press). In addition, in common with other female staff in Lower School, she was held to be a liability because she was not prepared to hit pupils and so was dismissed as 'soft' by staff and boys alike. I refer frequently to the temporal context (starting-the-year), and the pedagogical and institutional/historical contexts can best be sketched in by quoting Mr Changeable, the headmaster. He described himself as a 'secondary modern man' and was distrustful of what he regarded as the 'grammar school types' who held the senior positions in Middle and Upper School. A number of writers have noted how, even within the comprehensive school, earlier divisions between teacher professional groups (for example, that between the University graduate and the BEd holder) are being perpetuated (David Hargreaves 1980, 1982; Riseborough 1981; Ball 1984; and Beynon 1985b). Mr Changeable, the head of Lower School, was an advocate of what he termed 'old-fashioned schoolmastery', which included uncompromising

146

(physical) discipline and highly traditional teaching methods. His philosophy, his fears for the future, and the type of school he ensured he presided over are made clear in the statement below:

> I would describe Lower School as *a school for men*. By that I mean quite simply that it is a large boys' school, the majority of the staff are men and the ethos is male. Women often prove to be a liability and that is why they are shunted off down to me in Lower School. I have to find them jobs because they can't cope with the bloody-minded third, fourth, and fifth years! In my view a lot of the women and – let's be fair! – some of the men, especially some of the younger, more irresponsible ones, let the side down. They're no longer schoolmasters or schoolmistresses, but teachers who couldn't give a damn as long as the cheque is waiting for them at the end of the month. The old skills, the old self-respect, are fast disappearing and the motivation for excellence on all scores just isn't there. They may have better paper qualifications then my generation of teachers, but that doesn't make them better teachers. Many of them would never have survived in the old Sec. Mods. They're sloppy and some are prepared to let the kids get away with murder. Well, that's not my way: I run this school like clockwork and, as a result, they're either with me or against me, depending on their competence as schoolteachers. I'm a stickler for no-nonsense, old-fashioned schoolmastery and if that means cuffing a boy across the head, so be it!

3 The life history method has recently been applied to the study of teachers' lives and careers (Ball and Goodson 1985).
4 An excellent review and discussion of issues relating to fieldwork and theory (to which I am indebted) is that by Hammersley and Atkinson (1983).
5 For a lucid exploration of the different origins and subsequent development of American and British traditions of educational ethnography, see Atkinson and Delamont (1980).
6 Seatown was the site of a large holiday complex and most boys were frequent visitors.
7 All terms in inverted commas were used by teachers and/or pupils (for example, 'bodybuild', 'suss', 'laughing', 'show hard', 'old fashioned schoolmastery', and so on.
8 There is now considerable literature on typifications (Schutz 1972) in schools (see, for example, Werthman 1963; Nash 1976; Furlong 1977). In spite of the fact that they researched in different areas at different times a broad concensus emerges of the main attributes of 'good' and 'bad' teachers.
9 This naturally posed a dilemma for me as a 'neutral' researcher as, on occasions, I witnessed considerable violence and petty vandalism on school property (Beynon 1983). As I write, pupil violence is again in the news, with the leading article of the *Times*

Educational Supplement of 22 August 1986, entitled 'L.e.a. told of fighting in Comprehensive School's corridors – Break-time violence appals inspector.' Although the article details the nature of the violence ('he saw pupils at a Manchester Comprehensive trying to throw each other over a balcony and fighting on the floor . . . boys hitting each other with heavy schoolbags during the breaks and tripping others up . . .'), it makes no attempt to investigate its purposes.

10 I focus on myths relating to violence, but there were others: for example, some stories related to sex. Mr Dancer was repeatedly portrayed as homosexual and Ms Floral as promiscuous; similarly boys were portrayed as 'queers', 'straights', 'screw-ups', and 'perverts'. Sets of myths interacted and the unfortunate Mr Dancer was stigmatized and ostracized on a number of counts.

11 Seatown was in depressed, post-industrial South Wales with its main employer, the docks, now lying idle. New jobs in the area were few and most employment was in Cityton, a dozen miles away. Many of the boys came from a huge 1960s housing estate noted for its high unemployment rate. There was, in Lower School, a heavy emphasis upon 'teaching basics' and ensuring boys learned how to take orders and 'produce goods on time'. This, it was argued, would render them more reliable and employable when they came on to the job market.

REFERENCES

Atkinson, P. and Delamont, S. (1980) 'The two traditions in educational ethnography: sociology and anthropology compared', *British Journal of Sociology of Education* 1(2): 139–52.

Ball, S.J. (1981) *Beachside Comprehensive: A Case Study of Secondary Schooling*, Cambridge: Cambridge University Press.

—— (1984) 'School politics, teachers' careers and educational change', paper presented to Westhill College Conference, Birmingham, January.

Ball, S.J. and Goodson, I.F. (eds) (1985) *Teachers' Lives and Careers*, Lewes: Falmer Press.

Bernstein, B. (1973) *Class, Codes and Control, Volumes 1 and 2*, London: Routledge and Kegan Paul.

Beynon, J. (1983) 'Ways-in and staying-in: fieldwork as problem solving', in M. Hammersley (ed.) *The Ethnography of Schooling*, Driffield: Nafferton.

—— (1984) 'Sussing out teachers: pupils as data gatherers', in P. Woods (ed.) *Life in School: The Sociology of Pupil Culture*, Milton Keynes: Open University Press.

—— (1985a) *Initial Encounters in the Secondary School: Sussing, Typing and Coping*, Lewes: Falmer Press.

—— (1985b) 'Career histories in a Comprehensive School', in S.J. Ball and I.F. Goodson (eds) *Teachers' Lives and Careers*, Lewes:

Falmer Press.
—— (in press) 'The micropolitics of drama teaching', in L. Tickle (ed.) *The Aesthetic Curriculum*, London: Croom Helm.
Beynon, J. and Atkinson, P. (1984) 'Pupils as data gatherers: mucking and sussing', in S. Delamont (ed.) *Readings on Interaction in the Classroom*, London: Methuen.
Beynon, J. and Delamont, S. (1984) 'The sound and the fury', in N. Frude and H. Gault (eds) *Disruptive Behaviour in Schools*, Chichester: Wiley.
Blumer, H. (1969) *Symbolic Interactionism: Perspective and Method*, Englewood Cliffs: Prentice-Hall.
Delamont, S. (1973) 'Academic conformity observed: studies in the classroom', unpublished PhD thesis, University of Edinburgh.
—— (1980) *Sex roles and the School*, London: Methuen.
—— (1983) *Interaction in the Classroom* (2nd edn), London: Methuen.
Denzin, N.K. (1978) *The Research Act: A Theoretical Introduction to Sociological Methods* (2nd edn), New York: McGraw Hill.
Furlong, V. (1977) 'A Nancy goes to school: a case study of pupils' knowledge of their teachers', in P. Woods and M. Hammersley (eds) *School Experience*, London: Croom Helm.
Glaser, B. and Strauss, A. (1967) *The Discovery of Grounded Theory*, Chicago: Aldine.
Goffman, E. (1968) *Asylums*, Harmondsworth: Penguin.
—— (1971) *The Presentation of Self in Everyday Life*, Harmondsworth: Penguin.
Gold, R.L. (1958) 'Roles in sociological fieldwork', *Social Forces* 36: 217–23.
Grace, G. (1978) *Teacher, Ideology and Control*, London: Routledge and Kegan Paul.
Hammersley, M. and Atkinson, P. (1983) *Ethnography: Principles in Practice*, London: Tavistock.
Hargreaves, A. (1978) 'Towards a theory of classroom coping strategies', in L. Barton and R. Meighan (eds) *Sociological Interpretations of Schooling and Classrooms*, Driffield: Nafferton.
—— (1979) 'Strategies, decisions and control: interactions in a Middle School classroom', in J. Eggleston (ed.) *Teacher Decision-Making in the Classroom*, London: Routledge and Kegan Paul.
—— (1980) 'Synthesis and the study of strategies: a project for the sociological imagination', in P. Woods (ed.) *Pupil Strategies*, London: Croom Helm.
Hargreaves, D. (1967) *Social Relations in a Secondary School*, London: Routledge and Kegan Paul.
—— (1972) *Interpersonal Relations and Education*, London: Routledge and Kegan Paul.
—— (1978) 'Whatever happened to symbolic interactionism?', in L. Barton and R. Meighan (eds) *Sociological Interpretations of Schooling and Classrooms*, Driffield: Nafferton.
—— (1980) 'The occupational culture of teachers', in P. Woods

(ed.) *Teacher Strategies*, London: Croom Helm.

——— (1982) *The Challenge for Comprehensive Schools: Culture, Curriculum and Communication*, London: Routledge and Kegan Paul.

Lacey, C. (1970) *Hightown Grammar*, Manchester: Manchester University Press.

Lofland, J. (1976) *Doing Social Life: The Qualitative Study of Human Interaction in Natural Settings*, New York: Wiley.

Mead, G.H. (1934) *Mind, Self and Society*, Chicago: University of Chicago Press.

Measor, L. and Woods, P. (1983) 'The interpretation of pupil myths', in M. Hammersley (ed.) *The Ethnography of Schooling*, Driffield: Nafferton.

Nash, R. (1976) 'Pupils' expectations of their teachers', in M. Stubbs and S. Delamont (eds) *Explorations in Classroom Observation*, Chichester: Wiley.

Pollard, A. (1980) 'Teacher interests and changing situations of survival threat', in P. Woods (ed.) *Teacher Strategies*, London: Croom Helm.

——— (1982) 'A model of classroom coping strategies', *British Journal of Sociology of Education* 3: 19–37.

——— (1984) 'Coping strategies and the multiplication of differentiation in infant classrooms', *British Educational Research Journal* 10: 33–48.

Riseborough, G.F. (1981) 'Teacher careers and Comprehensive schooling', *Sociology* 15: 352–80.

Schatzman, L. and Strauss, A. (1973) *Field Research: Strategies for a Natural Sociology*, Englewood Cliffs: Prentice Hall.

Schutz, A. (1964) 'The stranger: an essay in social psychology', in A. Schutz (ed.) *Collected Papers, Vol. II*, The Hague: Martinus Nijhoff.

——— (1972) *The Phenomenology of the Social World*, London: Heinemann.

Turner, G. (1983) *The Social World of the Comprehensive School*, London: Croom Helm.

Walker, R. and Goodson, I.F. (1977) 'Humour in the classroom', in P. Woods and M. Hammersley (eds) *School Experience*, London: Croom Helm.

Walker, R., Goodson, I.F., and Adelman, C. (1975) 'Teaching, that's a joke', Centre for Applied Research in Education, Norwich, University of East Anglia.

Werthman, C. (1963) 'Delinquents in school', in B.R. Cosin *et al.* (eds) *School and Society*, London: Routledge and Kegan Paul.

Woods, P. (1977) 'Teaching for survival', in P. Woods and M. Hammersley (eds) *School Experience*, London: Croom Helm.

——— (1980a) *Teacher Strategies*, London: Croom Helm.

——— (1980b) *Pupil Strategies*, London: Croom Helm.

——— (1983) *Sociology and the School*, London: Routledge and Kegan Paul.

Part Three

APPLICATIONS TO SOCIAL PROBLEMS INVOLVING AGGRESSION

Chapter 7

ANGER-MANAGEMENT METHODS IN RELATION TO THE PREVENTION OF VIOLENT BEHAVIOUR

KEVIN HOWELLS

INTRODUCTION

Human aggression has long been the focus of considerable theoretical analysis and research effort amongst psychologists (Geen and Donnerstein 1983). It is likely that much of this effort has been stimulated by a desire to apply knowledge directly to the prevention of violence in the natural environment. It is my own experience that the work of many of the professionals most involved in the management of violence in everyday life (social workers, probation officers, doctors, and nurses) is relatively untouched by contemporary theoretical ideas or research findings. Feldman suggested in 1982 that 'the time is now ripe for social scientists to apply the results of our studies to real life problems of violence'.

In this chapter I discuss the potential utility of one particular approach to violence prevention – the clinical use of anger-management methods. Firstly, anger management will be briefly set in the context of other approaches to prevention. How violence might be understood and modified in terms of anger will then be demonstrated by the description of an individual clinical case, 'Jim'. In the course of this clinical description reference will be made to theoretical ideas, particularly those of Novaco (1975, 1978, 1979). The problems and limitations of the use of anger-management methods will be illustrated by a second clinical case, 'Brian'. Some difficulties in the implementation of these methods will be discussed.

KEVIN HOWELLS

THE CLINICAL APPROACH

Anger-management interventions form part of what might be labelled a 'clinical' orientation to the prevention of violent and other forms of offending behaviour. The essential attribute of this approach is that psychological characteristics of the violent person him/herself are given a causal status in the aetiology of the behaviour and are seen as targets in producing change. The clinical approach can be contrasted with situational, sociological, and economic approaches to the explanation and prevention of offending behaviour (Schur 1979; Bartol 1980; Clarke 1980; West 1980, 1986). From this latter viewpoint, broad social and economic change may be seen as more appropriate interventions than individual therapy. It would be a mistake to identify the clinical approach with the medical model of social deviance (Schur 1979) since the psychological processes which are the focus of study are not 'pathological' in any medical sense.

Few psychologists working clinically or therapeutically with violent individuals would claim that clinical methods are appropriate for all forms of violence. Violent behaviour may not pose a problem for the violent person in that it is construed as acceptable and even necessary conduct. A person may learn, for example within a prison, that violence is an effective strategy for dealing with the environment in terms of achieving status and goods and preventing victimization. Such a person is unlikely to seek therapeutic help to change his or her behaviour. Contingency management procedures can be used to encourage non-violent behaviour but such interventions do not typically involve or require a therapeutic alliance between the violent person and professional helper.

A distinction is commonly made in the theoretical literature on aggression between 'instrumental' and 'angry' or 'incentive-motivated' and 'annoyance-motivated' aggression (Buss 1961; Bandura 1973, Zillman 1979; see Chapter 1 of this volume). For instrumental, incentive-motivated aggression, emotional arousal of an angry sort is not present and the behaviour is motivated by the rewards potentially achieved in the environment (for example, using violence to rob a bank). For angry aggression, on the other hand, emotional arousal is present and the reward for the aggression may be the infliction of hurt itself (for example, a husband being violent to his wife in the course of an angry 'provoking' argument).

Acts of violence which are purely instrumental require a different therapeutic strategy than those which are anger-induced. For the former the focus will be on changing environmental contingencies and on providing the client with alternative ways of securing reinforcers from the environment. For the latter the focus may be on self-control of the anger-response. Not all angry aggressors, of course, have a need or a willingness to exert control over their anger. Anger-management methods are most relevant, then, for that proportion of violent offenders for whom violence is anger-induced and who also have a subjective sense of loss of control over the anger response and/or are dissatisfied with their habitual ways of dealing with anger. A sense of loss of control or dissatisfaction may be situational rather than dispositional, in that particular life circumstances may induce a person who previously did not question their control of, or the appropriateness of, their anger to re-evaluate his or her behaviour. A dramatic example of this is provided by the person who first 'discovers' that he/she has an anger problem following an explosive act of violence. The origins of the violence are poorly understood by the person and the violence itself is deemed unacceptable. The two circumstances are sufficient to lead the person to construe him or herself as 'having a problem' requiring therapeutic help.

What proportion of violent offences/offenders meet these two criteria of anger induction and loss of control/dissatisfaction is unknown. Serious violence appears to be frequently associated with strong anger. Voluntary manslaughter, the most common form of homicide, is often induced by anger and rage (Averill 1982). Rape has been shown to be triggered by anger in a significant proportion of cases (Groth 1979; Marques 1981). Violence between marital partners is commonly preceded by arguments and disputes involving sexual possessiveness and disagreements over domestic tasks (Dobash and Dobash 1984).

Physical abuse of children *may* occur for instrumental reasons. Frude (1989) quotes particular cases in which deliberate injury has been inflicted on a child in order to produce some change in the environment (to get the child put into care), but such motivation appears to be rare, with the vast majority of abusive incidents being triggered by angry situations. Gardner and Gray's review (1982) of the antecedents of abuse again highlights the importance of factors such as general stress, marital conflict, and frustrating behaviour on the part of the child. The context of abuse strongly suggests the presence of angry affect in the vast majority of cases.

There is a clear need for future research to establish methods for systematically classifying violent events as 'instrumental', 'angry', or 'mixed', so that quantitative estimates might be made of the proportion of violent acts that are anger-mediated. It also needs to be determined in what percentage of cases the perpetrator sees the incident as caused by his or her difficulties in controlling anger, rather than as acceptable and justified.

In summary, clinical methods such as anger management are not appropriate for all forms of interpersonal violence. Research into various forms of interpersonal violence suggests, indirectly, however, that anger is a common antecedent.

A CASE FOR ANGER-MANAGEMENT TRAINING: JIM

Amongst violent people will be found those who meet the criteria of anger mediation and construing themselves as having an anger problem.

Jim is 30 years old and was referred to an anger-management group. He had a long history of scrapes with other people and with social institutions. He had frequently appeared in court and had been admitted to penal and psychiatric facilities on a number of occasions. The offending behaviour leading to court appearances was mainly acquisitive (minor theft) and violent in nature. His violent offences were the main reason for admission to prison and psychiatric clinics. He had been in a number of fights since his childhood. For the vast majority of these the outcome was non-serious, Jim and his adversary suffering minor bruises and lacerations. Occasionally, however, he has lost control entirely in a confrontation and caused serious damage to the other person.

Jim admits to frequently being very angry and violent, the two normally being interrelated. In an interview he reports a history of confrontations with his family, teachers, the police, prison officers, and hospital nurses. He admits to being particularly sensitive to criticism and that this is often the start of a violent episode. He describes himself as being easily carried away by his anger. Provocations make him physically tense and he sweats. He expresses considerable dissatisfaction with his tendency to 'blow his top'. He feels he does not understand how or why this occurs and he wishes he had more control over his temper. He clearly identifies his temper as a major reason for his general difficulties.

Jim's family and social background is viewed by professionals as 'disturbed'. In childhood he was admitted to a series of children's homes because of family disturbance. He hated, and still hates, his father, who frequently beat him. He has a strong sense of always having been 'picked on' and criticized by his father. When beaten he was frightened, but later in childhood had fought back successfully.

Jim is currently in a psychiatric hospital and is described in case notes as impulsive and 'easily angered', though generally he is amenable and co-operative with hospital staff. Jim himself construes himself as having a problem of 'blowing his top' and was referred to an anger-management group at his own request. How might an anger problem of this nature be assessed, formulated, and treated?

THEORETICAL UNDERPINNINGS

Anger and anger problems have been the subject of analysis both by those with a general theoretical interest in emotion (Averill 1982; Feshback 1986) and by those concerned to provide a basis for clinical interventions (Novaco 1975, 1985). Without any doubt, it is the work of Raymond Novaco (1975) that has most influenced clinical practice with violent people. Novaco's initial model of the components of anger (Novaco 1978) has provided a general framework for assessment and intervention. The following discussion in this chapter owes much to Novaco's work.

Novaco (1978) identifies four components to the anger-aggression syndrome: (1) external triggering events; (2) cognitive processing; (3) anger arousal itself, which includes

157

physiological arousal and the labelling of the arousal; and (4) behavioural reactions. It is an important feature of Novaco's analysis that bi-directional reciprocal relationships exist between these components (see Fig. 11.1, p. 276).

Triggering events

Angry violence appears to have particular environmental antecedents or triggers but specification and classification of common triggering events is no easy task. Not all triggers for anger are 'frustrations' if the latter are defined in terms of a failure to achieve an accustomed reward or to reach a valued goal, though frustration does feature as an important instigator in most surveys (Hall 1899; McKellar 1950; Averill 1982). McKellar (1950) suggested that two categories of triggering event can be discerned in natural environments: (1) 'interference with the pursuit of a goal, under the influence of some primary and secondary need', including, for example, missing a bus; (2) 'felt encroachment upon values, possessions, status, or habitual relations and attitudes towards other persons', including criticism of the person's ideas, work, clothing, or friends (cf. the discussion in Chapter 5 of this volume by Blanchard and Blanchard).

Berkowitz (1982, 1983) has argued from laboratory work that the stimuli which elicit angry forms of aggression are simply *aversive* and that frustrations are anger-inducing to the extent that they are aversive. Indeed, a range of aversive stimuli can be shown to produce aggression in laboratories, including pain, high temperature, noise, and 'disgusting' visual stimulation (ibid.).

In naturalistic studies, however, it is clear that the major triggers for anger are predominantly *interpersonal* and often embedded in close affectional relationships. One of the most comprehensive naturalistic studies has been that of Averill (1982), whose results suggest that instigators commonly involve frustration (interruption of ongoing or planned activity), loss of pride/self-esteem and violated expectations, wishes and socially accepted rules. Averill's data also reveal the important cognitive dimension of triggering events. Anger is induced when the aversive social behaviour is construed as voluntary and unjustified or as the result of negligence or carelessness (see below for further discussion of cognitive factors).

Studies of real-world violence (as opposed to anger) between men and their female partners reveal that arguments and disputes precede the violent act and that the arguments often have a particular theme, such as jealousy or financial concerns (Dobash and Dobash 1984). For violence to children within families, aversive crying on the part of the child, in the context of general stress, social isolation, and marital conflict, may be an important antecedent for the violent act (Gardner and Gray 1982; Frude 1989).

How are triggers for angry violence to be identified in clinical work? The full range of cognitive-behavioural assessments (Hersen and Bellack 1981) has some relevance in this task. A detailed history of the client, covering previous incidents of heightened anger, aggression, and violence may help to identify common triggers, though clients may need some form of preliminary training in behavioural analysis to help them distinguish external triggers from internal processes such as hostile cognitions. Such a history can sometimes be supplemented by interview material from relatives or others who have known the client over an extended period. A wife or mother, for example, may sometimes be more able to identify what the client's triggers are more easily than the client himself.

Inventories of common elicitors of anger (such as Novaco's Anger Inventory) (Novaco 1975) have some value in allowing an economical screening of a wide range of potentially important triggering events. Clients who have encountered the psychiatric system may have extensive written case histories which may be helpful in revealing long-term themes for triggers for anger.

Cognitive processes

There is now an extensive experimental and theoretical literature suggesting that the nature of the cognitive processing of aversive events is a crucial determinant of the affective and behavioural reactions they elicit. Novaco's original model (1978) highlighted the importance of three facets of cognition: expectations, appraisal, and private speech. Since this suggestion was put forward a large social psychological literature has confirmed, in particular, that appraisal processes of an attributional nature are very relevant to anger induction (Dyck and Rule 1978; Kremer and Stephens 1983; Nasby *et al.* 1980; Ferguson and Rule 1983); Forsterling 1984; Dodge 1985). Ferguson and Rule's analysis (1983) reveals that complex social judgements of intention, motivation (goals), and foreseeability are involved when we appraise the aversive behaviour of others and that such appraisals affect subsequent anger. Such work would clearly lead the clinician to assess social judgements and appraisals of responsibility and blame by angry violent people.

The cognitive dimension to anger and aggression has been analysed from a rational emotive perspective (Grieger 1982), again highlighting the centrality of cognition and particularly of cognitive rules and rule violation for anger.

Physiological arousal

Physiological arousal is an important component of most theories of emotion (Izard 1977), though theories clearly vary in the causal status given to arousal. Marked physiological activation accompanies state anger and the physiological changes may differ from those accompanying other emotions such as fear (Ax 1953; Funkenstein *et al.* 1957). Rise of diastolic blood pressure seems to be a particular feature of arousal produced by anger.

The work of Shield (1984) suggests that differences do exist between anger and anxiety and sadness in terms of the person's *perceived* pattern of symptoms, with particular symptoms (for example, temperature changes) being distinctive to anger.

It is a reasonable inference from the experimental literature that physiological activation will often accompany the anger state in angry violent people and that for some the physiological changes will be a major part of the subjective experience of anger.

Behavioural reactions

A range of behavioural reactions, including violence, may occur following anger arousal. Averill's results (1982) suggest that violence is a very low frequency response to anger in the normal population. Where violence does occur it is often the product of an escalating sequence of social exchanges with the potential victim (Toch 1969, 1985; Patterson 1985). In this sense violence may be an interactional or 'transactional' problem (Toch 1985), with attention needing to be paid in clinical settings to the contribution of the other person (victim) to the chain of behaviour that culminates in violence.

What behaviours escalate anger to behavioural violence are not known, though it is likely that very aggressive reactions to internal anger will provide an aversive stimulus for others in the environment, who in turn may escalate their level of aversive behaviour.

'Overcontrolled' patterns of anger expression have been identified amongst violent offenders (Blackburn 1968, 1971; Megargee 1971, 1984) who appear to be characterized by very low levels of anger expression but who may be at risk for extreme acts of violence in the long term. The reciprocal nature of the relationship between behavioural reactions and the environment itself is stressed in Novaco's model (Novaco 1978), and it is possible to construe overcontrol in this way. The overcontrolled person's failure to express anger at all may fail to produce change in the environment, so that the sources of frustration persist until they are responded to in an inappropriate and explosive manner.

APPLYING CONCEPTS TO THE CLINICAL CASE: JIM

A number of methods were used to identify the triggers for Jim's episodes of angry violence.

He completed a modified form of the Novaco Anger Inventory, a ninety-item inventory of hypothetical anger-inducing situations. Anger intensity was rated on a five-point Likert scale (Novaco 1975). Some items were modified from Novaco's original list in order to cover provoking situations commonly experienced in psychiatric and prison settings. Amongst items given a maximum rating of 5 for anger intensity were (1) being called a liar; (2) being called a 'stupid idiot' in an argument; (3) being criticized in front of others; (4) being teased or joked about; (5) being called names; (6) being the subject of personal remarks, and so on. High-scoring items related to the general theme of criticism and personal derogatory comments.

Jim also completed an anger diary over a two-week period. For the diary he was asked to recall experience of anger during the day and to provide written answers to the following questions:

(1) What was the situation that made you angry? What happened?
(2) When and where did this happen?
(3) How exactly did you feel?
(4) What thoughts were going through your mind?
(5) What irritated you most?
(6) What did you actually do?
    (a) Did not show any anger at all;
    (b) Showed any anger in words only;
    (c) Became aggressive (for example, hitting, punching);
    (d) Left the situation.

The diary also involved ratings of anger intensity and of whom/what anger was directed at. Finally the diary asked whether and how Jim had tried to control his angry feelings in the situation.

Jim reported between three and five angry experiences on most days. The triggers he identified were predominantly comments of a critical, disparaging nature from other patients, particularly in a group context. A typical incident was one in which Jim was 'slagged off' by another patient in a ward meeting. Jim perceived the patient as 'making him look an idiot'. He described his feelings as 'seething' angry and his cognitions at the time were of the sort 'He's a bastard . . . he's trying to turn everyone against me . . . he's always showing me up'. On this particular occasion he expressed his anger mainly in verbal abuse but acknowledges 'pushing' the other patient when the argument continued after the meeting. On other occasions Jim reacted with physical aggression (mainly punching) to similar triggers. He generally rates his anger as 'very strong', and as directed against 'other people' or 'things in general' rather than himself. His diaries indicate that he is typically highly aroused physically in angry situations. He reports wanting to maintain control for many incidents but not knowing how to do it.

During the two weeks that Jim completed his diary he was also rated on a parallel observation schedule by nursing staff. The items on the schedule were similar to those in his own diary, covering the nurses' perception of what made Jim angry on a daily basis, how he behaved in these situations, on what basis they judged him to be angry, the intensity and direction of his anger, and so on. The triggers appearing in the diaries and the observation charts were not identical as nurses were not always present in all the situations that Jim encountered. The general themes, however, were similar for diary and observation incidents. A typical incident recorded by nurses involved Jim being provoked to anger by being laughed at and joked about by another patient in an occupational therapy setting. He was observed to get 'tense and fidgety' in the situation, to have 'furrowed eyebrows', and eventually to swear, call names, and threaten the patient involved. Anger intensity was again rated as 'very strong' and as manifesting itself verbally (for example, shouting abuse), nonverbally (facial expression, tone of voice), and behaviourally (punching, hitting, slapping).

In addition to these measures, Jim completed the trait scale Spielberger State-Trait Anger Inventory, on which he obtained virtually the maximum score possible (Spielberger *et al.* 1983).

In summary then, information from case records, interviews, diaries, and staff observations suggested with some consistency that particular triggers existed for anger. Critical comments, particularly in a group setting, and if made in what Jim perceived as a 'joking or humiliating' way, were particularly likely to elicit a reaction.

Analysis of the cognitive component of Jim's anger was based in part on his self-reported thoughts which preceded angry incidents, as revealed by his diary. The major themes from recorded thoughts were that critical remarks from others were perceived as malevolent. A critical comment, for example, tended to be seen as part of a general attempt to humiliate and show him up in front of others. A second theme revealed in the diaries was the tendency to construe some aversive social behaviours as deliberate social *exclusions*. On one occasion, for example, a member of nursing staff baked a cake for patients on the ward, as part of a birthday celebration. In the course of distributing slices of cake to patients Jim was inadvertently omitted. He did not speak up and his exclusion was not perceived. Jim's interpretation was that he had been *deliberately* excluded and victimized and this left him hurt and angry.

Similar cognitive themes were elicited when previous anger-inducing situations were re-enacted in role plays or in imagination and Jim was asked to 'speak aloud' his thoughts. Role plays also revealed that the thought sequence following a provocation also involved cognitive rehearsal of the consequences of *not* responding aggressively. Typically the sequence included self-statements of the sort 'If I don't do something now . . . I will look weak, be picked on in future; never be respected by others', and so on.

The arousal component of the anger response was highly salient for Jim. In his diaries he reported that physical arousal was strong, even for minor provocations. The most frequently reported sensations were of physical tension, sweating, and of legs trembling. He found this physical state to be aversive and typically labelled himself as 'angry and upset' when he was in this state. His main concern was that the arousal state would sometimes persist for the rest of the day, or even longer, leaving him irritable and likely to respond to other minor provocations, and also creating sleep problems. Apparently high physiological reactions were also reported in staff ratings. It was not possible to monitor physiological activation directly, but there were good reasons to believe that heightened physiological arousal contributed to the inappropriateness of Jim's behaviour in angry situations.

Observational, self-report role-play and case-record data suggested that Jim had a limited repertoire of behavioural reactions to provocation. Some angry incidents resulted in Jim becoming violent. The violent act itself rarely occurred immediately but followed an escalating sequence of angry social exchanges. The assessment task was to identify the verbal, nonverbal and paralinguistic features of Jim's social behaviour that produced the escalation effect. In essence the need was to define the difference between Jim's aggressive social style and appropriate assertion in such situations (Hollandsworth 1977; Hollandsworth and Cooley 1978; Hull and Schroeder 1979; Kirchner *et al.* 1979; Hedlund and Lindquist 1984). The task of microanalysis of aggressive social behaviour is akin to that undertaken in the context of social skills training (Howells 1976; Trower *et al.* 1978; Hollin and Trower 1986), though the focus is on identifying aggression-inducing behaviours rather than those leading to social failure or inadequacy. In Jim's case, the following verbal behaviours were identified as escalating the situation: (a) Jim's tendency to respond to mild criticism with counter-criticism of an aggressive sort. 'Aggressive' counter-criticism comprised statements which were *generally* disparaging and abusive; (b) Jim's tendency to *swear* in disagreements ('You ignorant bastard, what do you know about . . .'); (c) Jim's tendency, later in the interaction, to issue a *threat* ('Say that again and I will down you').

In the paralinguistic channel the following behaviours were identified: (a) very high voice volume early in the interaction. Jim was perceived as shouting angrily in disputes even when his subjective sense of anger was low; (b) threatening voice tone. In the non-verbal channel the following were identified: (a) 'angry' facial expression early on in the sequence; (b) excessive proximity (standing too close) in the course of the dispute; (c) if the other person was seated, Jim 'stood over' the person in a way that was threatening; (d) aggressive gesticulation (hand-waving, likely to be perceived as in incipient punch); and (e) excessive eye contact (staring). Jim was unaware of any of these behaviours and of his role in escalating the interaction towards violence.

OTHER ASSESSMENT METHODS

Jim's case illustrates the general range of variables that need to be assessed and investigated in the clinical setting but the methods described are far from exhaustive. The whole range of cognitive-behavioural assessment methods is potentially applicable to violent people with anger problems (Hersen and Bellack 1981). Feindler and Ecton (1986) have recently published a wide-ranging review of assessment methods for anger problems, including self-monitoring methodologies, self-report inventories, rating scales, role-play assessments, direct observation, and other techniques. Amongst Feindler and Ecton's own contributions to assessment methodology are a 'Hassle Log' and a direct observation recording method. The

Hassle Log is a brief diary-type self-monitoring device for adolescents. These authors recommend interval recording of direct observations of angry behaviour in real-life settings, using recording categories such as 'tease', 'argue', 'threat', 'hit', 'in fight', 'start fight', and 'damage'.

In recent years there has been some progress in devising brief psychometric measures of anger processes. I have already discussed the State-Trait Anger Scale (Spielberger *et al.* 1983). This scale assesses the *experience* of anger, rather than its expression. An important extension of this scale has been the development of an Anger Expression (AX) Scale (Spielberger *et al.* 1985), with anger in/anger out sub-scales. Siegel (1985) has also developed a Multidimensional Anger Inventory (MAI) which distinguishes frequency, magnitude, mode of expression, and other aspects of the anger experience. Such scales have been used mainly in the area of anger-related cardiovascular disease, but there is a clear need for such measures in the assessment of violent people.

TREATMENT PROGRAMMES AND THEIR OUTCOMES

Jim's case can be used to illustrate the broad principles of the anger-management treatment approach. Theoretical analyses such as those of Novaco (1975, 1978, 1979, 1985) suggest a comprehensive and broad-based approach to treatment in which triggering events, cognition, arousal, and behaviour become targets for change.

An essential feature of anger-management therapy with violent people is the attempt to convey to the client an understandable model of anger and its relationship to triggering events, thoughts, and violent behaviour itself. Novaco (1975, 1978) labels this the *cognitive preparation* phase. In Jim's case this would involve enabling him to understand that his anger experiences do have particular accompanying triggers (for example, criticism), cognitive appraisals, and physiological changes, and also that anger can be distinguished from its behavioural expression in the form of violence.

The identification of triggering events can suggest therapeutic strategies. In Jim's case the fact that his anger occurred only in response to particular forms of criticism raises the possibility of removing triggering events themselves as a strategy for violence reduction. This was unlikely to be productive in Jim's case as criticism was likely to be an endemic social response to his behaviour and one that could not, realistically, be modified. On the other hand, much of the criticism he encountered was 'normal' social reaction to his unacceptable behaviour. In particular, his propensity for stealing and his general unreliability at work provoked criticism from acquaintances and colleagues. Although Jim amplified criticism, through his appraisal of it as, for example, an attempt to humiliate him, it was objectively true that others did indeed criticize him at a high frequency. In this sense, producing general change in the area of stealing and behaviour at work might be a relevant, though indirect, component of anger-management training in this case (for other examples of 'stimulus control' methods see Howells 1987).

Jim's hostile cognitive appraisals, expectations, and self-talk also suggest therapeutic interventions. Producing affective and behavioural change by means of changing cognitions is the central task of 'cognitive therapy' methods, which have been widely used in relation to problems of anxiety and depression (Beck *et al*. 1979; Clark 1986).

Novaco's cognitive methods (1975, 1978) focus mainly on the modification of anger-inducing appraisals and on constructive use of self-instructions (private speech) so as to deal with provoking situations successfully. Jim underwent a cognitively oriented group anger-management training of this sort, with particular attention being paid to demonstrating the habitual 'automatic' nature of his appraisals of other people as malevolent and intent on doing him deliberate harm. The details of a programme of this sort, with descriptions of a range of practical exercises, can be found in Feindler and Ecton (1986) There was a strong element of attributional retraining in Jim's therapy (Forsterling 1985) involving attempts to encourage him to generate and test alternative hypotheses as to why people responded to him as they did.

In Jim's therapy his increasing appreciation that his thoughts and self-statements played a role in producing and maintaining his anger, and that he had an element of choice in deciding which thoughts were helpful and which were harmful (and hence needed change), proved to be major steps in changing his violent behaviour.

The physiological arousal component of Jim's anger suggested that relaxation training might also be useful. In a group setting, deep muscle relaxation was taught and used in a variety of ways, particularly (1) to use as a self-control technique when he found his arousal to be escalating; (2) to teach him to monitor internal physiological changes and use these changes as a cue for taking preventative action; and (3) to use as an antagonistic response in desensitization to visualized anger-inducing scenes (Hearn and Evans 1972; Evans and Hearn 1973).

Finally, an attempt was made to produce change in his overt behaviour itself in angry situations. Social skills training methods (Hollin and Trower 1986) were used, including instruction, modelling, video-feedback, and role-play rehearsal, to change his social repertoire in response to provocation and to reduce the frequency of the escalating verbal, nonverbal and paralinguistic behaviours identified above. Social skills methods were used as part of a problem-solving orientation (D'Zurilla and Goldfried 1971; Platt *et al.* 1986), with an emphasis on generating alternative strategies for achieving goals and on evaluating the short- and long-term advantages and disadvantages of particular ways of behaving. In practice, maintaining low voice-volume and eliminating verbal threats proved to have the most obvious impact on actual angry encounters, in terms of reducing the probability of a violent outcome.

The above constitutes little more than a sketch of anger-management methods. It can be seen that in practice, such methods have a large number of components. This complexity creates problems in the evaluation of the effectiveness of anger-management methods. Where a programme can be shown to be effective it may be unclear as to whether it is the cognitive, behavioural, arousal, or other aspects of the programme that are crucial to its effectiveness. (For a full review of outcome studies and methodological issues, see Novaco 1985.)

Outcome studies have been broadly encouraging, some evidence suggesting that Novaco's stress inoculation methods have therapeutic effects (Novaco 1975, 1976a, b, 1977a, b). Not all studies, however, deal with populations who have explicit problems of violence. Moon and Eisler (1983) and Hazaleus and Deffenbacher (1986) report therapeutic gains for cognitive and other components of anger management, but anger problems rather than violent behaviour were the dependent variables assessed.

Studies with child-abusing parents have reported improvements with cognitive anger-management methods (Denicola and Sandler 1980; Nomellini and Katz 1983). In a series of studies Feindler and colleagues have reported controlled evaluation of the effects of a comprehensive multi-faceted anger-management programme with delinquent and aggressive adolescents (Feindler *et al.* 1984, 1986; Feindler and Ecton 1986). These latter studies involve genuine clinical client groups, rather than angry students. In the 1984 study (Feindler *et al.* 1984) this group of workers showed that bi-weekly anger-control training over fourteen sessions produced greater changes than a control condition on measures of disruptive and aggressive behaviour. In a subsequent study (Feindler *et al.* 1986) aggressive adolescents in an inpatient psychiatric facility were exposed to an eleven-week anger-control training programme, and a reduction in aggressive and disruptive behaviour was demonstrated, as well as change in the area of self-control, problem-solving and social skills.

Hearn and Evans (1972), Evans and Hearn (1973), and Hazaleus and Deffenbacher (1986) have produced some evidence as to the effectiveness of relaxation training in anger management but this is a relatively undeveloped area of research. Social skills methods have been described (Howells 1976; Goldstein 1981) and evaluated in both single-case (Kaufman and Wagner 1972; Foy *et al.* 1975; Frederiksen *et al.* 1976; Rahaim *et al.* 1980) and group comparison studies (Rimm *et al.* 1974; Fehrenbach and Thelen 1981; Moon and Eisler 1983).

The outcome studies reported to date provide some encouragement for those wishing to use anger management in violence prevention, but it must be said that the essential studies remain to be conducted – namely, controlled evaluations of the effects of anger-management methods in populations that are seriously violent and where violence itself is assessed as the major outcome variable. As suggested earlier, anger has a relationship to major social problems, and it is in relation to such real-world problems that therapeutic methods need to be evaluated.

LIMITATIONS AND PROBLEMS OF ANGER-MANAGEMENT THERAPY

Although it has been argued so far that there is a role for these methods in the prevention of violence, they present no panacea. There are a number of limitations on the usefulness of anger management and problems in its implementation. Some of these can be illustrated through an account of a clinical case.

BRIAN

Brian was referred for assessment of his suitability for anger-management therapy. He had been admitted to a psychiatric facility following the development of an acute psychiatric condition while in prison. Two years previously he had been admitted to prison after being convicted of murder. Prior to this crime he had never been involved in criminal or violent behaviour and had no psychiatric history. Available information suggested he had always been a quiet, retiring person who did not make friends easily. He had been brought up in a conventional, middle-class family and did well at school and in his subsequent career. He had few significant relationships, and none with women until meeting Linda in his early thirties. This he reports to have been the 'perfect' relationship. He was very much in love with his partner and relieved to have made a long-term relationship. His feelings were reciprocated and the relationship continued over several years.

One morning he received a telephone call 'out of the blue' to tell him she had met someone else and that it was 'all over'. He pleaded with her, but to no avail. He describes himself as having been distressed and depressed but not angry at the time. This state lasted over several months. On the day of the murder, he called at the house of his former fiancée. What followed next could not be established with any certainty but the outcome was that in the course of an argument between the two she was stabbed.

Brian himself reports that this was the only occasion on which

170

he had ever been violent, an account confirmed by a variety of sources. He claims to abhor violence and anger itself: 'It (anger) is the wrong way to conduct yourself.' His violent crime was regarded by himself and those that knew him as extremely out of character.

Currently, he is conforming, quiet, and apparently adjusted to hospital life, his psychiatric disturbance having disappeared since his transfer from prison. He has never been observed to have been involved in any aggressive behaviour in the hospital setting.

Brian completed an anger diary over two weeks, but recorded no anger experiences over this time. This failure to record appeared to be a genuine perception of not having been angry, rather than an attempt to present himself as non-aggressive or a failure to co-operate with the requirements made of him. His anger diaries were annotated to the effect that he 'never feels angry' and regards anger as a 'waste of time' and 'silly'. Virtually all items on the Novaco Anger Inventory were rated as 1 (would not make him at all angry) and he obtained virtually the lowest score possible on the State-Trait Anger Inventory (Spielberger *et al.* 1983). Staff observations on the anger chart were revealing. Nurses were 'unsure' as to whether or not they had observed him to get angry. They identified what appeared to have been triggering situations (another patient deliberately bumping into Brian and spilling his coffee). In response to such incidents he appeared to be physically tense (jaw clenching) but he typically said nothing and left the situation. He occasionally muttered under his breath in these situations but nurses were uncertain as to whether this was angry behaviour. Nurses were unable to rate the intensity or duration of his anger.

Structured interviews with Brian, focusing on his perceptions of apparently angry situations, confirmed the picture painted by more formal measures, that he failed to perceive or label himself as becoming angry in what appeared to be provoking situations and, further, that Brian strongly disapproved of anger as 'wrong'.

Brian was considered by the author not to be suited to anger-management therapy, at least of the conventional sort, and to illustrate some general limitations to the applicability of these treatment methods. What Brian illustrates is a not uncommon desynchrony of the anger response. He responds to apparent provocations with apparent high arousal, but aggressive behaviour is entirely inhibited and more importantly, he fails to label his affective state as anger. This pattern seems to have also existed prior to the murder itself. The abrupt ending of the relationship might have been expected to produce intense anger and resentment, and he was agitated and disturbed in the months following his rejection, but again, as far as we can ascertain, his affective reaction was never acknowledged as anger. In the murder the behavioural manifestation of anger finally occurred, but was construed by Brian as an 'accident' and not as an expression of how he felt.

Desynchronies of this sort have some similarity to the pattern of 'overcontrol' identified as common in homicides and extreme acts of violence by Megargee, Blackburn, and others (Megargee 1966, 1971, 1984; Blackburn 1968, 1971; Arnold and Quinsey 1977; Howells 1983). This form of desynchrony differs from that in which high internal anger is reported but behavioural expression of it is inhibited. It is feasible that overcontrolled violent offenders show both patterns, but, I would argue, the problem of desynchrony seen in Brian is likely to be resistant to directive cognitive and behavioural methods. From his own viewpoint, Brian has no 'problem' and has no motivation to acknowledge angry feelings or to change. The preconditions for anger-management therapy of the conventional sort are thus not met and some longer-term psychotherapeutic method intended gradually to reveal 'repressed' or 'submerged' (Howells 1983) angry feelings and cognitions may be required. In the author's experience such people are very resistent to short-term, structured anger-management programmes.

Brian's case illustrates violence which may be anger-mediated but where anger is not acknowledged. A second class of violent offenders not suited to anger-management therapy will be those violent people for whom violence is not emotionally mediated but of a more instrumental and sadistic quality (see above). There are clear dangers in assuming that all violent people *ipso facto* have an anger problem requiring therapeutic attention. The tendency to apply blanket treatment programmes indiscriminately to offender populations has been noted elsewhere in relation to social skills training programmes with offenders (Henderson and Hollin 1986; Howells 1986). Careful individualized assessment of suitability for such methods is clearly required.

A third group amongst violent people who would need to be excluded from consideration for anger-management therapy are those whose violent behaviour is entirely congruent with their short-term and long-term goal structure. Such persons cannot be considered *affectively incompetent* and it is proposed here that affective incompetence is a major criterion for suitability for anger-management therapy. The notion of affective incompetence has been adapted from the concept of social incompetence as elaborated by McFall (1982). Social incompetence is defined by McFall as a major task/performance mismatch, a task being a goal or the 'behavioural programme' in which the person is engaged. From this viewpoint a particular form of anger expression can be evaluated as incompetent only in relation to the person's tasks, goals, and intentions. Evaluations are, therefore, *criterion-referenced* rather than *norm-referenced*. It is the fact that a particular way of expressing anger disrupts the achievement of the person's tasks, rather than that their behaviour is more aggressive than that of most other people, which is important in judging whether or not they are incompetent and in need of therapy. The point being made here is that many forms of angry behaviour are not incompetent, even though they may be judged by others to be excessively aggressive and socially unacceptable. Thus, extreme angry behaviour may be functional for the person whose behaviour is organized in terms of the goal, for example, of 'intimidating others'. In clinical settings, as McFall suggests, skills training needs to be preceded by identification of the important life tasks for the individual, and by an analysis of the effectiveness of the person's existing behaviour in achieving those tasks.

McFall also introduces the notion that tasks may be hierarchically organized. Thus, the task of 'controlling my temper' may be nested within the task of 'getting on well with others' or 'keeping out of trouble with the law'. From this perspective some angry/violent people may not be affectively incompetent but may have a task system incompatibility. Thus, for example, a person may enjoy the fact that his or her outburst of temper coerces others into doing what he or she wants but not fully aware that this task is incompatible with the person's longer-term, superordinate task of wanting the friendship and companionship of others. Task system problems can be addressed within anger management therapy but the nature of the therapeutic interventions will be very different from those with people with true affective incompetences, the latter group requiring the teaching of molecular skills so as to reduce the task/performance mismatch. Finally, some people may express anger in extreme and violent ways which are deemed unacceptable by society, but which, nevertheless, are entirely in agreement with both the person's subordinate and superordinate tasks. Clearly, such people are not suitable for anger-management therapy. It is people of this kind who are typically labelled as 'unmotivated' for the therapeutic endeavour.

McFall's analysis, if extended to anger problems, would suggest a threefold typology of angry violent problems: (1) violence associated with affective incompetence; (2) violence associated with task system incompatibilities; and (3) task-congruent violence. It would, of course, be possible for an individual to show more than one type of violence in different settings.

FURTHER PROBLEMS

Many seriously violent offenders and psychiatric patients may be resident in secure institutions. Environments of this sort can pose problems for the implementation and evaluation of anger-management methods. In such settings violence has not only to be treated but to be contained. Ostapiuk and Gentry (1989), working in an institution for violent adolescents, stress the importance of the distinction between containment and long-term therapy, and suggest that a coherent and effective containment policy is a prerequisite for therapy. It is difficult to use anger-management methods with potentially seriously violent clients unless therapists and other institutional staff are confident as to what is to be done in the event of a violent incident and also clear as to how an incident is to be handled effectively. Anger-management may need to be conducted, then, in a coherent and consistent organizational framework.

174

In institutional settings the generalization and maintenance of treatment effects may be difficult to establish. The fact that violence can be prevented in an institution through anger-management does not guarantee that this effect will generalize to community settings or maintain over time so as to prevent violence in the long term. Feindler and Ecton (1986) have suggested a number of useful methods of enhancing generalization and maintenance of anger-control effects, including varying training tasks, using generalized rather than specific self-statements, preparing clients for non-reinforcing or punishing contingencies, booster sessions, and use of significant others in training.

The low baseline frequency of violent behaviour in highly controlled institutions may make evaluation of the effects of therapy on violent incidents almost impossible, as suggested by Alves (1985) in relation to conducting anger management with seriously violent mentally abnormal offenders. Alves and Bonham (1982) illustrate the low baseline frequency problem in their discussion of a patient in anger-management therapy who had attacked and killed a child when in the community but who, over a six-year period in an institution, had been antagonistic on only six occasions, only one of these involving physical violence, and that being to his own property.

CONCLUSIONS

Anger-management methods derived largely from the seminal work of Novaco (1975, 1978, 1979, 1985) form part of what might be called the clinical, therapeutic approach to violence prevention. What evidence is available suggests that anger is functionally important for many forms of violent behaviour. Anger-management requires a multifaceted analysis of angry violence in terms of the environmental, cognitive, physiological, and behavioural components specified by Novaco. In this chapter the anger-management approach to more serious forms of violence has been illustrated. Controlled outcome studies are encouraging but few studies have been conducted in which serious violence itself has been the outcome assessed. Anger-management is not a panacea for the prevention of violence and some of the limitations of the approach and difficulties in implementation and evaluation have been discussed. It is concluded that these methods have undeniable potential in the field of violence prevention but that we are at an early stage in assessing their actual therapeutic impact.

REFERENCES

Alves, E.A. (1985) 'The control of anger in the "mentally abnormal" offender', in E. Karas (ed.) *Current Issues in Clinical Psychology, Vol. II*, New York: Plenum.

Alves, E.A. and Bonham, E.M. (1982) 'Issues in the use of anger management procedures with aggressive offenders', paper presented to the British Association for Behavioural Psychotherapy Conference, Brighton.

Arnold, L.S. and Quinsey, V.L. (1977) 'Overcontrolled hostility among men found not guilty by reason of insanity', *Canadian Journal of Behavioral Science* 9: 330–40.

Averill, J.R. (1982) *Anger and Aggression: An Essay on Emotion*, New York: Springer-Verlag.

Ax, A.F. (1953) 'The physiological differentiation between fear and anger in humans', *Psychosomatic Medicine* 15: 433–42.

Bandura, A. (1973) *Aggression: A Social Learning Analysis*, Englewood Cliffs, NJ: Prentice-Hall.

Bartol, C. (1980) *Criminal Behavior: A Psychological Approach*, Englewood Cliffs, NJ: Prentice-Hall.

Beck, A.T., Rush, A.J., Shaw, B.F., and Emery, G. (1979) *Cognitive Therapy of Depression*, New York: Guildford Press.

Berkowitz, L. (1982) 'Aversive conditions as stimuli to aggression', in L. Berkowitz (ed.) *Advances in Experimental Social Psychology, Vol. 5*, New York: Academic Press.

—— (1983) 'Aversively stimulated aggression', *American Psychologist* 38: 1135–44.

Blackburn, R. (1968) 'Personality in relation to extreme aggression in psychiatric offenders', *British Journal of Psychiatry* 114: 821–8.

—— (1971) 'Personality types among abnormal homicides', *British Journal of Criminology* 11: 14–31.

Buss, A.H. (1961) *The Psychology of Aggression*, New York: Wiley.

Clark, D.M. (1986) 'Cognitive therapy for anxiety', *Behavioural Psychotherapy* 14: 283–94.

Clarke, R.V.G. (1980) 'Situational crime prevention: theory and practice', *British Journal of Criminology* 20: 136–47.

Denicola, J. and Sandler, J. (1980) 'Training abusive parents in cognitive-behavioural techniques', *Behavior Therapy* 11: 263–70.

Dobash, R.E. and Dobash, R.P. (1984) 'The nature and antecedents of violent events', *British Journal of Criminology* 24: 269–88.

Dodge, K.A. (1985) 'Attributional bias in aggressive children', in P.C. Kendall (ed.) *Advances in Cognitive-Behavioral Research and Therapy, Vol. 4*, New York: Academic Press.

Dyck, R.J. and Rule, B.G. (1978) 'Effect on retaliation of causal attributions concerning attack', *Journal of Personality and Social Psychology* 36: 521–9.

D'Zurilla, T. and Goldfried, M. (1971) 'Problem solving and behavior modification', *Journal of Abnormal Psychology* 8: 107–26.

Evans, D.R. and Hearn, M.T. (1973) 'Anger and systematic desensitization: a follow-up', *Psychological Reports* 32: 569–70.

Fehrenbach, P.A. and Thelen, M.H. (1981) 'Assertive-skills training for inappropriately aggressive college males: effects on assertive and aggressive behaviors', *Journal of Behavior Therapy and Experimental Psychiatry* 12: 213–17.

Feindler, E.L. and Ecton, R.B. (1986) *Adolescent Anger Control: Cognitive Behavioral Techniques*, New York: Pergamon.

Feindler, E.L., Marriott, S.A., and Iwata, M. (1984) 'Group anger control training for junior high school delinquents', *Cognitive Therapy and Research* 8: 299–317.

Feindler, E.L., Ecton, R.B., Kingsley, D., and Dubey, D. (1986) 'Group anger control training for institutionalized psychiatric male adolescents', *Behavior Therapy* 17: 109–23.

Feldman, M.P. (1982) 'Overview', in M.P. Feldman (ed.) *Developments in the Study of Criminal Behavior, Vol. 2: Violence*, Chichester: Wiley.

Ferguson, T.J. and Rule, B.G. (1983) 'An attributable perspective on anger and aggression', in R.G. Green and E.L. Donnerstein (eds) *Aggression: Theoretical and Empirical Reviews, Vol. I*, New York: Academic Press.

Feshbach, S. (1986) 'Reconceptualizations of anger: some research perspectives', *Journal of Social and Clinical Psychology* 4: 123–32.

Forsterling, F. (1984) 'Importance, attributions and the emotion of anger', *Zeitschrift fur Psychologie* 192: 425–32.

—— (1985) 'Attributional training: a review', *Psychological Bulletin* 98: 495–512.

Foy, D.W., Eisler, R.M., and Pinkston, S.G. (1975) 'Modeled assertion in a case of explosive rage', *Journal of Behavior Therapy and Experimental Psychiatry*, 6: 135–7.

Frederiksen, L.W., Jenkins, J.O., Foy, D.W., and Eisler, R.M. (1976) 'Social skills training to modify abusive verbal outbursts in adults', *Journal of Applied Behavior Analysis* 9: 117–25.

Frude, N. (1989) 'The physical abuse of children', in K. Howells and C.R. Hollin (eds) *Clinical approaches to Violence*, Chichester: Wiley.

Funkenstein, D.H., King, S.H., and Drolett, M.E. (1957) *Mastery of Stress*, Cambridge: Harvard University Press.

Gardner, J. and Gray, M. (1982) 'Violence towards children', in M.P. Feldman (ed.) *Developments in the Study of Criminal Behavior,*

Vol. 2: Violence, Chichester: Wiley.

Geen, R.G. and Donnerstein, E.L. (eds) (1983) *Aggression: Theoretical and Empirical Reviews, Vols I and II*, New York: Academic Press.

Goldstein, A.P. (1981) 'Social skills training', in A.P. Goldstein, E.G. Carr, W.S. Davison II, and P. Wehr (eds) *In Response to Aggression*, Oxford: Pergamon.

Grieger, R. (1982) 'Anger problems', in R. Grieger and I.Z. Grieger (eds) *Cognition and Emotional Disturbance*, New York: Human Sciences Press.

Groth, A.N. (1979) *Men Who Rape*, New York: Plenum.

Hall, G.S. (1899) 'A study of anger', *American Journal of Psychology* 10: 516–91.

Hazaleus, S.L. and Deffenbacher, J.L. (1986) 'Relaxation and cognitive treatments of anger', *Journal of Consulting and Clinical Psychology* 54: 222-6.

Hearn, M. and Evans, D. (1972) 'Anger and reciprocal inhibition therapy', *Psychological Reports* 30: 943–8.

Hedlund, B.L. and Lindquist, C.V. (1984) 'The development of an inventory for distinguishing among passive, aggressive and assertive behavior', *Behavioral Assessment* 6: 379–90.

Henderson, M. and Hollin, C.R. (1986) 'Social skills training with delinquents', in C.R. Hollin and P. Trower (eds) *Handbook of Social Skills Training, Vol. I*, Oxford: Pergamon.

Hersen, M. and Bellack, A.S. (1981) *Behavioral Assessment: A Practical Handbook (2nd edn)*, New York: Pergamon.

Hollandsworth, J.G. (1977) 'Differentiating assertion and aggression: some behavioral guidelines', *Behavior Therapy* 8: 347–52.

Hollandsworth, S.G. and Cooley, M.L. (1978) 'Provoking anger and gaining compliance with assertive versus aggressive responses', *Behavior Therapy* 9: 640–6.

Hollin, C.R. and Trower, P.T. (eds) (1986) *Handbook of Social Skills Training, Vols I and II*, Oxford: Pergamon.

Howells, K. (1976) 'Interpersonal aggression', *International Journal of Criminology and Penology* 4: 319–30.

—— (1983) 'Social construing and violent behaviour in mentally abnormal offenders', in J. Hinton (ed.) *Dangerousness in Problems of Assessment and Prediction*, London: Allen & Unwin.

—— (1986) 'Social skills training and criminal and antisocial behaviour in adults', in C.R. Hollin and P. Trower (eds) *Handbook of Social Skills Training, Vol. I: Applications Across the Life Span*, Oxford: Pergamon.

—— (1987) 'The management of angry violence: a cognitive-behavioural approach', in W. Dryden and P. Trower (eds) *Developments in Cognitive Psychotherapy*, London: Erlbaum.

Hull, D.B. and Schroeder, H.E. (1979) 'Some interpersonal effects of assertion, non-assertion and aggression', *Behavior Therapy* 10: 20–8.

Izard, C.E. (1977) *Human Emotions*, New York: Plenum.

Kaufman, L.M. and Wagner, B.R. (1972) 'Barb: a systematic treatment technology for temper control disorders', *Behavior Therapy* 3: 84–90.

Kirchner, E.P., Kennedy, R.E., and Draguns, J.G. (1979) 'Assertion and aggression in adult offenders', *Behavior Therapy* 10: 452–71.

Kremer, J.F. and Stephens, L. (1983) 'Attribution and arousal as mediators of mitigation's effect on retaliation', *Journal of Personality and Social Psychology* 45: 335–43.

McFall, R.M. (1982) 'A review and reformulation of the concept of social skills', *Behavioral Assessment* 4: 1–33.

McKellar, P. (1950) 'Provocation to anger and the development of attitudes of hostility', *British Journal of Psychology* 40: 104–14.

Marques, J.K. (1981) 'Effect of victim resistance strategies on the sexual arousal and attitude of violent rapists', in R.B. Stuart (ed.) *Violent Behavior: Social Learning Approaches to Prediction, Management and Treatment*, New York: Brunner-Mazel.

Megargee, E.I. (1966) 'Undercontrolled and overcontrolled personality types in extreme antisocial aggression', *Psychological Monographs* 80 (Whole No. 611).

—— (1971) 'The role of inhibition in the assessment and understanding of violence', in J.E. Singer (ed.) *The Control of Aggression and Violence: Cognitive and Physiological Factors*, London: Academic Press.

—— (1984) 'Recent research on overcontrolled and undercontrolled personality patterns among violent offenders', in I. Jacks and S.G. Cox (eds) *Psychological Approaches to Crime and its Correction*, Chicago: Nelson-Hall.

Moon, J.R. and Eisler, R.M. (1983) 'Anger control: an experimental comparison of three behavioral treatments', *Behavior Therapy* 14: 493–505.

Nasby, W., Hayden, B., and De Paulo, B.M. (1980) 'Attributional bias among aggressive boys to interpret unambiguous social stimuli as displays of hostility', *Journal of Abnormal Psychology* 89: 459–68.

Nomellini, S. and Katz, R. (1983) 'Effects of anger control training on abusive parents', *Cognitive Therapy and Research* 7: 57–68.

Novaco, R.W. (1975) *Anger Control: The Development and Evaluation of an Experimental Treatment*, Lexington: D.C. Heath and Co.

—— (1976a) 'The function and regulation of the arousal of anger', *American Journal of Psychiatry* 133: 1124–8.

—— (1976b) 'Treatment of chronic anger through cognitive and relaxation controls', *Journal of Consulting and Clinical Psychology* 44: 681.

—— (1977a) 'Stress inoculation: a cognitive therapy for anger and its application to a case of depression', *Journal of Consulting and Clinical Psychology* 45: 600–8.

────── (1977b) 'A stress inoculation approach to anger management in the training of law enforcement officers', *Journal of Community Psychology* 5: 327–46.

────── (1978) 'Anger and coping with stress', in J.P. Foreyt and D.P. Rathjen (eds) *Cognitive Behavior Therapy*, New York: Penguin.

────── (1979) 'The cognitive regulation of anger and stress', in P. Kendall and S. Hollon (eds) *Cognitive Behavioral Interventions: Theory, Research and Procedures*, New York: Academic Press.

────── (1985) 'Anger and its therapeutic regulation', in M.A. Chesney and R.H. Rosenman (eds) *Anger and Hostility in Cardiovascular and Behavioral Disorders*, New York: Hemisphere Publishing Co.

Ostapiuk, E.B. and Gentry, M. (1989) 'Violence in institutions for young offenders', in K. Howells and C. Hollin (eds) *Clinical approaches to Violence*, Chichester: Wiley.

Patterson, G.R. (1985) 'A microsocial analysis of anger and irritable behavior', in M.A. Chesney and R.H. Rosenman (eds) *Anger and Hostility in Cardiovascular and Behavioral Disorders*, Washington: Hemisphere Publishing Co.

Platt, J.J., Prout, M.F., and Metzger, D.S. (1986) 'Interpersonal cognitive problem-solving therapy (ICPS)', in W. Dryden and W. Golden (eds) *Cognitive-Behavioural Approaches to Psychotherapy*, London: Harper and Row.

Rahaim, S., LeFebvre, C., and Jenkins, J.O. (1980) 'The effects of social skills training on behavioral and cognitive components of anger management', *Journal of Behavior Therapy and Experimental Psychiatry* 11: 3–8.

Rimm, D.C., Hill, G.A., Brown, N.N., and Stuart, J.E. (1974) 'Group assertive training in treatment of experience of inappropriate anger', *Psychological Reports* 34: 791–8.

Schur, E.M. (1979) *Interpreting Deviance*, New York: Harper and Row.

Shield, S.A. (1984) 'Reports of bodily change in anxiety, sadness and anger', *Motivation and Emotion* 8: 1–21.

Siegel, J.M. (1985) 'The measurement of anger on a multidimensional construct', in M.A. Chesney and R.H. Rosenman (eds) *Anger and Hostility in Cardiovascular and Behavioral Disorders*, Washington: Hemisphere Publishing Co.

Spielberger, C.D., Jacobs, G.A., Russell, S., and Crane, R.S. (1983) 'Assessment of anger: the state-trait anger scale', in J. Butcher and C.D. Spielberger (eds) *Advances in Personality Assessment, Vol. 2*, Hillsdale, N.J.:Erlbaum.

Spielberger, C.D., Johnson, E.H., Russell, S.F., Crane, R.J., Jacobs, G.A., and Worden, T.J. (1985) 'The experience and expression of anger: construction and validation of an anger expression scale', in M.A. Chesney and R.H. Rosenman (eds) *Anger and Hostility in Cardiovascular and Behavioral Disorders*,

Washington: Hemisphere Publishing Co.
Toch, H. (1969) *Violent Men*, Harmondsworth: Penguin.
—— (1985) 'The catalytic situation in the violence equation', *Journal of Applied Social Psychology* 15: 105–23.
Trower, P., Bryant, B., and Argyle, M. (1978) *Social Skills and Mental Health*, London: Methuen.
West, D.J. (1980) 'The clinical approach to criminology', *Psychological Medicine* 10: 619–31.
—— (1986) 'Clinical approaches to criminology', in C. Hollin and K. Howells (eds) *Clinical approaches to Criminal Behaviour. Issues in Criminological and Legal Psychology, No. 9*, Leicester: British Psychological Society.
Zillmann, D. (1979) *Hostility and Aggression*, Hillsdale, NJ: Erlbaum.

Chapter 8

THE NATURALISTIC
CONTEXT OF
FAMILY VIOLENCE
AND CHILD ABUSE

KEVIN BROWNE

INTRODUCTION

During the past decade, family violence has been increasingly reported in our daily newspapers and news bulletins. These accounts painfully describe acts of violence between spouses, or from adults towards their own children or their defenceless elderly relatives. This has forced us to recognize that violence within the family is a common phenomenon of modern society. Indeed, Gelles and Cornell (1985) began their recent book, *Intimate Violence in Families*, by stating that 'people are more likely to be killed, physically assaulted, hit, beaten up, slapped or spanked in their own homes by other family members than anywhere else, or by anyone else in our society' (p. 12).

Family violence is not a 'new' problem. Historically, violence has been regarded as an acceptable way for the family man to exert control over the behaviour of his dependents. This aggressive control is still evident today: for example, a husband has the legal right to rape his wife and physically punish his children. Thus, rather than condemn violent acts, law and social policy attempts to discriminate between socially acceptable 'normal' violence and unacceptable 'abusive' violence in the family. This has confounded most attempts to deal with the pervading problem.

This chapter aims to explain the usefulness of naturalistic approaches for the recognition and treatment of family violence. To demonstrate the relevance of a naturalistic framework, it is first necessary to describe what is known about violence in the family and to discuss the existing theories and models used to understand its causes. The application of an ethological approach to the study of relationships in child-abusing families is then presented as a specific example of a naturalistic perspective to the problem. The limitations of this perspective are also discussed.

THE TYPES OF FAMILY VIOLENCE
AND THEIR INCIDENCE

In Chapter 1 we described violence as the exercise of physical force so as to cause injury or forcibly interfere with personal freedom. When applied to the family this definition embraces three broad areas of violence by adults, child abuse, spouse abuse, and elder abuse, and two areas of violence by children, sibling abuse and parent abuse. Research has examined each type of abuse separately, one possible reason being that each one evolved as a recognized social problem at a different time. Each type of abuse can, however, be characterized in the same way, and dichotomized into 'active' and 'passive' forms: active abuse involves violent acts (as defined above) in a physical, emotional, or sexual context; passive abuse refers to neglect, which can only be considered violent in the metaphorical sense, as it does not involve physical force (see Chapter 1). Nevertheless, it can cause both physical and emotional injury, such as non-organic failure-to-thrive in young children.

Victims of family violence are unlikely to be subjected to only one type of abuse: for example, sexual abuse and physical abuse are always accompanied by emotional abuse. Emotional abuse may take a number of recognizable forms, principally: verbal assault, including threats of sexual or physical abuse; close confinement, such as locking a child in a room; and other adversive treatment, such as withholding food.

The lack of consensus concerning the definitions of various forms of abuse account for the wide variations in reports on the prevalence and incidence of violence in the family. Besharov (1982), for example, claims that estimates of child abuse cases in the USA range from 60,000 to 4,500,000 each year, depending upon the definition of abuse adopted. Despite these wide discrepancies the following summary of the available statistics attempts to illustrate the wide extent of family violence within modern society.

Violence by adults

1 Child abuse and neglect

In the UK there are no truly accurate estimates, as no mandatory system of recording has been adopted. One of the few government attempts to assess the problem of child abuse, the House of Commons Select Committee on Violence in the Family (1977), reported that there is one severely injured child per thousand children under four years of age. Approximately 10 per cent of these severely physically abused children, with deep tissue injuries (bone fractures, etc.) will die and a further 10 per cent will suffer from brain damage or other severe handicaps. It was concluded from this assessment that child abuse was the fourth commonest cause of death to pre-school children in the UK.

It is more difficult to estimate the number of moderate cases with subcutaneous injuries (bruises, burns, etc.) or mild cases with surface injuries (scratches, weals, etc.), since these children may not be sent to hospital. However, the government report gives an annual figure of as many as 40,000 children in this category for England and Wales alone, which gives a rate similar to that of the USA (Gil 1970), of four physically abused children in every thousand. It is generally accepted that most of these cases of moderate or mild non-accidental injury occur in children under five years old, with those under one year old being most seriously harmed. Furthermore, it is estimated from the National Society for the Prevention of Cruelty to Children's (NSPCC) special unit registers in England and Wales, that over a six-year period from 1979–1984 the physical abuse of children increased by 70 per cent (Creighton 1987). The above figures are based on an operational definition which emphasizes the *physical* nature of child maltreatment, physical child abuse being defined as 'the intentional, non-accidental use of force on the part of the parent or other caretaker interacting with a child in his or her care aimed at hurting, injuring or destroying that child' (Gil 1970). However, since 1980 cases of other types of abuse, sexual abuse, and non-organic failure-to-thrive have been included in registers of child-abusing families. By 1984 these groups accounted for 22 per cent of child-abuse cases (Creighton 1987). Sexual abuse showed the most dramatic increase, from 1 per cent in 1980 to 11 per cent in 1984.

Kempe (1980) defines sexual abuse as 'the involvement of dependent, developmentally immature children and adolescents in sexual activities that they do not fully comprehend, to which they are unable to give informed consent or that violate the social taboos of family roles' (p. 198). A postal survey to relevant professionals in the UK, conducted by Mrazek *et al.* (1981), revealed that 1,065 reported cases of sexual abuse could be classified into 3 types:

Type 1: battered children whose injuries were primarily in the genital area (4 per cent),
Type 2: children who have experienced attempted or actual intercourse, or other inappropriate genital contact with an adult (69 per cent); and
Type 3: children who have in some other way been involved with an adult in sexual activities (16 per cent).

Some 10 per cent of the children with type 2 and 3 abuse had also suffered a physical injury. Unlike physical abuse, however, most of the children were over 6 years of age (87 per cent) and most were female (85 per cent). It was concluded from the study that a minimum of three children in every thousand would be sexually abused by the time they reached adulthood.

The NSPCC reported 9,590 physical-abuse cases and 6,330 sexual-abused cases for 1986 (NSPCC Press Release 1987) and concludes that as many as 200 children die per year as a direct or indirect result of maltreatment by their parents (NSPCC 1985).

2 Spouse abuse

The problem of marital violence emerged as a significant issue in the early 1970s. However, Binney *et al.* (1981) state that there is still widespread ignorance about the nature of spouse abuse and the form it takes. Gelles and Straus (1979) have defined it as 'any act carried out with the intention of or perceived as having the intention of physically hurting another person'

KEVIN BROWNE

(p. 554). This definition, therefore, includes both physical and psychological assault, which involves such acts as throwing objects near a person or destroying pets and other belongings (Purdy and Nickle 1981). Often, these acts are associated with sexual abuse of the spouse where forced sex or 'marital rape' is accompanied by some form of threat or actual violence (Straus *et al*. 1980).

Studies have shown that 'marital violence' occurs once a year or more in at least one in six American families (ibid.), and it has been estimated that one woman in twenty-two is physically assaulted (Straus 1980). It should be pointed out, however, that this violence is not always unidirectional (men to women). Straus *et al*. (1980) reported that 5 per cent of the wives surveyed had engaged in violence towards their husbands. They suggest that sometimes the 'marital violence' is bidirectional, with similar rates of 'hitting' for husbands and wives. Nevertheless, because husbands are usually stronger and larger than their wives, with more social resources at their command, the physical or social consequences of marital violence are limited when the man is the victim. Thus, 'Marital violence is primarily a problem of victimised women' (Gelles and Cornell 1985).

In the UK there are no regularly updated statistics on wife abuse but the problem is extensive. From police records Dobash and Dobash (1979) found that the second largest category of interpersonal violence was assault on wives (25 per cent), the most common form of violence being between unrelated males (38 per cent). Of the 1,051 cases of violence within the home recorded by the police 'wife-beating' represented 77 per cent, 'child-beating' 11 per cent, and 'husband-beating' 1 per cent of cases.

In their book *Leaving Violent Men*, Binney *et al*. (1981) reported a survey of 150 refuges in England and Wales. From this, they estimate that 11,400 women and 20,850 children used the accommodation in a one-year period (September 1977 to September 1978). A survey of 656 women who were in the 150 refuges at the time of their study showed that the majority of women had left home to escape physical violence to themselves (90 per cent) and sometimes to their children (27 per cent). Other forms of ill-treatment were also mentioned, such as psychological or mental abuse and not being given enough

186

money to live on. Many of the women had experienced several kinds of ill-treatment. In their follow-up study of eighty-four women they found that 34 per cent had suffered life-threatening attacks or had been hospitalized for serious injuries (for example, broken bones). Assaults included being kicked, pushed into fires or through glass, thrown against walls or down stairs, being punched, or having their hair pulled out.

Dobash and Dobash's in-depth study (1979) of 106 'battered' women shows that violence during a typical physical assault falls into the following categories: punching the face and/or the body, 44 per cent; kicking, kneeing or butting, 27 per cent; pushing into a non-injurious object, 15 per cent; hitting with an object, 5 per cent; and attempted smothering or strangling, 2 per cent. In 89 per cent of cases the violence started after marriage, or after the woman began living with the man. In some cases, it was only when the violence also began to be directed at the children that the woman felt justified in leaving home. Whereas Binney *et al.* (1981) reported that 68 per cent of the women they interviewed claimed that 'mental cruelty' was one of the reasons they left, usually this happened in conjunction with physical violence, although 10 per cent said they had suffered mental cruelty on its own. In some cases the women had been kept virtual prisoners, and in others they had been verbally tormented and threatened, until they were confused about their own sanity.

In another refuge study by Pahl (1985), a detailed examination of forty-two violent couples revealed the following findings. In thirty-eight (90 per cent) of the couples there was *a child under five* in the household when the violence was taking place. For fifteen (36 per cent) of these families the woman was *pregnant* when the violence began. In eleven of the cases, this was the first child for the prospective parents. In the remaining four households the mother had had other children by a previous husband.

In the majority of surveyed cases (81 per cent), the women were aged between 20 and 34 years old with an average of two to three children. The violence these women suffered had often occurred for a considerable length of time, the average length of time being seven years (ranging from a few months to 30–40 years). Over half the sample (59 per cent) had been abused for three years or more.

3 Elder abuse

Physical abuse of the elderly most frequently manifests itself in neglect (Steinmetz 1978) for example, tying an elderly person who needs constant watching on to a bed or chair in order to complete the housework or shopping, or the excessive use of sleeping medication or alcohol in order to make them more manageable. It is important to recognize that this type of neglect may not necessarily be intended to harm the elderly person. There is a lack of knowledge about how to care for the elderly and in some cases abuse is not intentional.

It is clear why there are difficulties in assessing the prevalence of elder abuse. Elderly people are not involved in social networks such as schooling or employment. They are on average even more isolated from the mainstream of society than younger adults. Victims are also unwilling to report maltreatment. Only one in four known cases of abuse are reported by the victims themselves (Legal Research and Services for the Elderly, 1979.

According to Gelles and Cornell (1985) there are several reasons why the elderly are reluctant to report their abuse. They may be too embarrassed to admit to having raised a child capable of such behaviour (assuming that a son or daughter is involved). They may also assume the blame for the abuser's behaviour, a trait that is also common in wife- and child-abuse victims. Often the love for the abuser is stronger than the desire to leave. Despite these difficulties, it is estimated that 7 per cent of the elderly US population are abused (Pierce and Trotta 1986). Indeed, Press (1979) has reported that at least 500,000 elderly persons aged 65 or over who live with younger members of their families are physically abused each year in the US. Block and Sinnott (1979) place the figure closer to one million victims annually. Although there are no reliable estimates for the UK, both Renvoize (1978) and Freeman (1979) suggest that 'granny bashing', as they call it, may be increasing in Britain as a result of the increase in numbers of elderly dependent individuals in our society. This is especially true for very elderly people (i.e. aged 75 or over), many of whom are mentally infirm and/or physically disabled (see Browne 1984). The economic and social burden of caring for these old people has fallen more and more on the relatives, with more than 50 per cent living with their immediate families (DHSS 1978). The stress of increased caregiving responsibility within the family and the resulting problems, such as relatives resenting the unwanted intrusion into their lives of 'granny sitting', places a heavy strain on family relationships (Renvoize 1978). Indeed, in a study of fifty adults who had parents living with them, 75 per cent reported a variety of familial difficulties due to their parents ageing (Simos 1976). Pierce and Trotta (1986) report that it is this stress associated with caring for the elderly relative which is the precipitating factor for violence in the majority of cases (63 per cent). A more detailed review of this aspect of family violence follows in the next chapter (Chapter 9), which concludes that there is now a growing awareness of the problem of 'old-age abuse'.

Violence by children

It is generally thought that children are not physically capable of seriously injuring others. However, research has demonstrated that violence towards siblings and parents are common forms of family problems.

1 Sibling abuse

Sibling rivalry is considered to be a 'normal' part of family life (Dunn 1984; Dunn and Kendrick 1982). Aggressive interactions are found by parents to be annoying but they do not perceive these events as dangerous or leading to serious conflict (Steinmetz 1977). Previous research has mainly dealt with the most extreme forms of sibling violence such as murder (for example, Adelson 1972), but recently more attention has been directed towards the 19 million children in the USA who seriously injure their brothers and sisters every year (Straus *et al.* 1980). In general, the latter research suggests that four out of five children (3 to 17 years of age) with one or more siblings are involved in at least one violent conflict annually with their brother or sister. Their findings also confirm the widely held beliefs that as children grow older, the use of violence to resolve sibling conflict decreases (Maccoby 1980), and that boys were more aggressive than girls (Archer and Lloyd 1985). It should be pointed out, however, that although boys were more violent than girls at all ages, the difference was relatively small. Overall, 83 per cent of boys and 74 per cent of girls were physically aggressive towards their brother or sister (Straus *et al.* 1980).

2   Parent abuse

Warren (1978) investigated fifteen adolescents (between the ages of 12 and 17), who were admitted to a psychiatric hospital for violence towards their parents. She states that these adolescents used weapons and speed to combat the greater physical strength of their parents. Thus, for example, a 12 year old 'poured gasoline in the bathroom while his mother was in there, threw a match and shut the door'. The problem is difficult to estimate because of the common denial by parents that they have abusive children (Harbin and Madden 1979). Nevertheless, the findings of surveys conducted in the USA indicate that one in ten parents report at least one act of violence by their teenager (Cornell and Gelles 1982) and that 3 per cent of these incidents resulted in serious assault to the parent (i.e. kicked, punched, bit, knifed, or shot).

This problem is not necessarily confined to lower socio-economic groups, the mentally ill or mentally handicapped, since Mulligan (1977) reports that 12 per cent of US college students admit one act of violence towards a parent when they lived at home during the senior year of high school.

Common factors in family violence

Similarities have been found between those who physically and sexually abuse their children, those who abuse their wives, and those who abuse their aged relatives. These include: a misperception of the victim, low self-esteem, sense of incompetence, social isolation, a lack of support and help, lack of empathy, marital difficulties, depression, poor self-control, and a history of abuse or neglect as a child.

Several characteristics found within the victims of abuse are common to all types of abuse. These include: a poor relationship with the abuser; dependency; emotional and social isolation; and ill health.

It is not surprising, therefore, to find reports that suggest wife abuse and child physical abuse are closely linked (Stark and McEvoy 1970; Milner and Gold 1986), or that wife abuse occurs in families where there is child sexual abuse (Julian and Mohr 1979). Thus, it is important to consider whether these common factors relate to common causes for the various forms of violence in the family.

THE CAUSES OF FAMILY VIOLENCE

In a general survey of types of family violence, it is evident that physical violence does not encompass the whole range of harmful acts which are described under the term 'abuse'. Hence, some authors distinguish between acts of physical violence and other forms of abuse, because the causes, and their potential solutions, are different (see Etzioni 1971). While all harmful acts have some causes in common, other factors are unique to physical violence. Therefore, I consider the following outline of causal factors in relation to family violence to be more relevant to physical abuse and neglect than to other forms of abuse.

In seeking to understand the many causal factors involved in family violence, several theoretical models have been proposed.

Psychopathic model

This psychiatric analysis focuses on the abnormal characteristics of the abuser, emphasizing the psychological dysfunctions characteristic of certain abusing adults (see Elmer 1967). However, Kempe and Kempe (1978) suggested that only 10 per cent of child abusers can accurately be labelled as mentally ill. Nevertheless, the model has been useful in recognizing certain predispositions of abusive individuals. These include a tendency to have:

(1) distorted perceptions of their dependents (Spinetta and Rigler 1972; Rosenberg and Reppucci 1983);
(2) difficulty dealing with aggressive impulses as a result of being impulsively immature, often depressed, and self-centered (Kempe *et al.* 1962; Steele and Pollock 1968; Hyman 1977);
(3) a history of having been abused, neglected or witnessing

violence as children (Wasserman *et al.* 1983; Spinetta and Rigler 1972; Hunter *et al.* 1978).

The emphasis of this model is on the abuser's 'abnormal' personality, which is the result of adverse socialization experiences that produce a 'psychopathic' character, with a predisposition to behave violently (see Figure 8.2).

One form of this predisposition is referred to as 'transference psychosis' (Galdston 1965). Involving transference from parent to child, for example: the parent often interprets the child as if he/she were an adult and perceives the child as hostile and persecuting, projecting that part of their own personality they wish to destroy (Steele and Pollock 1968). Thus, the child is seen as the cause of the parent's troubles and becomes a scapegoat to which all anger is directed (Wasserman *et al.* 1983). Authors who promote the psychopathological model claim that social variables do not enter into the causal scheme of family violence. This is of course a narrow viewpoint, and a major fault of the model is its failure to examine the possible social causes of psychological stress that may lead to violent interactions within families.

The social and environmental models

By contrast, this approach focuses on the social and environmental factors which can promote family violence, such as low wages, unemployment (O'Brien 1971; Krugman 1986), social isolation (Garbardino 1977) overcrowding, and poor housing (Skinner and Castle 1969). Indeed, Gelles (1973) claimed that violence is an adaptation or response to structural and situational stress, which is not confined to families in lower socioeconomic groups.

A broader perspective is put forward by Gil (1970) who emphasized the 'macrosystem' of cultural values and beliefs which affect the standards of caregiving and the acceptance of physical punishment as an appropriate way of control and violence as a form of emotional expression. This is said to influence the social structure of the neighbourhood community and the microsystem of the family itself (see Chapter 1).

Dobash and Dobash (1979) recognized the contribution of

patriarchy to family violence, and proposed that the source of violence lies in society and how it is organized, rather than within individual families or communities. Indeed, Gelles and Cornell (1985) point out that an individual's general acceptance of violence as the 'norm' may influence the extent to which they exhibit or tolerate aggressive behaviour.

The special victim model

In direct contrast with the viewpoints considered so far are suggestions that the victims themselves may be instrumental in some way in eliciting attack or neglect. Friedrich and Boroskin (1976) review the complex reasons why a child may not fulfil the parent's expectations or demands. The dependent may in some way be regarded as 'special': for example, studies have found prematurity, low birth weight, illness and handicap to be associated with child abuse (Elmer and Gregg 1967; Lynch and Roberts 1977; Starr 1988). As pointed out by Berkowitz the physical unattractiveness of these children may be an important factor for child abuse (see Chapter 3).

The psychological model

Frude (1980) takes a psychological perspective and puts forward the notion of a causal chain leading to an incidence of abuse: first, the objective stressful situation which is usually long-term, such as poverty; second, abusing parents may assess a situation differently from non-abusing parents, i.e., as threatening; third, anger and emotional distress are more likely as responses to these situations; and fourth, lack of inhibitions with regard to violent expression, together with a lower threshold of tolerance. Together these result in the caregiver being more easily provoked to take physical action against their dependents (see Figure 8.1).

In Chapter 7 of this volume, Howells outlines the work of Novaco (1978) in relation to anger arousal. This work emphasizes the role of cognitive processes such as appraisal and expectations of external events in the above causal chain (see Fig. 11.1, p. 267).

193

KEVIN BROWNE

Figure 8.1 A causal psychological model of abuse

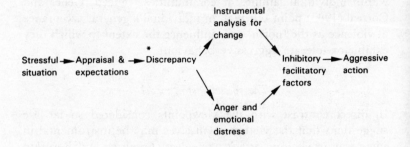

Source: Modified from Frude (1980).

* Discrepancy between what is perceived to be real in the current situation and what is perceived to be the desired goal and the degree of change required.

The psychosocial model

Each model has been useful and together they have served to emphasize the diverse nature of the variables involved in family violence. It must, therefore, be concluded that family violence cannot be explained by a single factor and that it is a multi-factorial phenomenon. Simple explanations make the solution of this pervasive problem appear too easy. Thus, the first Report from the House of Commons Select Committee on Violence in the Family (House of Commons 1977) laid special emphasis for child abuse on 'bonding' in the days immediately following the birth of a baby. However, we know from follow-up studies of infants who have suffered early post-natal separation that most observable effects disappear within the first eighteen months (Leiderman and Seashore 1975; Sluckin *et al.* 1983). Furthermore, many abused infants are not so separated.

This has led to a 'psychosocial model', which is a combination of the above models, emphasizing the 'social-situational approach' to family violence. Originally proposed by American researchers (for example, Gelles 1973; Gelles and Cornell 1985), this model suggests that certain stress factors and adverse background influences may serve to predispose individuals to

194

Table 8.1 Relative importance of screening characteristics for child abuse (as determined by step-wise discriminate function analysis)

	Abusing families (n = 62)	Non-abusing families (n = 124)	
	%	%	
1 Parent indifferent, intolerant or over-anxious towards child	83.9	21.8	*
2 History of family violence	51.6	5.6	*
3 Socio-economic problems such as unemployment	85.5	34.7	*
4 Infant premature, low birth weight	24.2	3.2	*
5 Parent abused or neglected as a child	43.5	6.5	*
6 Stepparent or cohabitee present	35.5	4.8	*
7 Single or separated parent	38.7	8.1	*
8 Mother less than 21 years old at the time of birth	40.3	23.4	*
9 History of mental illness, drug or alcohol addiction	61.3	21.8	*
10 Infant separated from mother for greater than 24 hours post delivery	17.7	5.6	*
11 Infant mentally or physically handicapped	1.6	0.8	
12 Less than 18 months between birth of children	22.6	15.3	
13 Infant never breast fed	46.8	40.3	

* Significant difference $p < 0.05$.

Source: From Browne and Stevenson (1983).

violence, which will occur in the presence of precipitating factors, such as a child misbehaving. It has been claimed that the 'predisposing' factors may form a basis for identification of families 'at risk' of abusing their children (see Pringle 1980). However, a more pertinent question is why the majority of such families under stress do *not* abuse their children.

From our own work (Browne and Saqi 1988a) involving a sample of over 14,000 births we have found that 6.7 per cent of Surrey families with a new-born have a high number of 'predisposing' factors for child abuse (see Table 8.1).

On follow-up only one out of seventeen of these 'high risk' families went on to abuse their child within two years of birth. On the basis of the predictions from the psychosocial model and of the known incidence of infant maltreatment within the Surrey area (approximately one-third of abused children in Surrey are maltreated before the age of 2 years old – statistics cited in Hyman 1978) this figure should have been considerably higher – that is, six out of seventeen.

Thus, we conclude that background influences and situational stress factors associated with 'high risk' families are not a sufficient causal explanation for family violence.

The limitations for Gelles's psychosocial model is that he neglected the transactions that occur between abuse-prone caretakers and vulnerable dependents. It may be that additional stress will only lead to family violence when adverse family interactions exist. Belsky (1980) and Parke (1976) have taken a more integrated approach to child abuse. They conceptualize child maltreatment as a social-psychological phenomenon that is 'multiply determined by forces at work in the individual, the family, as well as in the community and the culture in which both the individual and the family are embedded' (Belsky 1980: 320). Given a particular combination of these three factors, an interactional style develops within the family and it is in the context of this interaction that abuse occurs. This approach will be adopted to explain child, spouse, and elderly abuse.

AN INTEGRATED APPROACH TO THE CAUSATION OF FAMILY VIOLENCE

In Chapter 1, we commented that the study of social interactions and relationships can be seen as occupying a central and potentially integrating place in the study of aggression (Figure 1.2). In relation to violence between family members, Figure 8.2 presents a tentative model of the causes of family violence. It assumes that the 'situational stressors' are made up of the following four components:

(A) Relations between Parents and Grandparents – intermarriage, marital disputes, stepparent/cohabitee or separated/single parent.
(B) Relations to Children, such as spacing between births, size of family, parental attachment to child, and parental expectations of child.
(C) Structural Stress – poor housing, unemployment, social isolation, threats to parental authority, values, and self-esteem.
(D) Stress generated by the child (or other dependent) – for example, an unwanted dependent; one who is incontinent,

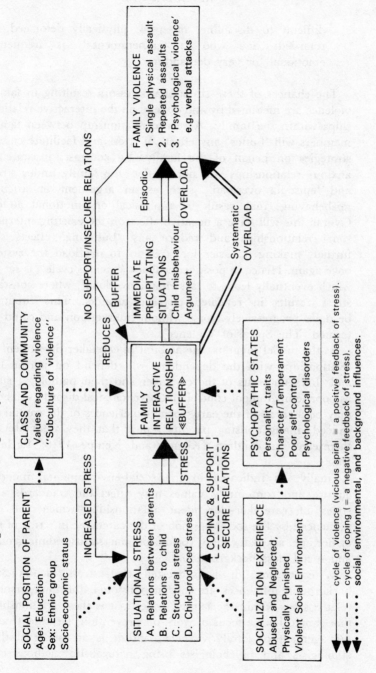

Figure 8.2 An integrated psychosocial model of the causes of family violence

difficult to discipline, often ill, physically deformed, or retarded; one who is temperamental, is frequently emotional, or very demanding.

The chances of these situational stressors resulting in family violence are mediated by and depend on the interactive relationships within the family. A secure relationship between family members will 'buffer' any effects of stress and facilitate coping strategies on behalf of the family. By contrast, insecure or anxious relationships will not 'buffer' the family under stress and 'episodic overload', such as an argument or a child misbehaving, may result in a physical or emotional attack. Overall this will have a negative effect on the existing interpersonal relationships and reduce any 'buffering' effects still further, making it easier for stressors to overload the system once again. Hence, a positive feedback ('vicious cycle') is set up which eventually leads to 'systematic overload', where constant stress results in repeated physical assaults. This situation becomes progressively worse without intervention and could be termed 'The Spiral of Violence'.

As the model suggests, the amount of caretaker investment in relationships with the dependents will depend on personality and character traits of the caretaker and their pathology, such as poor temperament control and psychological disorders. These may be a result of the early social experiences of the caretaker. Indeed, many abusing parents report that they were abused themselves as children (Kempe and Kempe 1978; Egeland 1988).

Finally, as indicated in the social-environmental models, culture and community values may affect the standards and styles of caretaker–dependent relationships which will be influenced by the social position of the caretaker in terms of his or her age, sex, education, socio-economic status, ethnic group, and social class background.

In conclusion, it is suggested that stress factors and background influences are mediated through the interpersonal relationships within the family. Indeed, it is these relationships that should be the focus of work on prevention, treatment, and management of family violence, and it is at this level that ethologists and psychologists using naturalistic methods can make a significant contribution. This point will be emphasized in relation to studies on child abuse.

AN ETHOLOGICAL APPROACH TO THE STUDY OF SOCIAL RELATIONSHIPS IN CHILD-ABUSING FAMILIES

The previous section has identified social interactions within the family as mediating stress factors and background influences for family violence. This section reviews the application of one naturalistic approach to the study of social relationships in child-abusing families, that of ethological observations as described by Smith in Chapter 4.

Observational studies of child-abusing families

To date, observational studies of child-abusing families have described the behaviour of mothers and their children in either structured playroom settings or unstructured home environments. Most of this research has been carried out in the United States, and the majority of the studies have focused primarily on the mother's behaviour (see Aragona and Eyberg 1981; Mash *et al.* 1983; Wasserman *et al.* 1983).

In general, studies carried out in structured playrooms have shown abusing and neglectful mothers to be more directive and more negative in their interactions with their children than non-abusing mothers, matched for socio-economic status. However, Dietrich *et al.* (1980) stated that the abusing mothers in their study were not easy to distinguish from 'matched control' mothers and that they were not grossly depriving, but just stimulated their infants less. A similar lack of distinction between the behaviour of abusing and non-abusing mothers has also been reported by Relich *et al.* (1980).

In the home environment, Disbrow *et al.* (1977) observed that abusive parents ignored, intervened and punished more often than non-abusive parents, whereas neglectful parents were found to fall between the abusers and controls in their behaviour. Furthermore, Burgess and Conger (1977, 1978) noted that abusive parents in comparison with control parents showed less physical play and less compliance in interaction with their children at home. There were fewer verbal interactions from abusive mothers, with 'affectionate' and 'supportive' interactions occurring 50 per cent less often than in control mothers. In addition, there was a higher number of 'threatening' and 'complaining' interactions from abusive parents, although this difference from control parents was not statistically significant. Clearer differences were evident for neglectful parents, who showed a similar pattern of interaction to abusive parents but in a more extreme fashion. Corresponding findings were reported by Reid et al. (1981). However, they noted that the highest level of aversive behaviour in their families was exhibited by the abused children themselves. The researchers concluded that the children were not passive participants in the abuse process and were observed to be extremely difficult to handle.

The problem with most of the above studies is that they fail to describe the reciprocal nature of the mother–child relationship or lack or it. In contrast, observational research projects concerned primarily with the behavioural characteristics of abused infants have utilized methods broadly based on the 'strange situation procedure' (Ainsworth and Wittig 1969) to investigate this reciprocity. The methods used all involve at least three phases of observation: the infants' behaviour and interaction before separation from the mother, during separation, and on reunion.

Overall, these research studies (Hyman et al. 1979; Lewis and Schaeffer 1981; Gaensbauer 1982; Browne and Saqi 1987, 1988b) indicated that prior to separation there was less interaction and less positive affect between abusing mother–infant dyads, in comparison with non-abusing dyads. During separation, abused infants showed less interest in strangers and objects around the room and were less upset than their matched controls. However, abused infants that did display distress and discomfort persisted in this, long after their mother's return. By contrast, the matched non-abused infants showed immediate recovery. On reunion, the abused infants showed less positive affect and greeting behaviour and again mother–infant interaction in abusing dyads was less reciprocal than controls with fewer visual and vocal exchanges.

In addition to reporting the frequency of behaviours, Browne

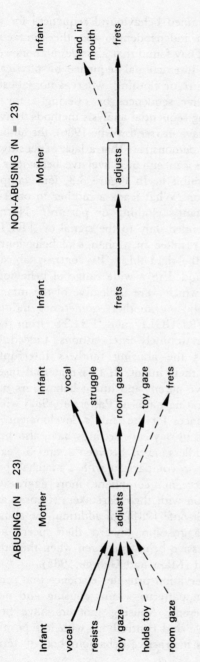

Figure 8.3 Infant-to-mother interaction

ABUSING (N = 23)

NON-ABUSING (N = 23)

Source: Browne and Saqi (1987).

z > 3.10, p < 0.001

z > 2.34, p < 0.01

z > 1.96, p < 0.05

and Saqi (1987) also examined behavioural sequences for the mothers and the children independently and the interactive behaviour between them. They found that abusive mothers were more likely to disrupt an interactional sequence by physically adjusting the infant's posture or clothing, whereas non-abusive mothers extended interactive sequences by offering a toy or smiling at their child. Using sequential analysis methods derived from studies on animal behaviour (see Browne 1986), the authors (op. cit.) were also able to demonstrate that a lack of sensitivity shown by abusing mothers can enhance aversive behaviour in their infant rather than inhibit it. In Figure 8.3, for example, the authors ask the question 'What leads a mother to obstrusively "ADJUST" her infant's clothing or posture?' Normal mothers significantly responded only to the signal of 'FRETS' from their infants, which resulted in a change of behaviour if they successfully adjusted the right thing. By contrast, abusing mothers significantly responded to a wide range of behaviours with 'ADJUST', none of which were indicative of the infant's distress. Ironically, the abusing mothers sometimes induced distress in the form of 'STRUGGLE' and 'FRETS' from their infants as a result of their untimely interventions. Indeed, on the majority of occasions the abusing mothers interrupted exploratory behaviour on their infant. If this maternal insensitivity persists, the coercive parent and infant behaviours may form a cyclical and accelerating pattern (Patterson 1982) which will have serious consequences for the child's development.

Naturalistic observations in day-care settings have also been carried out on abused toddlers, aged between 1 and 3 years. Studies have reported that in comparison with a matched peer group, abused children were non-compliant, more aggressive, and initiated less interaction with their caretakers (George and Main 1979; Egeland and Stroufe 1981). In addition, the abused children directed more aggression toward their peers and continued with their aggressive behaviour even when the other child was visibly distressed (Main and George 1985).

In summary, direct observation provides evidence that social behaviours and interaction patterns within abusing and non-abusing families are different. Abusing mothers have been described as being negative and controlling, with less positive effect. They also show less interactive behaviour both in terms of sensitivity and responsiveness to their children. This may result in infants developing an insecure attachment to their abusive mothers, which in turn produces 'marked changes in the abused children's socio-emotional behaviour' (Rutter and Garmezy 1983), in accordance with the predictions of attachment theory.

Studies of attachment in child-abusing families

In considering social interactions between parents and children from an ethological perspective, the concept of 'attachment patterns' developed by Ainsworth and her colleagues (1978) is crucial. This concept is based on the view that children are predisposed to form close attachments to their 'primary caregiver' during infancy (Bowlby 1969), which has considerable importance for the study of child abuse. The literature contains numerous reports regarding the high number of abusive parents who were themselves victims of abuse as children (see Oliver and Cox 1973; Smith and Hanson 1974; Steele 1976; Egeland 1988). It has been suggested that in some cases the link between experience of abuse as a child and abusing as a parent is likely to be the result of an unsatisfactory early relationship with the principal caretaker and a failure to form a secure attachment (Browne and Parr 1980; DeLozier 1982; Bowlby 1984). Evidence for this notion has been provided by Crittenden (1985), who found that all of the abused and neglected infants in her study showed an insecure pattern of attachment toward their mother. However, Browne and Saqi (1988b) have demonstrated that only a greater proportion of maltreated infants are insecurely attached to their caregiver (70 per cent) in comparison with infants who have no record of maltreatment (26 per cent) (see Table 8.2).

Recent studies carried out at Harvard University (Schneider-Rosen and Cicchetti 1984; Schneider-Rosen et al. 1985) have investigated attachment behaviour of abused and non-abused infants longitudinally at 12, 18, and 24 months of age. At 12 months the abused infants were significantly different from the non-abused group and from norms extrapolated from Ainsworth's data (Ainsworth et al. 1978). Indeed, 71 per cent of the abused group were insecurely attached compared with 33 per

Table 8.2 Attachment patterns derived from the brief separation and reunion of mother and infant in a strange environment

Attachment pattern	Ainsworth category		Abusing families (n = 23)	Non-abusing families (n = 23)
Avoidant	A1	A2	10	3
Secure (1)	B1	B2	4	11
Secure (2)	B3	B4	3	6
Ambivalent	C1	C2	6	3
Total number of insecure attachments			16	6

$x^2 = 9.04$, p < 0.03

Source: From Browne and Saqi (1988b).

cent of the non-abused group and 30 per cent of Ainsworth's sample (op. cit.). At 18 months the figures for insecure attachments were 77 per cent of the abused group and 33 per cent of the non-abused group and at 24 months, 68 per cent of abused and 34 per cent of non-abused infants. An interesting trend was observed longitudinally, at 12 months the insecurely attached abused children tended to be ambivilant (resistant) rather than avoidant (42 per cent vs. 20 per cent), at 18 months they tended to be avoidant rather than ambivalent (31 vs. 46 per cent) and this pattern was again observed at 24 months (21 vs. 46 per cent). Contrary to expectations there was no relationship observed between the type of attachment observed and the type of abuse experienced by the child, i.e. neglect, emotional abuse, or physical abuse.

More recently, however, Lyons-Ruth *et al.* (1987) have correlated maternal behaviour in the homes of abusing families with the insecure attachment pattern shown by abused infants during the 'strange situation procedure'. They found that avoidant infants were experiencing more covertly hostile mothering whereas ambivalent (resistant) infants had less communicative mothers.

In conclusion, Schneider-Rosen *et al.* (1985) suggest that even for abused infants, compensatory background factors will increase the probability of a secure attachment, while under normal circumstances, stressful environmental factors will increase the likelihood of an insecure attachment. They point out that these background and environmental influences may be either transient or enduring, and emphasize that attachment behaviour is best understood in terms of the child, the caregiver, and the environment. This viewpoint supports an integrated approach to the causation of family violence, as outlined earlier.

Limitations of ethological studies

The ethological approach emphasizes the importance of description as a basis for the analysis of behaviour. However, this purely behavioural approach is unlikely to be adequate for studies of family violence and child abuse as other techniques are often necessary to elucidate the meaning of behaviour. Browne (1986) outlines four main approaches to data collection concerned with parent–child behaviour and interaction: permanent recording of film, direct observation, indirect reports and self-reports.

For both indirect and self-reports it should be noted that reported events may not correspond to actual ones. Nevertheless, how a respondent thinks or feels may be crucial: for example, Browne and Saqi (1987) used a questionnaire for abusing and non-abusing parents to rate their child's pattern of sleeping, eating, activity, controllability, and interaction. The responses to the questionnaire demonstrated that abusing parents have more negative conceptions about their child's behaviour than non-abusing parents.

From observational studies it has previously been suggested that the child contributes to its own abuse (Kadushin and Martin 1981). The work of Browne and Saqi (1987) does not support this notion. They consider that abuse may be attributed to the fact that parents have unrealistic expectations of their children *in addition* to psychosocial stress. As a consequence, abusing parents have more negative conceptions of their infant's behaviour than non-abusing parents, they perceive their infant to be significantly more irritable and demanding and interpret certain age appropriate behaviour of their infants as deliberate or intentional non-compliant behaviour. This may produce the coercive pattern of parenting many authors observe, which in turn promotes parental insensitivity and an anxious/insecure attachment from the infant to the mother.

Thus, when time and finances permit, a research study should contain data collected using all four approaches. This multi-method technique allows interview/questionnaire data to be validated against directly observed behaviour and vice versa. Indeed, it is essential for the complete assessment of dimensions in the parent–child relationship, especially if one considers that a substantial amount of parental behaviour and caregiving responses are under minimal conscious control (Papousek and Papousek 1983). Hence, being unaware of their actions, the parent cannot report on them in a questionnaire.

TREATMENT OF CHILD ABUSE USING NATURALISTIC APPROACHES

Ethological studies using direct observation have provided the impetus for a number of behavioural intervention programmes with abusive families, which have been reviewed both in the UK (Hutchings 1980; Smith 1984) and in the USA (Isaacs 1982; Blythe 1983).

Many behavioural intervention programmes are based on the principle of parent skills training (see Kelly 1983). This may involve setting the abusing parent training targets to increase the number of positive verbal statements and physical gestures directed towards the child (for example, Crimmin *et al.* 1984; Reavley *et al.* 1985). Alternatively, the parent is instructed in the use of behavioural techniques of child management such as 'time out' and 'positive reinforcement', which are rehearsed in role plays (Crozier and Katz 1979). Such interventions are usually carried out in the family home, over a number of days or weeks. Direct observations are used both to assess the problems to be addressed and to monitor the progress of each family. Thus, for example, Nicol *et al.* (1985) compared positive and negative child and parent behaviours (defined by Patterson 1982) and used them as 'dependent measures'. The study demonstrated that, as the parent's behaviour towards their children became more positive and less negative, the children reduced their aversive behaviours. A similar finding has been reported by Crozier and Katz (1979) with no incidents of abusive behaviour occurring for a follow-up period of seven months.

Wolfe *et al.* (1981) reported the evaluation of group training for eight abusive parents compared with a comparison group of abusers who received only casework intervention. Training group parents were taught child management skills and techniques of problem solving and self-control. Improved skills were only observed in the treatment group and further incidents of abuse were neither reported nor suspected in the following year. The comparison group did not meet with the same success.

Behavioural interventions have also been carried out with failure-to-thrive children and their families. Iwaniec *et al.* (1985) reported that behavioural social work directed toward improving the feeding performance and parent–child relationship had a high success rate and that observed improvements were maintained for one year or more.

In a recent study involving both abusive and neglectful families, Brunk *et al.* (1987) evaluated the comparative effectiveness of parent training and multisystematic therapy over eight weekly (1½-hour) sessions. They assessed the effects of treatment at the three levels associated with an integrated approach to child maltreatment: individual functioning, family relations, stress and social support. Both treatment approaches were found to be effective in reducing the severity of identified problems at all three levels. It should be pointed out, however, that the authors found that multisystematic therapy was more effective at restructuring parent–child relations, while parent training was more effective at reducing social and behavioural problems.

Thus, it is suggested that those involved in the treatment of abusive families should be concerned with the development of a 'secure' relationship between parent and child. It is not sufficient to evaluate treatment programmes on the basis of the occurrence or non-occurrence of subsequent abuse. Training parents to inhibit aggressive behaviour towards their children may still leave quite unchanged the harmful context in which the initial abuse occurred. It should also be recognized that in some cases treatment with the child remaining in the family may be ineffective and may in fact serve to perpetuate the 'abused becoming abuser' cycle (Kempe and Kempe 1978).

An alternative approach to the problem of child abuse is that of prevention. Ethological studies place more emphasis on the importance of early parent–child relationships and the extent to which attachment behaviours influence later social and interpersonal development. Thus, Hyman *et al.* (1979) aimed to develop behavioural indicators to alert clinicians to families of child abuse, from comparative studies of mother–infant inter-action in abusing and non-abusing families.

PREVENTION OF FAMILY VIOLENCE USING NATURALISTIC APPROACHES

For social and background factors to be of use in the recognition and prediction of family violence they must be considered with the context of the family's interpersonal network. Affectionate familial relationships act as a buffer against internal and exter-nal stress factors (Belsky 1980; Browne and Saqi 1987). An awareness and concern for other family members characterizes affectionate relationships (Hinde 1979). It is important to consider abuse in the light of these family dynamics, whereby each family member gives moral and physical support to one another. If both parents are independent of one another and yet mutually supportive, they are complementary and can cope with the stress of caring for an ageing relative. The same mechanism can be seen to work with regards coping with parenthood (Browne and Saqi 1987). If the parents have a poor relationship with their child there is no 'buffer' against stress, and violence may occur (given adversive background factors) between the parents or against the child or grandparent.

The key to preventing family violence is the monitoring of family dynamics by direct observation and interview techniques. Evaluation of high-risk families at regular intervals is proposed and any adverse change of family circumstances assessed for positive help and intervention. Only in this way can preven-tative strategies be targeted towards helping families avoid a potentially abusive situation.

As far as the individuals are concerned there is a clear distinc-tion to be made between child abuse, elder abuse, and spouse abuse. Stopping child abuse and elder abuse must involve the promotion of safe dependence for children and elderly dependents. Stopping spouse abuse must involve the promotion of safe independence for women.

CONCLUSION

The study of family violence cannot be considered in isolation from the total picture of violence in society. It is related to philosophies of dependent care and training, society's perceptions of the family, and the status of women and children within it. British society no longer views the wife as a possession of the husband or the children as the possession of the parents. Legislation now permits the removal of children from homes where their personal safety is at risk and has given licence to perform this function to social workers through the courts. Voluntary organizations, such as the National Society for the Prevention of Cruelty to Children, the National Women's Aid Federation, and Age Concern exist to provide help and to intervene where elderly dependents, women, or children suffer from violence or abuse. Nevertheless, the difficult decision as to whether to allow children or other dependents to stay in an extremely disruptive and sometimes life-threatening family environment, or to place them in care, is continually faced by the social services.

Naturalistic approaches to the study of family violence will *not* provide all the answers, but will serve to provide ways in which a fuller understanding of family dynamics and interactions may be developed. This will allow a more precise appreciation of the difficulties involved in preventing, identifying, and treating pathological relationships within the family and thereby improve the health and social services.

REFERENCES

Adelson, L. (1972) 'The battering child', *Journal of the American Medical Association* 222: 159–61.

Ainsworth, M.D.S. and Wittig, B.A. (1969) 'Attachment and exploratory behaviour in one-year olds in a strange situation', in B.M. Foss (ed.) *Determinants of Infant Behaviour, 4*, London: Methuen, pp. 113–36.

Ainsworth, M.D.S., Blehar, M.C., Waters, E., and Wall, S. (1978) *Patterns of Attachment: A Psychological Study of the Strange Situation*, New Jersey: Lawrence, Erlbaum Assoc.

Aragona, J.A. and Eyberg, S.M. (1981) 'Neglected children: mothers' report of child behaviour problems and observed verbal behaviour', *Child Development* 52: 596–602.

Archer, J. and Lloyd, B.B. (1985) *Sex and Gender*, New York: Cambridge University Press.

Belsky, J. (1980) 'Child maltreatment: an ecological integration', *American Psychologist* 35: 320–35.

Besharov, J.D. (1982) 'Toward better research on child abuse and neglect: making definition issues an explicit methodological concern', *Child Abuse and Neglect* 5: 383–90.

Binney, V., Harkell, J., and Nixon, J. (1981) *Leaving Violent Men*, London: National Women's Aid Federation (NWAF).

Block, R. and Sinnot, D. (1979) *The Battered Elder Syndrome: An Exploratory Study*, Maryland: University of Maryland Center on Aging.

Blythe, B.J. (1983) 'A critique of outcome evaluation in child abuse treatment', *Child Welfare* 62: 383–90.

Bowlby, J. (1969) *Attachment and Loss, Volume. 1. 'Attachment'*, London: Hogarth.

—— (1984) 'Violence in the family as a disorder of the attachment and caregiving systems', *American Journal of Psychoanalysis* 44: 9–31.

Browne, K.D. (1984) 'Confusion in the elderly', *Nursing* 2: 698–705.

—— (1986) 'Methods and approaches to the study of parenting', in W. Sluckin and M. Herbert (eds) *Parental Behaviour*, Oxford: Blackwell, pp. 344–73.

Browne, K.D. and Parr, R. (1980) 'Contributions of an ethological approach to the study of abuse', in N. Frude (ed.) *Psychological Approaches to Child Abuse*, London: Batsford Press, pp. 83–99.

Browne, K.D. and Saqi, S. (1987) 'Parent–child interaction in abusing families: possible causes and consequences', in P. Maher (ed.) *Child Abuse: An Educational Perspective*, Oxford: Blackwell, pp. 77–104.

—— (1988a) 'Approaches to screening families high risk for child abuse', in K.D. Browne, C. Davies and P. Stratton (eds) *Early Prediction and Prevention of Child Abuse*, Chichester: Wiley, pp. 57–85.

—— (1988b) 'Mother–infant interaction and attachment in physically abusing families', *Journal of Reproductive and Infant Psychology* 6(3) (in press).

Browne, K.D. and Stevenson, J. (1983) 'A checklist for completion by health visitors to identify children "at risk" for child abuse', Report to the Surrey County Review Committee on Child Abuse (unpublished, cited in Browne and Saqi 1988a).

Brunk, M., Henggeler, S.W., and Whelan, J.P. (1987) Comparison of multisystematic therapy and parent training in the brief treatment of child abuse and neglect', *Journal of Consulting and Clinical Psychology* 55(2): 171–8.

Burgess, R.L. and Conger, R.D. (1977) 'Family interaction patterns related to child abuse and neglect', *Child Abuse and Neglect* 1:269–77

—— (1978) 'Family interaction in abusive, neglectful and normal families', *Child Development* 49: 1163–73.

Cornell, C.P. and Gelles, R.J. (1982) 'Adolescent to parent violence', *Urban Social Change Review* 15: 8–14.

Creighton, S.J. (1987) 'Quantitative assessment of child abuse', in P. Maher (ed.) *Child Abuse: An Educational Perspective*, Oxford: Blackwell, pp. 23–34.

Crimmin, D.B., Bradlyn, A.S., Lawrence, J.S., and Kelly, J.A. (1984) 'A training technique for improving the parent–child interaction skills of an abusive–neglectful mother', *Child Abuse and Neglect* 8: 533–9.

Crittenden, P.M. (1985) 'Maltreated infants: vulnerability and resilience', *Journal of Child Psychology and Psychiatry* 26: 85–96.

Crozier, J. and Katz, R.C. (1979) 'Social learning treatment of child abuse', *Journal of Behaviour Therapy and Psychiatry* 10: 213–20.

DeLozier, P.P. (1982) 'Attachment theory and child abuse', in C.M. Parkes and J. Stevenson-Hinde (eds) *The Place of Attachment in Human Behaviour*, London: Tavistock Publication, pp. 95–117.

Department of Health and Social Security (DHSS), UK (1978) *Elderly at Home*, London: HMSO.

Dietrich, K.N., Starr, R.H., and Kaplan, M.G. (1980) 'Maternal stimulation and care of abused infants', in T.M. Field, S. Goldberg, D. Stern and M. Sostek (eds) *High Risk Infants and Children: Adult and Peer Interactions*, New York: Academic Press, p. 25–41.

Disbrow, M.A., Doerr, H., and Caulfield, C. (1977) 'Measuring the components of parents' potential for child abuse and neglect', *Child Abuse and Neglect* 1: 279–96.

Dobash, R.E. and Dobash, R. (1979) *Violence Against Wives: A Case Against Patriarchy*, London: Open Books.

Dunn, J. (1984) *Sisters and Brothers*, London: Fontana.

Dunn, J. and Kendrick, C. (1982) *Siblings*, Oxford: Blackwell.

Egeland, B. (1988) 'Intergenerational continuity in parental maltreatment of children', in K.D. Browne, C. Davies and P. Stratton (eds) *Early Prediction and Prevention of Child Abuse*, Chichester: Wiley.

Egeland, B. and Stroufe, L.A. (1981) 'Attachment and early maltreatment', *Child Development* 52: 44–52.

Elmer, E. (1967) *Children in Jeopardy: A Study of Abused Minors and their Families*, Pittsburg: University of Pittsburgh Press.

Elmer, E. and Gregg, G. (1967) 'Developmental characteristics of abused children', *Pediatrics* 40: 596–602.

Etzioni, A. (1971) 'Violence', in R.K. Merton and R. Nisbet (eds) *Contemporary Social Problems*, New York: HBJ, pp. 709–41.

Freeman, M.D. (1979) *Violence in the Home*, Farnborough, Hampshire: Saxon, p. 237.

Friedrich, W.N. and Boroskin, J.A. (1976)'The role of the child in abuse: a review of literature', *American Journal of Orthopsychiatry* 46: 580–90.

Frude, N. (1980) 'Child abuse as aggression', in N. Frude (ed.)

Psychological Approaches to Child Abuse, London: Batsford, pp. 136–50.

Gaensbauer, T.J. (1982) 'Regulations of emotional expression in infants from two contrasting caretaking environments', *Journal of the American Academy of Child Psychiatry* 21(2): 163–71.

Galdston, R. (1965) 'Observations of children who have been physically assaulted by their parents', *American Journal of Psychiatry* 122: 440–3.

Garbardino, J. (1977) 'The human ecology of child maltreatment', *Journal of Marriage and the Family* 39: 721–35.

Gelles, R. (1973) 'Child abuse as psychopathology: a sociological critique and reformulation', *American Journal of Orthopsychiatry* 43: 611–21.

Gelles, R. and Cornell, C.P. (1985) *Intimate Violence in Families*, Beverly Hills: Sage.

Gelles, R. and Straus, M. (1979) 'Determinates of violence in the family', in W.R. Burr (ed.) *Contemporary Theories about the Family, Volume 1*, New York: Free Press, pp. 549–81.

George, C. and Main, M. (1979) 'Social interactions of young abused children: approach, avoidance and aggression', *Child Development* 50: 306–18.

Gil, D. (1970) *Violence Against Children*, Cambridge, MA: Harvard University Press.

Harbin, H. and Madden, D (1979) 'Battered parents: a new syndrome', *American Journal of Psychiatry* 136: 1288–91.

Hinde, R.A. (1979) *Towards Understanding Relationships*, London: Academic Press.

House of Commons (1977) *Violence to Children: First Report for the Select Committee on Violence in the Family*, Session 1976–1977, London: HMSO.

Hunter, R.S., Kilstrom, N,. and Kraybill, E.N. (1978) 'Antecedents of child abuse and neglect among premature infants. A prospective study of a newborn intensive care unit', *Pediatrics* 61: 629–35.

Hutchings, J. (1980) 'A behavioural approach to child abuse', in N. Frude (ed.) *Psychological Approaches to Child Abuse*, London: Batsford, pp. 181–91.

Hyman, C.A. (1977) A report on the psychological test results of battering parents', *British Journal of Social and Clinical Psychology*, 16: 221–4.

—————— (1978) 'Non-accidental injury: a research report to the Surrey Area Review Committee', *Health Visitor* 51: 168–74.

Hyman, C.A., Parr, R., and Browne, K.D. (1979) 'An observational study of mother–infant interaction in abusing families', *Child Abuse and Neglect* 3: 241–6.

Isaacs, C. (1982) 'Treatment of child abuse: a review of the behavioural interventions', *Journal of the American Biological Association* 15: 273–94.

Iwaniec, D., Herbert, M., and McNeish, A. (1985) 'Social work with failure-to-thrive children and their families; behavioural social work intervention', *British Journal of Social Work* 15: 375–89.

Julian, V. and Mohr, C. (1979) 'Father–daughter incest. A profile of the offender', *Victimology* 4: 10–17.

Kadushin, A. and Martin, J. (1981) *Child Abuse: An Interactional Event*, New York: Columbia University Press.

Kelly, J.A. (1983) *Treating Child-Abusive Families: Intervention Based on Skills-Training Principles*, New York: Plenum.

Kempe, C.H. (1980) 'Incest and other forms of sexual abuse', in C.H. Kempe and R.E. Helfer (eds) *The Battered Child, (3rd edn)*, Chicago: Chicago University Press, pp. 198–214.

Kempe, C.H., Silverman, F.N., Steele, B.B., Droegemueller, W., and Silver, H.K. (1962) 'The battered child syndrome', *Journal of the American Medical Association* 181: 17–24.

Kempe, T.S. and Kempe, C.H. (1978) *Child Abuse*, London: Fontana/Open Books.

Krugman, R.D. (1986) 'The relationship between unemployment and physical abuse of children', *Child Abuse and Neglect* 10: 415–18.

Legal Research and Services for the Elderly (1979) 'Elder abuse in Massachusetts. A survey of professionals and para-professionals' (unpublished, cited in Gelles and Cornell, 1985).

Leiderman, P.H. and Seashore, M.J. (1975) 'Mother–infant separation', in *Parent–Infant Interaction: Ciba Foundation Symposium, 33*, Amsterdam: Elsevier, pp. 213–39.

Lewis, M. and Schaeffer, S. (1981) 'Peer behaviour and mother–infant interaction in maltreated children', in M. Lewis and L.A. Rosenblum (eds) *The Uncommon Child*, New York: Plenum, pp. 194–223.

Lynch, M. and Roberts, J. (1977) 'Predicting child abuse', *Child Abuse and Neglect* 1: 491–2.

Lyons-Ruth, K., Connell, D.B., Zoll, D., and Stahl, J. (1987) 'Infants at social risk: relations among infant maltreatment, maternal behaviour and infant attachment behaviour', *Developmental Psychology* 23: 223–32.

Maccoby, E. (1980) *Social Development: Psychological Growth and the Parent–Child Relationship*, New York: Harcourt, Brace and Jovanovich.

Main, M. and George, C. (1985) 'Responses of abused and disadvantaged toddlers to distress in agemates: A study in a day-care setting', *Developmental Psychology* 21: 407–12.

Mash, E.J., Johnston, C., and Kovitz, K. (1983) 'A comparison of the mother–child interactions of physically abused and non-abused children during play and task situations', *Journal of Clinical Child Psychology* 12: 337–46.

Milner, J.S. and Gold, R.G. (1986) 'Screening spouse abusers for child abuse potential', *Journal of Clinical Psychology* 42: 169–72.

Mrazek, B.P., Lynch, M., and Bentovim, A. (1981) 'Sexual abuse of children in the United Kingdom', *Journal of Child Abuse and Neglect* 7(2): 147–53.

Mulligan, M. (1977) 'An investigation of factors associated with violent-modes of conflict resolution in the family', unpublished MA thesis, University of Rhode Island (cited in Gelles and Cornell, 1985).

National Society for the Prevention of Cruelty to Children (NSPCC) (1985) 'Child abuse deaths', *Information Briefing no. 5*, London: NSPCC.

Nicol, A.R., Smith, J., Kay, B., Hall, D., Barlow, J. and Williams, B. (1985) 'An evaluation of focus case work in improving interaction in abusive families', in J. Stevenson (ed.) *Recent Research in Developmental Psychopathology* (Suppl. to *Journal of Child Psychology and Psychiatry* 4), Oxford: Pergamon, pp. 151–67.

Novaco, R.W. (1978) 'Anger and coping with stress', in J.P. Foreyt and D.P. Rathjen (eds) *Cognitive Behaviour Therapy*, New York: Plenum.

O'Brien, J. (1971) 'Violence in divorce-prone families', *Journal of Marriage and the Family* 33: 692–8.

Oliver, J.E. and Cox, J. (1973) 'A family kindred with ill-used children: the burden on the community', *British Journal of Psychiatry* 123: 81–90.

Pahl, J. (1985) 'Violent husbands and abused wives: a longitudinal study', in J. Pahl (ed.) *Private Violence and Public Policy*, London: Routledge and Kegan Paul, pp. 23–94.

Papousek, H. and Papousek, M. (1983) 'Biological basis of social interactions: implications of research for understanding behaviour deviance', *Journal of Child Psychology and Psychiatry* 24(1): 117-29.

Parke, R.D. (1976) 'Child abuse: an overview of alleviation models', *Journal of Pediatric Psychology* 3: 9–13.

Patterson, G.R. (1982) *Coercive Family Process*, Eugene, Oregon: Castalia.

Pierce, R.L. and Trotta, R. (1986) 'Abused parents: a hidden family problem', *Journal of Family Violence* 1(1): 99–110.

Press, R. (1979) 'Battered grandparents: hidden family problem', *Christian Science Monitor* 5 December, p. 9 (cited in Pierce and Trotta, 1986).

Pringle, K.M. (1980) 'Towards the prediction of child abuse', in N. Frude (ed.) *Psychological Approaches to Child Abuse*, London: Batsford.

Purdy, F. and Nickle, N. (1981) 'Practice principles for working with groups of men who batter', *Social Work with Groups* 4: 111–22.

Reavley, W., Carver, V., and Gilbert, M.T. (1985) 'Behavioural approach to the treatment of child abusing families', *Behavioural Social Work Review* 6(3): 11–17.

Reid, J.B., Taplin, P.S., and Lorber, R. (1981) 'A social

interactional approach to the treatment of abusive families', in
R.B. Stuart (ed.) *Violent Behaviour: Social Learning Approaches to
Prediction, Management and Treatment*, New York: Brunner-Mazel,
pp. 83–101.

Relich, R., Giblin, P.T., Starr, R.H., and Agronow, S.J. (1980)
'Motor and social behaviour in abused and control children:
observations of parent–child interactions', *Journal of Psychology*
106: 193–204.

Renvoize, J. (1978) *Web of Violence: A Study of Family Violence*,
London: Pelican, pp. 128–42.

Rosenberg, M.S. and Reppucci, N.D. (1983) 'Abusive mothers:
perceptions of their own and their children's behaviour', *Journal
of Consulting and Clinical Psychology* 51(5): 674–82.

Rutter, M. and Garmezy, N. (1983) 'Developmental
psychopathology', in P.H. Mussen (ed.) *Handbook of Child
Psychology, 4: Socialisation, Personality and Social Development*, E.M.
Hetherington (vol. ed.), New York: Wiley, pp. 775–911.

Schneider-Rosen, K. and Cicchetti, D. (1984) 'The relationship
between affect and cognition in maltreated infants: quality of
attachment and the development of visual self recognition', *Child
Development* 55: 648–58.

Schneider-Rosen, K., Braunwald, K.G., Carlson, V., and
Cicchetti, D. (1985) 'Current perspectives in attachment theory:
illustration from the study of maltreated infants', in I.
Bretherton, and R. Waters (eds) *Growing Points in Attachment
Theory and Research: Monographs of the Society for Research in Child
Development* (No. 209), 50: 194–210.

Simos, G. (1976) 'Adult children and their aging parents', in J.
Davenport and J.A. Davenport (eds) *Social Services and the Aged*,
Washington DC: University Press, pp. 62–88.

Skinner, A. and Castle, R. (1969) *78 Battered Children*, London:
NSPCC.

Sluckin, W., Herbert, M., and Sluckin, A. (1983) *Maternal Bonding*,
Oxford: Blackwell.

Smith, J.E. (1984) 'Non-accidental injury to children: 1. A review
of behavioural interventions', *B.R.A.T.* 22: 331–48.

Smith, S.M. and Hanson, R. (1974) '134 battered children: a
medical and psychological study', *British Medical Journal* 3:
666–70.

Spinetta, J.J. and Rigler, D. (1972) 'The child abusing parent. A
psychological review', *Psychological Bulletin* 77: 296–304.

Stark, R. and McEvoy, J. (1970) 'Middle class violence', *Psychology
Today* 4: pp. 52–65.

Starr, R.H. (1988) 'Pre and perinatal risk and physical abuse',
Journal of Reproductive and Infant Psychology 6(3) (in press).

Steele, B.F. (1976) 'Violence within the family', in R.E. Helfer
and C.H. Kempe (eds) *Child Abuse and Neglect: The Family and the
Community*, New York: Ballinger Publications, pp. 3–23.

Steele, B.F. and Pollock, C.B. (1968) 'A psychiatric study of parents who abuse infants and small children', in R.E. Helfer and C.H. Kempe (eds) *The Battered Child*, Chicago: University of Chicago Press, pp. 103–47.

Steinmetz, S.K. (1977) *The Cycle of Violence: Assertive, Aggressive and Abusive Family Interaction*, New York: Praeger.

—— (1978) 'Battered parents', *Society* 15(5): 54–5.

Straus, M. (1980) 'A sociological perspective on causes of family violence', in M.R. Green (ed.) *Violence and the Family*, New York: Bould and Westview, pp. 7–31.

Straus, M., Gelles, R., and Steinmetz, S. (1980) *Behind Closed Doors: Violence in the American Family*, New York: Anchor Press.

Warren, C. (1978) 'Battered parents: adolescent violence and the family', presented to the Pacific Sociological Association (cited in Gelles and Cornell, 1985).

Wasserman, G.A., Green, A., and Allen, R. (1983) 'Going beyond abuse: maladaptive patterns of interaction in abusing mother–infant pairs', *Journal of the American Academy of Child Psychiatry* 22(3): 245–52.

Wolfe, D.A., Sandlet, J., and Kaufman, K. (1981) 'A competency based parent-training program for child abusers', *Journal of Consulting Clinical Psychology* 49: 633-40.

Chapter 9

STUDYING OLD AGE ABUSE

MERVYN EASTMAN

INTRODUCTION

In recent years, there has been a growing awareness about violence against older people (for example, Kosberg 1963). Such acts of aggression have been well publicized by the local and national media and include fraud, burglary, so-called mugging, and even murder. More recently, the media have highlighted the public's concern regarding maltreatment within residential care homes (for example, *Daily Mail* 1987). However, the abuse of elderly people by their relatives has received marginal attention: whilst an 80-year-old woman robbed and perhaps beaten makes 'good news-copy', the notion of a son or daughter over-medicating their senile ageing parent raises little interest. . ..

This chapter is concerned with the study of such conflicts which exist within a domestic setting, behind closed doors; consequently they are seldom open for public or professional investigation. The task of studying old age abuse is fraught with two major drawbacks. First, there is no agreed definition of what constitutes abuse, and second, there is no research which includes control groups of older people and carers who are not locked into violent reactions, yet are facing similar difficulties and dependency levels in their elderly parent or parents. Interestingly, there is one factor that has largely been ignored in the study of domestic violence related to old age abuse, namely that the abuse can, and frequently is, witnessed by other relatives and/or caring professionals or service providers.

Mrs Roberts, an 89-year-old woman, was often seen by the home help to be struck by her daughter. Not infrequently, the home help found her client sitting in the kitchen with a pair of rubber gloves pushed into her mouth. Other professional workers (district nurses, health visitors, and social workers) have witnessed their patients/clients being yelled at, pushed, shoved, and punched – as if they were actors in a play which the professional is called upon to witness.

I shall first deal with definitions; second, review the literature available on the subject since 1977; and third, describe my own study commencing in 1980. The discussion will cover the problems of identification, access, and stereotyping of older people, that preclude service providers from effectively intervening. It will also examine accounts of abuse from witnesses, and from collections of case histories and letters from relatives admitting abuse against their aging dependents. Finally, I shall examine briefly the legal implications, particularly in the United Kingdom, for those who abuse, witness the abuse, or are aware of it and for the older people themselves.

DEFINITION

Since 1975, when A.A. Baker first coined the phrase 'granny bashing', there have been a number of factors which have prevented professional workers and agencies knowing what to do when faced with the knowledge of old age abuse. Cloke (1983) wrote that among those factors 'stemming from considerable ignorance which exists about the subject' was that there was no agreement on a definition of old age abuse in either the UK or the US literature.

In the United Kingdom, 'Granny battering has been described as the systematic and continuous abuse of an elderly person by the carer, often, although not always, a relative, on whom the elderly person is dependent for care . . ..' (ibid.: 2). Interestingly, writers from the United States appear to include *all* abuse and violence, wherever the incident and whoever the perpetrator, in their definitions. Thus, the US House of Representatives Select Committee on Aging (1981) describes 'Elder Abuse' as 'The wilful infliction of physical pain, injury or debilitating mental anguish, unreasonable confinement, or wilful deprivation by a caretaker of services which are necessary to maintain mental and physical health'. My own definition

(Eastman 1984b), excluded mugging of an older person for personal gain, spouse abuse where there has been a history of family/marital violence, harassment against an older person being scapegoated by a local community or neighbourhood, and abuse by formal/paid carers in an institution. The latest article published on old age abuse in the UK at the time of writing (August 1987) cited case examples that included an elderly victim remarking 'of course he has always used me as a punch bag'. Within my definition, this case would have to be excluded from the study of old age abuse in that it demonstrates a history of spouse abuse. A husband does not necessarily stop beating his wife because he has reached retirement age!

Cloke (1983) argued that there has been a tendency to include such a wide range of abuses within the term "old age abuse" that the concept became almost meaningless as an heuristic tool.

Thus, the present understanding of old age abuse has the following features:

(1) physical assault such as punching, pinching, slapping, and forced feeding;
(2) threats of assault;
(3) neglect, such as locking an elderly relative in a room, refusing to provide meals, and refusing material, psychological, or emotional support;
(4) exploitation, such as financial abuse for the personal gain of the caregiver;
(5) abandonment – either to hospital, residential care, or the street;
(6) sexual abuse, including rape; and
(7) psychological abuse, including intimidation and frightening behaviour.

Furthermore, it may be justified to include abuse within residential-care homes, both public and private, where the factors leading to abuse are very similar, although not identical to, abuse within the domestic setting.

Finally, where the carer is abusing but is totally unaware that his or her behaviour constitutes abuse, this might also be included. Thus, a son who is supporting an inliving elderly mother and denies her food believing that she has already eaten has committed an abusive act within the present definition.

219

MERVYN EASTMAN

CURRENT AWARENESS

Prior to 1982, reports on old age abuse such as those by Burston (1975, 1977) and Baker (1975) received little attention in either the media or by policy-makers. Indeed, Cloke's (1983) review of the literature gives minimal attention to their work (op. cit.). He effectively argues that whilst interest in the subject first emerged in the mid-1970s in Britain, it did not receive the same amount of attention as in the United States until the early 1980s. Knowledge about the causes of abuse remained largely undeveloped because the study of old age was based on a limited number of reported incidents without effective sampling. Very few studies interviewed the victims of abuse. The research undertaken by Burston, Baker, Eastman, and others has primarily been within a health and social service, rather than a sociological or psychological perspective.

Cloke (1983) raises a number of extremely valid issues of concern when examining the study of old age abuse. These are as follows:

(1) Little attempt has been made to refine the concept of old age abuse (see above).
(2) Research has been based on small-scale studies of *known* cases about which it is difficult to generalize.
(3) Claims about the incidents of old age abuse are impossible to substantiate statistically.
(4) Speculations about the cause of old age abuse remain largely undeveloped and, therefore, as a result there is little upon which to base suggestions for solutions and preventative approaches.
(5) Comparisons with child abuse may have clouded some of the issues.
(6) The need to establish formal procedures and codes of practice for dealing with the problem has been questioned.

Hocking (1982) has identified three sets of circumstances common to old age abuse in her review of forty-two case studies:

(1) where violence is a method of communicating in the family;
(2) where the family perceive the elderly person as an 'inconvenient nuisance'; and

220

(3) among families which have been worn down by the very nature of the dependent's invalidity.

Although Cloke (1983) claims that we have successfully placed the item of old age abuse on the agenda for health and social service practitioners and to a lesser extent, for that of policy-makers, this opinion must now be revised. To date there has still been no formal and published research into old age abuse in the UK (cf. Hocking's unpublished research, above). Second, the public is still very reluctant to see old age abuse within a domestic setting as a cause for concern. This latter point has been picked up by Denis Marsden from Essex University (personal communication), who argues that, despite the occasional media attention, abuse has not been the subject of serious academic interest or public outcry in the UK. Mary Marshall (1984), Director of Age Concern in Scotland, makes a similar observation, suggesting that the reason may be linked to the public's denial of growing older and the possibility of themselves being abused by their adult children.

Although some recent publications on Old Age have included a section on abuse (Phillipson 1984), the awareness of the problem shown in these writings is minimal. This is exemplified by Murphy (1986), who states that 'Professionals occasionally come across tragic cases where one member of the family regularly physically abuses a relative . . .. But this kind of granny battering is rare.' Such opinions are in direct contrast to the evidence from the systematic surveys presented in the previous chapter (p.188).

However, a key publication in the USA by Kosberg (1983) entitled *Abuse and Maltreatment of the Elderly: Causes and Intervention* provides an overview of the causes and consequences of victimization, and suggests possible intervention by profes-sionals who have responsibility for 'maintaining the rights, safety and health of elderly individuals'. Discussing the various problems facing older people, notably crime and fear of crime, it goes on to examine elderly people who are vulnerable and concludes with discussions on a variety of interventive possibilities.

AN INVESTIGATION INTO OLD AGE ABUSE

My own interest in old age abuse arose out of fourteen years of social work experience with the elderly, collecting examples of families where the relationship had broken down to such an extent that violence has taken place. The various case histories and letters from relatives I have collected in the UK demonstrates that elderly abuse does occur in a domestic setting and that there appear to be common factors that are associated with this form of violence which can mostly be reduced by certain interventions. However, it is recognized that these apparent common factors may be suspect. The abuse is more likely to come to the attention of the statutory services if the family is on a low income, whereas, in my view, old age abuse has no economic boundaries (Eastman, 1982).

Case histories, and letters from relatives which describe elderly abuse in a domestic setting, appear to identify sixteen factors that, when accumulated, raise the possibility that abuse might occur. These are:

(1) physical and/or mental dependency on a 'key member of the family' – the caregiver;

(2) poor or negative communication between the elderly dependant and caregiver;

(3) that the caregiver is responsible for the support of 'another' member of the family (for example, husband, dependant child, etc.);

(4) the caregiver makes repeated visits to the General Practitioner;

(5) frequent periods of hospitalization of the elderly dependant, history of falls, facial bruising;

(6) vague explanations given by either the caregiver or elderly dependant;

(7) cramped living conditions;

(8) the elderly dependant had, in the past, cared for the caregiver (role reversal);

(9) a triggering behaviour or condition of the elderly dependant (for example, incontinence, spitting): this 'trigger' can be almost anything that produces a sense of anger or even rage in the caregiver;

(10) low self-esteem of the caregiver;

(11) that the dependency of the elderly person is perceived by the caregiver as 'childlike';
(12) the caregiver is experiencing multiple stress (for example, marital conflict, financial problems, and so on);
(13) the caregiver has a history of mental ill-health;
(14) unemployment of either caregiver or significant other in the family;
(15) drinking problems of either caregiver or dependant; and
(16) poor or inadequate social health provision.

These predisposing factors do not necessarily provide a definite list. Future research that includes comparison groups of relatives who do not abuse their parents may well lead to a complete re-evaluation of the factors outlined above.

However, in the mean time, an accumulation of these factors can provide a useful guideline in evaluating families at risk. Even where abuse has not initially been suspected, further probing of the interrelationships within the family may demonstrate that a 'pile-up' of stressors has led to abusive behaviour (see factor 12).

The way the relatives perceive the dependant behaviour or conditions is extremely important. If a daughter considers that her mother is not trying hard enough to walk, or, alternatively she is 'wetting herself' deliberately to get back at her, this could be a factor leading to abuse (see factor 11).

The triggering behaviour can be shown by the elderly dependant in the full awareness and knowledge of the caregiver's response. Many relatives claim that their dependants have 'deliberately' caused a row or have abused them (see factor 9). This interactive violence has been noted by American researchers but has received little attention in the UK and requires further investigation. Thus, for example, ignorance on the part of the carer about the exact nature of the mental and/or physical illness of the older person can result in the caregiver interpreting problem behaviour in a negative way. The recent growth in published material on the caregiver's role, and the sorts of stresses they experience, raises important issues in relation to the advice and education given by professionals. On numerous occasions relatives have written to me saying that if only they had understood why their elderly dependant had acted that way, they would have felt and responded differently. The elderly dependant becomes dehumanized, he or she is no longer seen as a mother, father or aunt, but as an 'object', somebody unrecognizable, alien to the family, an intruder, a usurper of the home and living space. Relatives may find that by denying their relationship to the dependant, abusive acts become easier.

A recurring question is why abuse in the domestic setting happens so frequently within say 7 per cent of families caring for older people (Pierce and Trotta 1986). There can be no definitive answers, only possibilities. The population over 60 is a growing proportion of modern society both in the UK and the United States (Selby and Schechter 1982). This section of society is denied basic rights to employment or adequate financial income because of old age, and they are perceived as dependants. 'Older people fall over'; 'old people are asexual'; 'old people are a drain on the National Health resources'. This stereotyping, in my view, has distorted the public's awareness of old age abuse. The focus of the social worker places the elderly person as a 'passive receipient' within the family network (Phillipson 1982) rather than a victim of low income, and inadequate housing and heating. This promotes the stereotype of elderly people as dependent and it may well be this dependency that produces aggression or even violence in the carer. If one scapegoats an individual (even within the family), one can rationalize abusive behaviour.

The fact that many relatives have witnessed the abuse of their parent by a caregiver, or that home helps and district nurses can witness an assault against their client or patient, raises the following interesting issues and questions:

(1) How far is the 'abuser' aware that his or her actions are perceived as abusive?
(2) Do the professionals who witness an act of domestic violence recognize it as such?
(3) Does the elderly victim excuse the act to the professional witness or other person?
(4) To what extent do the professionals intervene, given that they perceive the act as aggressive or violent?

Communications with relatives and professionals that have witnessed or have knowledge of abuse has indicated the following common responses.

— Informing their line manager (in the case of social services personnel) and allowing them to make a decision as to the appropriate action. This may mean no action or the worker being advised to 'counsel' the relative.
— Ignoring the action witnessed and not reporting it to their line manager.
— Intervention. Calling a case conference, thus following a similar procedure to child abuse.
— Informing the police who have, in most cases, either recommended no action (as a domestic assault) or occasionally attended a case conference, if that has been one of the responses.

These operations occur because there is no agreed definition of what constitutes abuse and most agencies have no procedure or policies to determine appropriate practice. A small questionnaire of 1,000 readers of a social work professional journal (Eastman 1984a), who were employed by a social services department, showed that two-thirds of hospital-based social workers reported the abuse to their line managers, as did approximately half of the officers in charge of residential homes for elderly people. Area-based or field social workers were far more diverse in their reactions to knowledge of abuse. Team leaders and senior social workers were more likely not to report the abuse and several considered that such reporting was 'not applicable'. It should be stressed that these results were not only based on 'witness abuse' by the professional but also suspected abuse during the course of their work with families.

The survey in terms of *responses* to families where abuse was known, evidenced, or suspected, was as follows:

Hospital Social Workers
Residential homes admission
Counselling
Domiciliary home-care support

Officers in Charge of Old People's Homes
Counselling
Notification to the police
Residential/hospital admission

Field Social Workers
Counselling, admission to hospital, or residential care
Domiciliary and day-care support
Notification to the police

At the time of the survey (1983) only one local authority responding to the questionnaire had a NAI (non-accidental injury) register for old age abuse. Whilst questions to professionals are fraught with problems, the survey did demonstrate the following points:

(1) that old age abuse exists and that it is not a localized problem to one geographical area in the UK;
(2) that most social workers (who responded) recognize the problem and have to deal with the whole range of abuses;
(3) that old age abuse must be defined in terms that encompass the whole range of abuse;
(4) that both health and socio-economic factors were perceived as being relevant;
(5) that lack of available services was not seen to be a contributory factor leading to abuse;
(6) that female members of the family are most likely to be the abusers (though one must recognize that males are rarely the key caregiver);
(7) removal from the family environment and counselling were seen as the most frequent responses in effective intervention;
(8) the lack of knowledge on the part of senior managers largely through the non-reporting of abuse cases which are known or suspected.

Case histories, questionnaires to service providers and relatives, relatives' letters, and diary extracts have over five years provided evidence that elderly people are commonly abused. The media, however, have only reacted at the times of publication of articles. The publication of *Old Age Abuse* (Eastman 1984), for example, produced a week of television and media interest which only occasionally resurfaces at Christmas or at national conferences that examine old age abuse. Beauvoir (1972) questioned, 'In what century the murder of old parents, by violence or privation, was proportionally most common?', but there are no facts or figures on which to base an answer.

However, abuse of the dependent elderly person is not a new phenomenon. Beckett, Shakespeare, and Zola have all written about non-accidental injury of elderly relatives in previous centuries. This suggests that there may be consistent factors through history that are as common today as then: these include, for example, society's attitude of the elderly as dependent, the stress that this dependency produces in the caregiver and family unit, and the lack of information concerning the prevalence and incidence of abuse.

The knowledge that a range of abuses of the elderly from shouting to murder commonly exists in society without the necessary practical guidelines and policy frameworks to combat it, should cause disquiet, certainly amongst professionals and voluntary agencies, if not the public. With such an uncomfortable situation the legal implications for abusers, abused, and professionals must be examined.

LEGAL IMPLICATIONS

Physical abuse is a criminal act, though prosecution can only be initiated if there is sufficient evidence available to identify the abuser. Within the domestic setting, the police have recently been allowed to view marital violence as if the assault had occurred in the street. Although this may well include violence between an elderly couple, it will not cover most victims of old age abuse. Age Concern (UK), recognizing that there is no requirement for statutory reporting of abuse and no system for intervention or support, proposes that a mechanism should be established which is both preventative and protective. It is argued that there should be a general power to promote the welfare of older people including 'advice, guidance, and assistance' together with providing (as with the 1983 Mental Health Act) a code of practice. However, this power would only be used to make services available. In addition, local authorities would have the power to investigate complaints and respond to requests for help from either the older person or the caregiver. In relation to old age abuse it is recommended (Age Concern 1987: 132) that local authorities be empowered to initiate assessment through intervention. In the US there are a number of states where there is mandatory reporting of old age abuse.

Such obligations offer an opportunity to deal with quantitative information and work appropriately.

An elderly person is often powerless, unwilling, or unable to initiate proceedings against their adult child. With increased obligations on the part of statutory agencies the Department of Health and Social Security is considering old age abuse within the legal context. However, the study of abuse to date has not provided sufficient evidence to support or reject increased powers of intervention by either local authorities or Health Service professionals. The rights of the individual must be safeguarded, especially privacy, but so must the rights of the vulnerable, mentally infirm elderly victim be safeguarded, as they have lost the ability to conceptualize the notion of risk. The balance is finely drawn and at the end of the day it must, as with all domestic violence, be a moral judgement made by Members of Parliament and professional workers. The fact that it is difficult to recognize old age abuse places the elderly victim in a dangerous and vulnerable position.

IN CONCLUSION

To date there have been no major government statements on old age abuse. However, there have been a few questions raised in the House of Commons. In answer to a question from Mr Andrew Bennett MP on whether it was possible to provide advice to authorities and social services departments on signs for the identification of abuse to elderly relatives, Geoffrey Finsburgh MP replied: 'I do not consider that it would be appropriate for the Department to give such advice. The identification of abuse to elderly people is essentially a matter of professional judgement in the individual case. . ..' (House of Commons Hansard, 25 November 1982, Column 565).

The study of old age abuse has not yet reached its infancy, but remains in an embryonic stage within the cosy world of the professional womb. Over the past few years I have attempted to encourage its birth in order that it can see the light of day and that we can recognize what it looks like and respond appropriately. However, there may be a reluctance to face this, particularly if all of us see in ourselves either the potential to become an abuser or potential victim.

REFERENCES

Age Concern (1987) *Vulnerable Elderly People and the Law*, England: Age Concern.

August, P. (1987) 'Threats to harm elderly people must always be taken seriously', *Social Work Today* 18(49): 14–15.

Baker, A.A. (1975) 'Granny bashing', *Modern Geriatrics* 5(8): 20–24.

Beauvoir, S. de (1972) *Old Age*, London: Weidenfield and Nicolson.

Burston, G. (1975) 'Granny bashing', *British Medical Journal* 3 (5983) 592, 3 September.

—— (1977) 'Do your elderly patients live in fear of being battered?', *Modern Geriatrics* 7(5): 54–5.

Cloke, C. (1983) Old Age Abuse in the Domestic Setting – A Review, England: Age Concern.

Daily Mail (1987) 'Staff helped old people die of cold, scandal at the Nye Bevan Lodge', *Daily Mail* (London), 22 July.

Eastman, M. (1982) 'Granny battering: a hidden problem', *Community Care* 27(413): 12–13.

—— (1984a) 'Honour thy father and thy mother', Appendix I in M. Eastman, *Old Age Abuse*, England: Age Concern, pp. 101–14.

—— (1984b) *Old Age Abuse*, England: Age Concern.

Hocking, E. (1982) 'Evidenced or suspected abuse in the catchment area of Swindon, Wiltshire, 1972–1982', unpublished study, cited in Eastman, M. (1984) *Old Age Abuse*, England: Age Concern, pp. 28–32.

Kosberg, J. (1983) *Abuse and Maltreatment of the Elderly: Causes and Intervention*, Bristol: Wright.

Marshall, M. (1984) 'Poignancy plus a few pointers', *Social Work Today* 16(5): 26.

Murphy, E. (1986) *Dementia as Mental Illness in the Old*, London: Macmillan.

Pierce, R.L. and Trotta, R. (1986) 'Abused parents: a hidden family problem', *Journal of Family Violence* 1: 99–110.

Phillipson, C. (1982) *Capitalism and the Construction of Old Age*, New York: MacMillan.

—— (1984) *Old Age Manifesto*, London: Pluto.

Selby, P. and Schechter, M. (1982) *Ageing 2000 – a challenge for society*, Boston: MTP.

US House of Representatives, Select Committee on Aging (1981) *Elder Abuse: An Examination of a Hidden Problem*, Washington DC: US Printing Office, Committee Publication, No. 97, p. 270.

Chapter 10

VIOLENCE
AND SOCIAL WORK

GLYNIS M. BREAKWELL AND COLIN ROWETT

INTRODUCTION

This chapter examines the advantages and disadvantages of adopting a naturalistic approach to the study of violent assaults on the social work staff of social services departments (SSDs) by the clients they are mandated to help. Although a current issue among caring professionals in Britain, the perceived increase in severity and frequency of physical assaults by clients on staff has generated remarkably little research. Small-sample surveys of social workers have reported some form of assault, physical or psychological, threatened or actual (Bute, 1979a, b, c; London Boroughs' Training Committee 1983; NALGO 1983; Brown *et al.* 1986; Crane 1986). With differing operational definitions of 'violence', widely differing population and sample groups, the absence of controls, little statistical manipulation other than data frequency counts, and an emphasis on description rather than analysis, it has not been possible to integrate knowledge that is capable of being of some practical use to the departments themselves, and of theoretical value for the study of aggression.

The only large-scale research on physical assaults on social workers employed by local authorities in Britain will be used here to illustrate some of the central issues in studying and explaining aggression (Rowett 1986). The chapter will also address wider issues generated by the research, such as the role of situational variables in human aggression, the carer as victim, the researcher as therapist, the ethical and practical issues involved when the subjects may be stigmatized by the research findings, the difficulties in validating data obtained in a naturalistic setting, and the problems in feeding back the findings in an effective but sensitive manner.

A common notion of what constitutes naturalistic research centres on the examination of situations which are outside the control of the experimenter. Though usually concerned with observing individuals *in situ*, there is no reason why it could not equally well be applied to the study of large-scale organizations, and it is with the latter focus that the present research will be reported. Direct observation will be replaced by direct questioning and the use of psychometric and scaling techniques. However, the emphasis will consistently be on the relationship of the individual with the organization, and on the development and importance of social norms, belief systems, and patterns of social attributions in influencing the behaviour of an individual in a given situation. The focus is upon violence which has occurred within a 'naturalistic setting', not manipulated by the researcher, but the methods of information-gathering do intrude upon that setting, changing it unintentionally. Control of the setting is achieved retrospectively through sampling in such a way as to get alternative perspectives on that 'setting' and the events occurring in it.

NOTIONS OF VIOLENCE

Whether an individual act is construed as being 'violent' is dependent upon a judgement of the meaning and social value of that act. This judgement will be influenced by such things as the perceived relationship between the reason for the act and the act itself, an evaluation of the aggressor's sense of responsibility for the act, and a more pervasive set of stipulative beliefs about the function of human aggression and of the social construction of morality. The way in which 'violence' is defined for theoretical or research purposes will significantly influence the conclusions drawn and thereby shape recommendations for its prevention and control (see Chapter 1 for a general discussion of problems of definition).

Establishing an operational definition for the study of violence in social work crystallizes a number of those issues. In Britain, and to a lesser extent in America, 'public' or local authority social work was established to provide for the administration of welfare capitalism. Although there is a strong element of 'caring' for those who are incapable of caring for themselves for physical or psychological reasons, the role also includes the rationing of scarce resources to those who are structurally disadvantaged, and the control of people whose behaviour is currently considered to be socially unacceptable. Examples of the 'control with care' aspects of social work would be:

(a) the compulsory admission of some mentally ill and mentally impaired people to psychiatric hospital;
(b) the removal of children from home against the wishes of the parents;
(c) the investigation of allegations of child abuse;
(d) the compulsory removal of elderly people from home to a general hospital; and
(e) the supervision of men and women in the community with a history of potential or actual violence.

There is considerable ambiguity about the respective roles of social worker and client. Many social workers have been taught that self-determination for the client, facilitated by the social worker's use of the self (BASW 1977), is paramount. It is difficult to reconcile this with the actual tasks which form the bulk of the social worker's workload that are typically concerned as much with control as with care. This ambiguity of purpose colours the recent concern about assaults by clients on social workers. The almost universal stance has been that in carrying out their legitimate tasks, social workers are experiencing more frequent assaults of greater severity than previously, and that something should be done to improve the situation. However, it is equally possible to argue that people who act as agents of state control should reasonably expect to be assaulted, and that in a sense the 'client' is morally correct so to do. Joxe (1981) argues, for example, that violence is essentially a structural response to oppression and that 'power is the application of the knowledge of violence'. From this perspective, by seeking research to reduce the amount of violence, social workers are hoping to use the knowledge gained to increase their power. Here, the researcher by accepting the brief, necessarily accepts the political stance of the dominant group. It is of course difficult for a researcher to do anything else if money, resources, and access are required from the same people who promulgate the perspective.

The focus is usually upon client violence against the social worker, yet of equal interest are those cases of social worker violence against the client. It has understandably been difficult to research this aspect, though what little research exists gives reason to believe that clients are as likely to be victims as aggressors (Tutt 1975; Hosie 1979). To date, there has been no substantial research which has looked at the incidence of violence between social workers and clients from both perspectives, and it would be unlikely that any SSDs would be prepared to allow a researcher to interview both social workers and clients involved in incidents of violence across a range of settings and in different legal and social contexts.

Confidentiality of information between a client and department, an uneasiness by departments to expose vulnerable clients to researchers with unknown and perhaps nonexistent counselling or therapeutic skills, and a reluctance to expose themselves or individual social workers to possible legal action, are powerful arguments against this type of research.

VIOLENCE AND THE CARING PROFESSIONS

In general, routine data collection is spasmodic, patchy, and enmeshed in a network of socio-political representations and self-interested stereotypes. It could be difficult, for example, to find a source of funding to investigate a possible increase in assaults committed by peopled discharged from long-stay psychiatric hospitals into the community as part of the community-care movement.

Drinkwater (1982) reviewed the available research on 'violence in psychiatric hospitals'. Most researchers had concentrated on patient-to-patient violence, closely followed by patient-to-staff violence, with some minor acknowledgement of the existence of staff-to-patient assault. Drinkwater noted that all of the available incidence figures had been based on routine record sheets, none had involved independent observation, and none had used experimental or quasi-experimental designs. Adopting a social learning approach she suggested that there was a 'high

)bability that the numbers and content of staff-patient inter-
.tions plays an important part in developing and maintaining
iolent behaviour on psychiatric wards'. After announcing a
major research programme to examine aspects of ward management of violence, she concluded: 'It is to be hoped that the
political sensitivity and hidden nature of this problem area will
not be allowed to prevent this work being done.' If Drinkwater's
approach is correct, and increased incidence is not necessarily
indicative of more violent patients but of more violence-
inducing staff–patient interactions, then this type of research is
clearly potentially threatening to staff practice, attributes, and
attributions.

NALGO (the National and Local Government Officers
Association) (1983) sent a short questionnaire in 1981 to all its
branches attempting to establish the number of assaults on
NALGO members by the public in 1979 and 1980, the jobs of
the assaulted members, the injuries suffered, and the difficulties
experienced in obtaining compensation or other help from the
employing agency. Some 221 (42 per cent) of the branches
responded. About half reported no incidents of violence. The
remainder had records of reported frequencies from one in two
years to one a week. The questionnaire did not define 'assault'
or distinguish psychological from physical violence. The main
job categories at risk were considered to be in housing, social
services (particularly in assessment centres and residential
homes), and in a number of posts which carried a responsibility
for inspection or enforcement such as environmental health
officers, building control inspectors, and traffic wardens.
Injuries ranged from verbal abuse to property damage, from
bruising to stab wounds and death. Some employers operated
formal compensation schemes; others expected the employee to
take legal action against the assailant and seek financial redress
through the Criminal Injuries Compensation Board Scheme.

Millham *et al.* (1976) examined 394 recorded incidents of
violence over thirty-six months in four community homes (the
average total number of boys per year was 339). The overall
incidence was low, most assaults were between boys, attacks on
staff were rare, and staff were more likely to assault boys than
vice versa.

Leavey (1978) examined 178 violent incidents in thirteen

community homes for children in London over a six-month period. Most of the assaults were minor. Some 5 per cent of the 44 per cent of the 165 children who were involved accounted for 37 per cent of all incidents. One-third of the assaults were on the staff, one-third between the children, and one-third involved staff using restraint.

The London Boroughs' Training Committee, Social Services Section (1983) distributed a postal questionnaire to the SSD of all twenty-nine London boroughs, with a 72 per cent response rate representing 41 of the possible 103 teams of social workers. Over a six-month period, fifteen teams reported no incidents; the remaining twenty-six teams reported a total of 113 incidents of which twenty-four occurred to members of one team. During the same period 349 threats of violence were recorded, 152 from three individuals.

Brown et al. (1986) carried out a postal survey of 560 staff of the 'personal social services' in Wessex in 1979, with a 60 per cent response rate, consisting of 177 fieldworkers (social workers in area teams, home help organizers, social workers in hospitals and clinics, probation officers, and others), 71 residential workers; 44 day-care workers (mainly from Adult Training Centres for the mentally handicapped); 21 'others' (mainly academic staff); 20 administrators; and five who did not reveal their occupation. Based on an analysis of the returns from the fieldworkers, residential and day-care workers (N = 292), and with a definition of violence as 'actual physical assault resulting in some injury or pain', and violence to property as 'actual damage', Brown et al. quote 98 (29 per cent of the total) reporting at least one assault over the preceding three years, with 62 of these staff (18 per cent of the total) being assaulted more than once. Some 134 (40 per cent) had been threatened at least once (no definition of threat provided). In total 180 (53 per cent) had at least once been either physically assaulted, threatened, or had family, close friends, or possessions subjected to violence over the preceding three years. While acknowledging some of the limitations of their own research (a biased sample, with likely self-selection of assaulted respondents), Brown et al. felt able to argue, first, that fieldworkers were most likely to be assaulted in the client's home, the most common occasions were during the taking of children into care and in carrying out compulsory admissions into psychiatric hospitals; and second, that more than half the assaults on residential staff occurred after staff had given 'advice or discipline' or had intervened to protect a third party. They concluded that 'The results would suggest then that men working in close contact with clients in day centres are the most likely group to be assaulted. . ..' Not surprisingly, when asked, the vast majority of staff wanted written guidelines from their employer on handling violence, clarification of their legal position when using restraint, and advice on the most effective restraint techniques.

Crane (1986) wrote to the directors of eight SSDs and asked to inspect the accident and report forms (where assaults are usually recorded) and to interview assaulted social workers nominated by the department with the permission of the line manager and the social worker. Four departments gave permission, and fifteen social workers were interviewed using content analysis of responses to open-ended and mainly unstructured questions. Although interesting descriptions of the assaults were provided, with all twenty incidents occurring in situations where the social worker was fulfilling a statutory role, the methodology obviously had substantial weaknesses which made generalizations difficult. Nevertheless, Crane was able to point out the following: a likely under-recording of assaults; specific training in the handling of violence was rarely available; there was a dearth of organizational support and an absence of procedural guidelines, and many of the incidents were what he termed the 'unpredictable'. What Crane did not do, however, was to draw together these system factors into some form of explanatory or descriptive model for the genesis of the incidents. Indeed, the absence of a theory-building perspective in this type of qualitative research can lead to what seems to amount to a sense of despair. Thus, the final words in Crane's monograph are perhaps more a reflection of the method than the issue: 'How does one train for the untrainable? How does one prepare for uncertainty? These are the implications for social work theory, practice and management.'

Assertions that the frequency and severity of assaults on carers in America is increasing mirrors that in Britain. Although there have been more research surveys than in Britain, few studies adopt experimental or quasi-experimental designs.

Whitman (1976) reported an incidence rate of 24 per cent of 101 mental health workers assaulted over a twelve-month period, 43 per cent of the total having received threats. Bernstein (1981) found 14 per cent of 422 psychotherapists (psychiatrists, psychologists, social workers and counsellors) reported an assault, 35 per cent of the total had been threatened, and 61 per cent had felt physically afraid. Star (1984) commented:

> Formal research into the topic of patient assaults on therapists is relatively new in this country. . ... Information comes from two main sources: studies of patient violence in inpatient settings and surveys of direct service mental health practitioners that focus on workers' experience with violent patients.

Her overview of the available research concluded that the two most likely targets of patient assault were psychiatrists and social workers, that younger and less experienced clinicians were at greater risk, and that the assaults were by only a small percentage of the clients. Lanza (1983) surveying the literature on patient–nurse violence up to 1980, found that it is almost non-existent

> the [literature] . . . that does exist usually denies that assaults on nurses are frequent, and focuses on how to care for the assaultive patient. When the issue of patient–nurse assault is discussed, blame for the assault is often placed on the nurse.

Here the stance of the researcher, herself a nurse, is clear-cut. The research focused on the type of emotional, cognitive, social, and biophysiological reactions of nurses as a result of being assaulted. Over a twelve-month period in one large Veterans Administration Neuropsychiatric Hospital in 1980 there were ninety-one recorded assaults on sixty-seven nurses. Forty of the assaulted nurses completed a questionnaire with a check list of 108 possible emotional, social, and biophysiological reactions to assault, each rated for intensity of reaction on a five-point scale. Cognitive responses were assessed through open-ended questions. The forty nurses had been assaulted on average seven times before the study period (range 0 to 112, with two nurses assaulted more than 80 times). During the survey period, twenty-four (60 per cent) of the nurses were assaulted by patients they had known for some months, all the patients were men, average age 58 (range 25–76), with main diagnoses of paranoid schizophrenia, Alzheimers disease, and chronic brain syndrome. The severity of assault was considerable (65 per cent of the assaulted staff required more than one week to recover, with 21 per cent of injuries being life-endangering), 'victims' most frequently reported only minimal reactions to the assault. Explaining this by a possible combination of suppression (displacement of affect from consciousness) and sensitization (over-familiarization producing indifference), Lanza outlines one of the main dilemmas facing the researcher using retrospective methods in naturalistic settings: since it is never possible to identify all the variables which might influence a specific behaviour such as assault, variance has to be explained by *post hoc* deductions often coloured by the researchers particular socio-political framework. In Lanza's study it may be the case that the nurses' psychological need to suppress emotions may explain the minimal reaction levels. It may equally be explained by the perceived relationship between the researcher and the employer, or the attitude of the nurses' union, pay differentials, or the policy of the insurance companies who offer personal indemnity cover, or the involvement of the nurses in provoking the incidents.

VIOLENCE IN BRITISH LOCAL
AUTHORITY SOCIAL WORK

Having identified an area which merits more detailed analysis, in this case the assertion that the incidence and severity of client assault on social workers was increasing, the development of a research methodology which was both academically respectable as well as politically and practically acceptable was paramount. The requirement was to adopt a design which would be essentially fact-finding, but would in addition be capable of examining some of the theoretical accounts of aggression occurring in a naturalistic setting. The quasi-experimental design adopted is shown in Figure 10.1.

The advantages of this design were that it would provide data and opinions from the directors of social services, usually after discussion with senior managers, about the level of violence they

Figure 10.1 The research design (Rowett 1986)

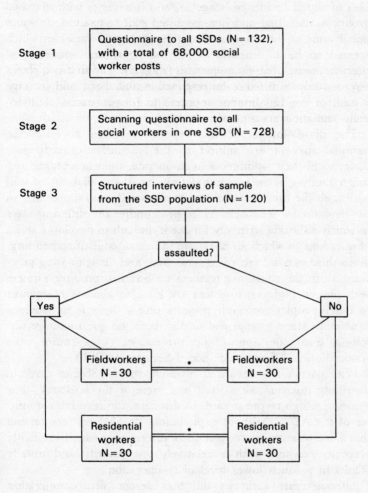

* Matched by sex, age, whether full or part-time, whether qualified, experience, location of workplace.

believed to be experienced by their staff (stage 1), blanket coverage of all social workers in one authority to provide some idea of actual incidence (stage 2), and interviews with matched groups of assaulted and non-assaulted staff to examine in more detail some of the situational and psychological variables which seemed to be of importance in the aggression sequence of precursors–incident–consequences (stage 3). The first two stages required approval from the responsible managers, and in stage 3 each of the 120 interviewees had to be approached individually and their consent negotiated.

The disadvantages of this type of research are that the national surveys are subject to the vaguaries of individual directors in their willingness to co-operate, their acceptance and understanding of the research definitions, the availability of staff with both the time and the data to answer the questions, and in the demand for feedback. More profoundly, the differing ways in which SSDs are structured make it difficult to develop a series of questions to which all SSDs are in fact capable of responding, given their varying recording, collating, and disseminating practices. With the constant pressures on SSDs to produce services with limited budgets, directors are loath to allocate manpower to other peoples' research projects unless there is an obvious benefit. In stage 1, approval to distribute the questionnaire was sought from the appropriate professional organization, the Association of Directors of Social Services (ADSS).

With particularly favoured research, the ADSS can agree to distribute questionnaires itself and monitor the feedback, thus assuring a high response rate. In this case, the research committee of the ADSS, without explanation, decided to 'recommend that Directors complete it at their discretion', which implicitly accredits research with a relatively low priority and usually results in a much lower level of co-operation.

Although one authority did provide complete co-operation with stage 2 and 3 of the research, it was not possible on ethical or practical grounds to either interview the clients who were involved in the violent incidents with the social workers or have access to their case files. Thus, the accounts of the violent incidents are inevitably biased and impossible to validate totally.

Research Definitions

'Violence' was defined as 'physical (including sexual) violence resulting in actual physical harm to the social worker. Threats, abuse or any other form of psychological violence are excluded.' It was more difficult to define what constituted a social worker. British local authorities are unique in that they employ an enormous range of staff, from occupational therapists and cooks who produce 'meals-on-wheels', to counsellors and psychiatric social workers, patchworkers, and team leaders, some or all of whom may from time to time be described as social workers. One basic distinction was imposed, based on work context, between those who work from an office base and usually leave the office to meet clients (fieldworkers), and those who are employed in a residential or day-care setting where clients come to them (residential workers).

Stage 1: the national survey

A questionnaire was sent to all Directors of SSDs in England, Wales, Scotland, and Northern Ireland (N = 132) in the autumn of 1983, seeking basic data on the number of social workers employed, how many had been assaulted, and how assaults were recorded and collated, for the five-year period 1978–1982. The return rate was low but acceptable (N = 41; 31 per cent representing 25,000 social worker posts). Some 49 SSDs did not reply and the remainder replied that they were either too busy to complete the questionnaire, had insufficient staff to extract the data required, or charged a fee for the service. The crude cumulative average incidence rate (1978–1982) of physical assault by clients on social workers was 1:259 (1:228 for residential social workers; 1:372 for fieldworkers). The incidence was highest in those SSDs which were predominantly urban (1:130 in the Metropolitan District Councils, 1:147 in the London boroughs), lower in the shire counties (1:434), and apparently negligible in Scotland and Northern Ireland (1:1415 and 1:5440 respectively). However, the quality of the available data was poor, with wide variations in practice between SSDs in the recording, collation, and dissemination of the data. Moreover, some of the returns were at distinct variance with other sources of information. Thus, the low level of reported violence from directors in Northern Ireland contrasted vividly with the accounts of high levels of severe violence to social workers reported in, for example, Darby and Williamson (1978). Clearly, the relatively low overall incidence levels were likely to be an artefact of wide variations in recording practice, compounded by an acknowledged gap between actual and recorded incidence. Not surprisingly, from the information available to them most directors considered the level of assault to be an 'acceptable' and 'tolerable' level.

Stage 2: the scanning survey (N = 450)

All 728 social workers with actual client contact in one shire county were given a short questionnaire to establish how often they considered they had been physically assaulted over the five-year period. The predicted incidence, based on the national rate, was a total of five assaults over the five years in the county. In fact 112 of the 450 social workers who replied (25 per cent) reported that they had been assaulted on at least one occasion, with forty-five (40 per cent) having been assaulted more than once. Most assaults were minor (bruising, cuts, sprains), though 24 per cent resulted in moderate (fractures, broken limbs) or severe injury (permanent physical damage such as scarring, loss of full functioning in a limb, hand or foot, and so on). Four variables distinguished assaulted from non-assaulted staff – sex of the worker (men were more likely to be assaulted even though most field and residential staff were women); whether field or residential (residential staff were more likely to be assaulted); whether full or part-time (full time staff were more likely), and whether consent to the subsequent interview had been given (the assaulted were more often prepared to be interviewed).

The scanning survey, as well as providing this basic data, was also intended to shed some light on aspects of Steadman's situational approach to the study of aggressive incidents. Steadman's argument, summarized diagrammatically in Figure 10.2, postulates the interaction of 'person', 'context', and 'situation' in the genesis of most acts of violence. Essentially, Steadman postulates that violence is influenced or mediated by a number

Figure 10.2 Steadman's general model for a situational approach to the study of violence

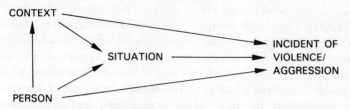

CONTEXT VARIATIONS: location, time, relationship, size, strength, age, alcohol use, drug use, number of persons present, dispute content.

PERSON VARIABLES: race, sex, education, socio-economic status, age, hospitalization, criminal histories, attitudes, life stress.

SITUATION VARIABLES: threats, insults, mediations, instigations.

Source: From Steadman 1982: 173.

of variables stemming from the interaction between 'aggressor' and 'victim' in certain situational contexts. However, the model does not distinguish differential probabilities of exposure to more serious incidents from differential reaction patterns when exposed to the same level of stimuli. These interactions are correlational and not causal, although the framework is useful for systematic data collection and an examination of the inter-relationships within and between the three major sets of variables. The scanning survey thus included an examination of the crude person and context variables of assaulted and non-assaulted social workers and found only four of significance – sex, workplace, hours employed, and willingness to discuss the incidents in more depth.

Stage 3:   structured interviews (N = 120)

Some 343 (76 per cent) of respondents to the scanning question-naire agreed to a subsequent interview. Thirty of the assaulted field social workers (FSWs) were matched with non-assaulted

243

FSWs by the criteria specified in Figure 10.1. This was replicated for thirty assaulted and thirty non-assaulted residential social workers (RSWs). It was not possible to make a complete four-way match. The schedule had five sections: section A elicited personal characteristics of the social workers; section B established the social workers' exposure to client contact; section C constituted a detailed description of the assault sequence; section D elicited the social workers' stereotypes of the most likely context of assault, most likely assaultive client, most likely type of assault, most likely response to assault, and the best response to assault. Thus, it established some of the attributions both assaulted and non-assaulted social workers held about the distinguishing characteristics of assaulted social workers; and section E consisted of the Hostility and Direction of Hostility Questionnaire (HDHQ) (Caine *et al.* 1967).

The sixty assaulted social workers reported that they had been assaulted a total of 588 times over the index six-year period. However, 378 of these assaults were on six residential social workers. If these are excluded the reported incidence rate was roughly 0.7 assaults per social worker per year.

The research did not compare the actual responses of assaulted and non-assaulted to the threat of assault, only their verbalized choice of what they considered should be the best responses in such a situation. Specific situational variables which might therefore distinguish assaulted from non-assaulted were not examined. Section C compared the reported behaviour of the assaulted groups. Though similar in terms of dispositional variables, basic social characteristics, verbal and actual response strategies, stereotypes, and attributions, they were distinguished on five variables:

(1) *Sex of the assaultive client*. RSWs were more likely to be assaulted by male clients, probably explained by the number of male adolescents in residential care with histories of violent assault. FSWs were most often attacked by women, again a reflection of context, likely to be related to the number of children being assessed for statutory care away from their parents.

(2) *Number of mentally ill clients*. Although a contextual artefact

(none of the RSWs were employed to work directly with the clinically mentally ill), it is noteworthy that most clients who assaulted FSWs had an acknowledged mental illness and that 38 per cent of all the assaultive clients had at least one admission to a psychiatric hospital.

(3) *Location of the assault.* FSWs were most likely to be assaulted in a client's primary territory, usually the client's home, and most RSWs in an area of secondary psychological importance, most often a communal area within a residency.

(4) *Severity of the injury.* Although one sixth of the assaults resulted in moderate or severe injury, usually to an RSW, staff rarely took time off work. Treatment was commonly sought in the workers' own time and at their own expense – that is, readily available National Health Service provision was ignored in favour of private medical or dental services. This may reflect the perceived negative characteristics attributed to assaulted social workers (see later).

(5) *Effect on practice.* Substantial numbers of staff (42 per cent), particularly FSWs, reported that the assault had adversely affected their subsequent practice, and 28 per cent felt less confident in their ability to do their job.

Remaining person and contextual variables seemed to be of little or no significance. Assaulted staff did not differ significantly from non-assaulted colleagues in terms of face-to-face contact with clients or size or type of caseload. At the time of the assault 92 per cent of all the clients were considered by the relevant social worker to have been experiencing some form of significant life stress, usually social. Some 60 per cent of all the clients had been known to the social worker for six months or more, and 47 per cent of the relationships were rated by the worker as having been 'good' or 'excellent' at the time, 45 per cent of the clients had at least one criminal conviction. There were no significant differences between the height and weight of the assaulted and non-assaulted social workers, and almost two-thirds of the assaultive clients were shorter and/or lighter than their respective social workers. Nine (15 per cent) of the sixty clients had been under the influence of drink or drugs at the time; none had taken both. The drug users were mainly glue sniffers and were 'high' without being out of control. The four who had been drinking were only mildly intoxicated. When asked to explain the reasons for the assault, most social workers interpreted it within the framework of the administration of authority, that is attempting to persuade or coerce the client into doing something against his or her wishes. However, this type of explanation often bore little relationship to the actual event, and nine workers were completely unable even to speculate as to why the assault might have occurred. In essence, the importance of most of the person and context variables in the genesis of client-to-social worker violence seems to be minimal, and increased emphasis falls upon the role of situational factors.

Situational factors in client-to-social worker violence

Precipitants

Social workers had difficulty in distinguishing the reasons for the assault from the precipitants immediately preceding the incident. Table 10.1 shows what was considered to have immediately preceded the assault. To examine the actual situational interaction patterns preceding the assault, a content analysis was completed of the social workers' descriptions of the events which led to the act of violence (Table 10.2). Some 42 per cent of the incidents were preceeded by verbal abuse, and 25 per cent by threats. On four occasions property was damaged, and six clients picked up an object to use as a weapon shortly beforehand. Some 30 per cent of the social workers attempted verbal reasoning, all of them clearly unsuccessfully: most staff simply watched and waited.

The large number of social workers unable to remember details was perhaps a consequence of three factors: the time lag between the incident and the interview; a reflection on a general lack of knowledge and skill in identifying and handling violent situations; and a not unreasonable wish to avoid 'disclosures' which might be held against them. It is of interest that no social worker was able to identify significant deviations in the client's behaviour which might correlate with impending aggression, at a stage before an actual aggressive outburst or act was carried out (Kaplan and Wheeler 1983).

VIOLENCE AND SOCIAL WORK

Table 10.1 Precipitants

	Total	%
Social worker upholding agency rules	15	25
Social worker controlling resources	4	7
Social worker acting as agent of the court	6	10
Client being generally aggressive	12	20
Client was mentally ill	13	21
Social worker was acting as therapist	2	4
Social worker was protecting the client	3	5
Other	5	8
Total	60	100

Table 10.2 Content analysis of descriptions of precursors to the assault

	Total	%
Verbal abuse	25	42
Threats	15	25
Damage to property	4	7
Expression of clients' psychosis	3	5
Social worker abused client	1	2
Client blocked exit to room	1	2
Client picked up a weapon	6	10
Social worker attempted reasoning	18	30
Social worker could not remember details	49	82

The incident

The most common types of assault were punching (34 per cent), kicking (14 per cent), use of a weapon (13 per cent), and pulling (13 per cent); 37 per cent of the incidents involved the use of more than one type of assault. Weapons ranged from an axe, an aerosol can, and a knife, to a shoe, a chain, and an iron bar. The most serious assault occurred in the client's home, and involved the use of an axe and strangulation with a rope, intermingled with considerable pulling and pushing. The episode lasted a number of hours and the social worker was severely injured. The incident had been preceded by a number of written and verbal death threats, specifying the type of assault being contemplated. Most of the assaults occurred in a location of

247

Table 10.3 Location of the assault

	Total	%
Client's primary territory	23	38
Client's secondary territory	29	48
Clients' public territory	3	5
Social workers' primary territory	2	4
Social workers' secondary territory	3	5
Social workers' public territory	0	0
	60	100

psychological importance to the client, and it was unusual for the assailant to seek out the social worker on 'home ground' (Table 10.3). The majority of the assaults were one-to-one, without bystanders, in isolation, and mostly without help being immediately available to the social worker.

The consequences

The consequences for a professional carer of being assaulted are likely to influence significantly the way in which the assault is evaluated, both personally and professionally. In harsh physical terms, 83 per cent of the social workers suffered only 'minor' harm, although nine of the thirty RSWs had moderate or severe injuries. Surprisingly, 92 per cent did not take any time off work as a direct and immediate consequence of the assault. Five of the moderately or severly injured staff received medical and/or dental treatment in their own time, and one social worker had a number of short-term hospital admissions over a period of years as a direct consequence of the assault. Staff were asked to recall their dominant emotion at the time of the assault: 47 per cent were shocked or surprised, 22 per cent angry, and 8 per cent afraid. The remainder remembered a sense of detachment, panic, or the absence of emotion.

It might be assumed that assaulted social workers would routinely inform managers and colleagues of the incidents. In fact, approximately one-fifth of managers and colleagues were never informed, and of the managers who were told, 33 per cent provided a response that the social workers found unsatisfactory. Colleagues were more helpful, with 82 per cent providing a satisfactory response. Social workers were asked whether the

Table 10.4 Evaluation of the incident

	Yes	No	Total
Completely unpredictable	30	30	60
Completely understandable	42	18	60
Entirely the workers' fault	2	58	60
Entirely the clients' fault	24	36	60
Both worker and client were partly responsible	34	26	60
I need further training	26	34	60
I remain wary of potential violence	36	24	60
I found it a valuable learning experience	40	20	60

incident had affected their confidence to fulfil their role. Some 18 per cent considered that their confidence had been temporarily impaired, and 10 per cent continued to feel less able to do their job. Seventeen social workers, therefore, construed the incidents as indicative of failure on their part.

To examine more closely how the social workers evaluated an incident which they viewed with some bewilderment and which they tended to seek to conceal, they were asked on a yes or no basis whether they considered a number of statements appropriate (Table 10.4). Although the workers were rarely responsible for the incident, and most were acknowledged to be a consequence of the interaction with the client, the violence itself was seen as being unpredictable. With most workers remaining wary of further violence but not considering they required further training, the potential existed for repeated episodes of violence against a number of those social workers.

Stereotypes and attributions

One of the interesting aspects of a tendency to decry the frequency of assaults, and the absence of normative data in the social work press, is whether or not the social workers in the sample held accurate stereotypes of client-to-worker violence, and what characteristics if any they attributed to social workers who had been assaulted. Stereotypes were elicited by asking social workers to rank eight cards on five topics on the basis of 'most likely'. Thus, for example, subjects were provided with eight types of client and asked to rank them on the basis of who they thought would be most likely to assault social workers. The remaining topics were: the most likely situation; the most likely type of violence; the most likely immediate response; and the best response strategies (the latter were elicited before being ranked). By comparing the stereotypes with the results of the surveys and main interview it was possible to establish whether these stereotypes were accurate or mismatched and thereby constituted social representations (Breakwell 1986). The results showed the striking similarities between assaulted and non-assaulted social workers along the topic headings. Although a number of the stereotypes were accurate, some were not. From the surveys and interview, the most likely aggressors are: parents whose children are being taken into care, children in residential care, and mentally ill people in the community. The interviewees also failed to identify elderly people in residential care as common aggressors, and included without justification mentally ill people in hospital.

The locations of assaults were accurately believed, for fieldworkers, to be in the client's home, and for residential staff to be in homes for children. However, all four groups inaccurately believed that, in addition, fieldworkers were often attacked at their office base.

Social workers considered that the most common types of assault were the least severe (pushing, holding, kicking, punching). In fact, the most often used means of violence were punching, kicking, use of a weapon, and pulling. Clients seemed to have been more determined to harm the social worker than the social worker had anticipated.

Most social workers, assaulted or not, had a dearth of response strategies that they accredited to others and were unable to indicate other than the most basic techniques of what they thought were optimum responses – usually 'move away or escape', 'verbal reasoning', 'passive self-protection', and 'retaliation'. This low awareness of possible responses is a reflection of their general inability to identify precursors to assault, and was exhibited in their actual responses which were largely consistent with these over-inclusive, non-analytic, and ineffective exhortations.

Social workers were asked whether assaulted social workers exhibited any characteristics which distinguished them from non-assaulted social workers. Interestingly, the substantial majority (78 per cent) of both assaulted and non-assaulted interviewees considered that there were distinguishing characteristics. The four characteristics consistently elicited were 'more provocative, incompetent, authoritarian and inexperienced': a stark contrast to the evaluation given to their own index of assaults which were almost never considered to be their own fault. Assaulted social workers, then, held a consistent and powerful negative image of assaulted workers. These interviewees were capable of giving inaccurate descriptions of themselves, and this raises the interesting question of how these incorrect views continued to be held. Perhaps they either did not consider their own assault as a test of the general rule that assaulted workers are more provocative and so on, or by tending not to report the incident they prevented other people from testing out the rule for them. It might, of course, be argued that assaulted social workers are indeed dispositionally different. To test this hypothesis, the total sample of 120 were given the HDHQ (Caine *et al.* 1967). Level and direction of hostility did not differentiate assaulted from non-assaulted. Moreover, social workers as a group were no more or less hostile than the general population. The position of the assaulted social worker is therefore particularly unenviable.

RECOMMENDATIONS FOR CHANGE

By adopting a comprehensive data collection framework within a quasi-experimental design, and utilizing a multi-method approach, the research enabled a number of important elements within a situational approach to be examined. From the available data (acknowledging the absence of information from the assaultive client), it would seem that Steadman's model had no particular explanatory power in the analysis of client-to-social worker violence. The social characteristics of assaulted and non-assaulted were basically the same, those of the clients were largely determined by context. Social workers as a group evaluated the violence along the same parameters, held the same attributions of those who were assaulted, and utilized the same

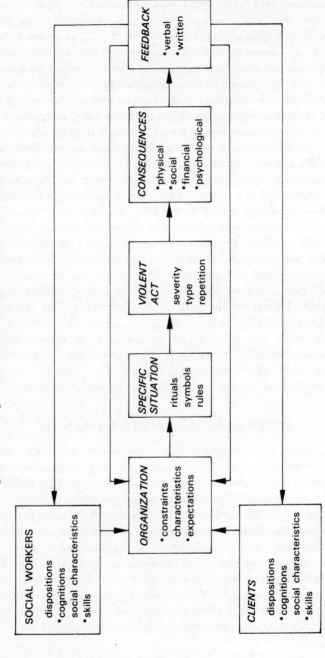

Figure 10.3 A process model of client-on-social worker violence

* = key change points

FEEDBACK
* verbal
* written

CONSEQUENCES
* physical
* social
* financial
* psychological

VIOLENT ACT
severity
type
repetition

SPECIFIC SITUATION
rituals
symbols
rules

ORGANIZATION
* constraints
* characteristics
* expectations

SOCIAL WORKERS
dispositions
* cognitions
social characteristics
* skills

CLIENTS
dispositions
* cognitions
social characteristics
* skills

sets of stereotypes. There were no differences in hostility level or direction. Physique, age, use of drug or alcohol were not significant, location was a consequent of work context and related to its psychological importance for clients and workers. Social workers were singularly unskilled in identifying the precursors to violence or in using effective response strategies once a violence sequence had been instigated. By taking no account of process, Steadman's model has no predictive power and cannot be invalidated. Figure 10.3 offers a simple process model analysis of client on social worker violence and identifies likely change points.

A detailed description of the various stages in this model is contained in Rowett (1986), and has led to the development of training packages aimed at the key change points specified above. In essence, social workers need to be made aware of the lack of differences between assaulted and non-assaulted, that violence largely occurs in a specific context, that the acquisition of basic skills by all social workers in the recognition and diffusion of interactions that induce violence is necessary, and that the recording of incidents should not therefore result in stigmatization.

The use of anxiety-management techniques, anger-management packages, and so on, when working with clients with a history of aggressive assault, needs to be more commonly developed. Line managers within the organization need to be made more aware of the consequences of assault for social workers and that institutional policy may have generated the situation which led to the violence. Senior managers should encourage routine recording of incidents and that information is collated and disseminated so that appropriate action is taken. The organization should have a clear and agreed policy towards violence, and established procedures. Some of the adverse consequences of assaults should be alleviated by, for example, the organization providing appropriate insurance cover, the provision of adequate recovery time, and of counselling and support when required. The quality and quantity of feedback between social workers and managers will only improve when both hold similar views on the genesis of violence, the importance of improving workers' ability to handle violence, and of the social workers' right to expect adequate training and adequate management support.

CONCLUSIONS

The research project summarized here represents an example of how a mixed-method, quasi-experimental design can be used to elucidate the features of violence occurring in a naturalistic setting. It illustrates the theoretical importance of studying aggression in its natural habitat since it is evident that there is a great schism between what people feel happens in their own lives and how they apply stereotypes and adhere to socially accepted attributions in describing what happens to others. The situational context of violence is recognized by those having to deal with it as paramount in determining its genesis, course, and consequences. Social psychological theories designed to predict and explain such violence must take account of these situational variables and can only do so if they incorporate data collected in the natural habitat of violent acts. The complex network of intermeshed situational precipitators and inhibitors (which may include ideological as well as material ones) cannot be modelled experimentally. They may be partially or singly recreated experimentally for minute examination but the essence of their impact stems from their interactions in their entirety.

Examining violence in its natural habitat may encourage the development of more integrated theoretical models, but it also modifies the research process. It inevitably pushes the researcher towards the Lewinian model of action research; towards intervention designed for change. This, in turn, brings into sharp relief powerful practical, ethical, and moral issues. The researcher then requires more awareness of his or her own political position and moral view about the research topic, an ability to assess and evaluate the socio-political constraints of funding or sponsoring agencies, a sensitivity to the consequences of the research for the participants, a willingness or otherwise to adopt a counselling or therapeutic role with those affected by the very methods used in the research, and the capacity to negotiate in advance adequate and appropriate feedback to all those influenced by the research.

POSTSCRIPT

Ethical and practical issues in the process of naturalistic research

Research in naturalistic settings can place the researcher in a plethora of complementary or contradictory roles and raises a number of difficult ethical issues.

Carer as victim

By identifying the subject of the research as a stigmatized individual, in this case a professional carer as a victim, the researcher from the outset is seeking to work with individuals who by co-operating run the risk of embarrassment, social stigmatization, and possible career impediments. Confidentiality between interviewee and researcher is ensured, but the act of contacting individuals through the management structure inevitably leads to an increased likelihood of identification. In a sense, the value of control groups as a means of avoiding identification of the experimental groups has as much value as their methodological importance.

Researcher as therapist

Researching emotionally 'difficult' areas, in private, with individuals who have had little opportunity to talk about the sources of the difficulty, inevitably places the researcher in a position where some form of 'therapy' will be expected from time to time, and on occasion demanded. In the present study, for example, a number of the more severely or more frequently injured became highly emotional when recounting the incidents, and on occasions broke down in tears. Although the researcher obviously has the choice of being therapeutically helpful or destructive on those occasions it is not possible to have no effect in either direction, in only because a relationship has been created. Whatever the researcher does will be construed in relation to the expressed emotion. This 'therapeutic' role has implications for the researcher as much as for the subject, ranging from the increased amount of time likely to be required, to the dilemma over whether to notify the subject's manager that more formal therapeutic help seems to be required.

Selecting and interviewing subjects

It is not immediately apparent why anyone should volunteer to co-operate with naturalistic research. The process is time consuming, usually tedious, adds to existing workload, has no immediate benefits, is not financially rewarding, and at worst can be embarrassing and threatening. The selection of subjects is usually made from a pool of such volunteers, who hopefully constitute a cross-section of the main demographic but not psychological variables to be examined. Once selected, the tracking down of individuals in their home or work-place, the negotiation of appropriate interview facilities, and the style of interview have all to be arranged and agreed. Last-minute refusal of one experimental subject to be interviewed may mean that the control subject will have to be deleted and another one interviewed, all of which may dramatically extend the overall time allocation of the project and may indeed threaten the research design.

Validating the data

Cross-checking of information provided by subjects can be time-consuming as well as difficult to negotiate. In the present study it was considered unethical and impractical to contact the assaultive clients or to look at relevant files. The only source of information was the victim, with obvious implications for the quality of the data elicited. If permission had been given, then the tracking down of the sixty individuals concerned (with the implications for the viability of the research design if a reasonable number refused to be interviewed) and the reading of the files scattered across an entire county, would in themselves have at least doubled the cost and length of the project, with a likely requirement for additional research staff and clerical support.

One way of dealing with this issue, which in retrospect should have been considered for use in this study, is to build in techniques within the interview itself, such as cross-questioning and confrontation (Brenner *et al.* 1985). Whether, however, the inevitable increase of emotional pressure in already highly emotional interviews is more or less likely to facilitate co-operation, accuracy of recall, and a therapeutic resolution, is questionable.

Feedback

Naturalistic research findings usually have to fill the dual requisites of being of some academic value and of actual use to the participating agencies and individuals. There are, however, remarkably few social science journals in Britain which are both academically respectable and widely ready by practitioners, a reflection of the dearth, perhaps, or practitioner-researchers. This dichotomy between academic and practice modes of publication places the researcher in the time-consuming and difficult position of having to submit articles to journals whose remits are only to publish certain aspects of the work, which may cause the central thrust of the argument to be lost or diluted. The alternative, that of submitting directly to the relevant agencies and ignoring publication, places the onus entirely on the agencies to disseminate the work appropriately, to have the staff capable of properly understanding the methodology and analyses, and avoids having the findings made available for wider criticism and debate.

Inevitable delays in publication and shortage of appropriate and accessible formats also have implications for the relationship between the researcher, subjects, and organization. Organizations, particularly in the state sector, reorganize frequently and rapid staff changes are endemic. Interviewees can be left in isolation, with different line managers, in an organization with a different structure, reading a research report about themselves two or three years after the interview. Organizations, which usually expect practical value from research within their ranks, can feel used by the researcher, without benefit to themselves.

REFERENCES

BASW (British Association of Social Workers) (1977) *The Social Work Task*, Birmingham: BASW.

Bernstein, B. (1981) 'Survey of threats and assaults directed towards psychotherapists', *American Journal of Psychotherapy* 34: (October).

Breakwell, G.M. (1986) *Coping with Threatened Identities*, London: Methuen.

Brenner, M., Brown, J., and Canter, D. (eds) (1985) *The Research Interview: Uses and Approaches*, London: Academic Press.

Brown, R., Bute, S., and Ford, P. (1986) *Social Workers at Risk, the Prevention and Management of Violence*, Basingstoke: Macmillan.

Bute, S.F. (1979a) 'The threat of violence in close encounters with clients', *Social Work Today* 11(4): (4 December): 14–15.
—— (1979b) 'Guidelines for coping with violence by clients', *Social Work Today* 11(5) (11 December): 13–14.
—— (1979c) *The Violent Client*, Hampshire Social Services and University of Bristol Social Work Department.
Caine, T.M., Foulds, G.A., and Hope, K. (1967) *The Hostility and Direction of Hostility Questionnaire*, London: University of London Press.
Crane, D. (1986) *Violence on Social Workers*, University of East Anglia, Norwich: Social Work Monographs, Monograph 46.
Darby, J. and Williamson, A. (eds) (1978) *Violence and the Social Services in Northern Ireland*, London: Heinemann.
Drinkwater, J. (1982) 'Violence in psychiatric hospitals', in M.P. Feldman (ed.) *Developments in the Study of Criminal Behaviour, Volume Two: Violence*, Chichester: Wiley.
Hosie, K. (1979) 'Violence in community home schools', *Child Abuse and Neglect* 3: 81–7.
Joxe, A. (ed.) (1981) *Violence and its Causes*, Paris: UNESCO.
Kaplan, S.G. and Wheeler, E.G. (1983) 'Survival skills for working with potentially violent clients', *Social Casework* 64(6): 339–47.
Lanza, M.L. (1983) 'The reactions of nursing staff to physical assault by a patient', *Hospital and Community Psychiatry* 34(1): 44–7.
Leavey, R. (1978) 'Violence in community homes', *Clearing House for Local Authority Social Services Research* 8: 1–81.
London Boroughs' Training Committee, Social Services (1983) 'Analysis of response to a questionnaire to ascertain the level of violence/unreasonably aggressive behaviour experienced by fieldworkers and other staff in area teams', unpublished report.
Millham, S., Bullock, R., and Hosie, K.M. (1976) 'On violence in community houses', in N. Tutt (ed.) *Violence*, London: HMSO Department of Health and Social Security.
NALGO (National and Local Government Officers Association) (1983) 'Survey and report on violence to members', unpublished report, 4 March.
Rowett, C. (1986) 'Violence in social work: a research study of violence in the context of local authority social work', *Institute of Criminology, University of Cambridge, Occasional Papers* 14.
Star, B. (1984) 'Patient violence/therapist safety', *Social Work* 29(3): 225–32.
Steadman, H.J. (1982) 'A situational approach to violence', *International Journal of Law and Psychiatry* 5: 171–86.
Tutt, N. (1975) 'So you think you know better', *Community Care* 20 August.
Whitman, R. (1976) 'Assault on the therapist', *American Journal of Psychiatry* 133 (April).

Part Four

CONCLUSIONS

Chapter 11

NATURALISTIC APPROACHES AND THE FUTURE OF AGGRESSION RESEARCH IN PSYCHOLOGY

JOHN ARCHER AND KEVIN BROWNE

OVERVIEW

In Chapter 1, we argued that psychological approaches to the study of aggression in relation to its social context occupy a central place between: (1) an individual or intrapsychic perspective which concentrates on the nature of aggressive motivation or aggressiveness as a trait; and (2) the study of aggression viewed from a wider societal perspective. We also argued that naturalistic rather than laboratory-based methods provide the most appropriate means of studying aggression and violence within its social context. Although laboratory experiments have until now been the most widely used form of methodology for studying aggression in social psychology, they were regarded as isolating the person from the social contexts in which most violent acts take place.

The debate about the appropriateness of laboratory or field studies in aggression research involves many of the same issues that have been raised in other areas. The major issue can be stated as follows: whether to control the variables experimentally in order to produce a 'harder' science, and hence to seek to elucidate causal relationships – but by so doing remove the behaviour from its usual context; or alternatively, to study behaviour in its social context, but by so doing forego experimental control over important variables, and hence limit the conclusions that can be reached about causal factors. In addition to this general issue, laboratory research on aggression raises the issue of whether the phenomenon *can* be studied in the

JOHN ARCHER AND KEVIN BROWNE

laboratory without substantially altering, or at least restricting it.

These and other questions raised by the laboratory–naturalistic debate on aggression research were discussed in Chapters 2 and 3 by Archer and Berkowitz respectively. Obviously, in a book devoted to naturalistic methods, the editors supported the view that the laboratory approach is limited, advanced in Chapter 2, rather than Berkowitz's defence of laboratory methods for researching aggression. We should, however, note that, as is often the case with such disagreements, there is more middle ground than may at first seem apparent. The aims of laboratory and naturalistic research are certainly different, and in Chapter 2 it was concluded that there has so far been too much emphasis on laboratory approaches to aggression research – to the detriment of the development of naturalistic methods – rather than laboratory research being of no value.

Our approach is consistent with the broad research strategy advocated by ethologists (cf. Tinbergen 1963; Blurton Jones 1972), that there is a place for the experimental analysis of causal factors, but that this should come *after*, and be informed by, a preliminary natural history phase. Our criticism of a social psychology of aggression, based largely on laboratory experiments, is that it has neglected such a preliminary natural history phase.

Most of this book is devoted to considering naturalistic methods of studying aggression and violence. In Chapter 2, such methods were introduced in general terms, and their limitations were considered. Obviously, official statistics form the least satisfactory way of obtaining information about aggressive acts: not only are there limitations in the frame of reference, and bias, but also many perpetrators of acts of violence are in a position to prevent their actions becoming officially recognized. One only has to contrast Davies's (1982) study of prison violence, which only involved violence *by* the prisoners, with Beynon's ethnographically based study of violence by teachers to pupils (Chapter 6) to realize that observations of, or accounts by, both participants are essential to obtain information which is not contaminated by the need to promote an acceptable self-image. Even so, accounts of

262

aggressive and violent acts will reflect the perceptions and cultural values of the person concerned. In cultural contexts in which the violent act confers status – for example, in the case of the football fans studied by Marsh *et al.* (1978) – the rhetoric has to be considered in the context of a culture which glorifies and exaggerates the extent of these acts. In cultural contexts in which the violent act is seen as a loss of control, and is associated with guilt, or where there is fear of official intervention, such as child or elder abuse (Chapter 8 and 9), steps may be taken to cover up the extent of the violent actions. Here, the rhetoric has to be considered in the context of a culture which seeks to deny that such acts take place at all.

The methods for studying aggression in a naturalistic setting clearly have to be viewed in the light of such considerations (as well as the other problems discussed in Chapter 2). The methods described in Parts 2 and 3 of the present book cover direct observations, both nonparticipant and participant, diary accounts in contexts where the respondent is seeking help from the researcher, questionnaires, and interview accounts. Ideally, a combination of several methods is useful for (at least partially) eliminating specific problems associated with any one of them.

Two contrasting examples of observational methods were described in Chapters 4 and 6. The ethological approach, discussed by Peter Smith, is characterized by direct nonparticipant observation. Whilst this may lead to more valid data than is obtained by other methods, the subject-matter suitable for this type of research is clearly limited by obtaining access. Many forms of aggression and violence within family and institutional settings would not be amenable to this method of study. In addition, as Smith points out, in many cases what people say about their actions may be as interesting as what they do. He therefore recommends a combination of ethological methods with others such as interviews.

One of the major advantages of ethological methods of observation, where they are appropriate, is that they provide a descriptive base of behavioural categories, which can readily be used in future investigations. Smith illustrates the importance of establishing such a descriptive base in relation to the crucial distinction between rough-and-tumble play and fighting in children. This distinction was not made in the often-cited study

263

of the imitation of aggression in young children by Bandura *et al.* (1961). Consequently, it is impossible to tell whether, as a result of observing aggressive behaviour, the children did show higher levels of fighting or whether they showed more rough-and-tumble play. Although this question has been raised in other contexts (cf. Chapter 3 by Berkowitz), only the descriptive base of the ethological approach provides a way of answering it.

In addition to initiating nonparticipant methods of observation, ethology has also provided a functional evolutionary framework for considering aggression (see also Chapter 4), and a rich source of both field and laboratory studies of animal aggression. Although the major focus of this book is human aggression, we have referred in passing to animal studies on several occasions, for example in the discussion of definitions and classification of aggression in Chapter 1. Chapter 5 concerns the more direct use of research on animal aggression for informing naturalistic studies of human aggression. Here, the influence is one of approach rather than methodology. It is important to note that in this chapter Caroline and Robert Blanchard are not simply extrapolating from the animal to the human case, but are concerned with the testing of hypotheses derived from an animal model but applied to human aggression. Since their approach to the analysis of animal aggression is essentially ethological, in that it is concerned with a detailed descriptive analysis and is sensitive to ecological context, when applied to humans it is relevant to naturalistic rather than laboratory contexts. Concepts and topics of interest derived from the detailed analysis of animal aggression, such as the distinction between offensive and defensive forms, assessment strategies prior to overt fighting, and the importance of a cognitive comparison process even in animals, can be used to direct descriptive research on human aggression. In this way, they help to place it in a broad comparative context, yet at the same time still focus on *human* studies.

In Chapter 6, we return to observational methods. John Beynon describes an ethnographic study of teacher–pupil violence in 11–12-year old children. Although this approach still casts the observer as a neutral 'fly on the wall', in other ways it provides a direct contrast with ethology, since the observer does not record the events as a series of objective behavioural categories which are amenable to quantitative analysis. Instead, Beynon sets out to investigate the transition to secondary school which takes place at these ages in the UK, by means of gaining the confidence of both pupils and teachers, the former because he was not an authority figure and the latter because he himself had been a teacher. In the course of his study, it became apparent that routine violence was one of the main ways in which teachers maintained the order in that section of the school. The ethnographic approach emphasizes the need to penetrate a cultural setting, so that the researcher becomes an 'insider', in order to have access to information normally hidden from view. Such information is gathered in the form of accounts which are checked and retaken over a period of time in an effort to minimize impression management. Analysis and presentation of the findings is in terms of a framework which emerges as the researcher becomes immersed in the cultural setting, i.e. order is imposed on the accounts by the researcher, who acknowledges his or her own personal involvement in the subject-matter.

In the third part of the book, several applications of naturalistic approaches are outlined in relation to social problems involving violence. In Chapter 7, Kevin Howells considers anger-management methods, which may be an appropriate way of dealing with some forms of real-life violence on an individual basis (he is, however, careful to point out its limitations to certain forms of aggression and to certain individuals). Underpinning such methods of anger-management is a view of uncontrolled anger as a major cause of violent acts, and interpersonal relations as the context for most episodes of anger. Interruption of plans or expectations, challenges to self-esteem and violation of accepted rules are highlighted as antecedents of aggressive acts (cf. a similar conclusion reached by the Blanchards in Chapter 5, and parallels with a model of aggression based on animal research: Archer, 1976). How such events are interpreted, particularly with regard to the perceived intentions of others, is crucially important in understanding the generation of anger and violent actions.

In applying anger-management methods to individual cases, it is first necessary to reveal the particular events which trigger that person's violence, and this was achieved through a combination of examination of case records, the Novaco Anger Inventory, a daily anger diary, and ratings based on observations by the hospital staff. As a result, it was possible not only to pinpoint the salient events which provoked anger, but also to understand how these were perceived by the person himself. This was further investigated by role-playing and asking him to speak his thoughts aloud. The aim of these methods in the clinical setting was to enable the person to understand the nature of the triggering events, his attributions and behavioural responses to these, and as a result, to suggest appropriate therapeutic intervention. However, as Howells remarks, crucial evaluation studies – notably, the controlled assessment of anger-management methods in seriously-violent populations – remain to be carried out. Nevertheless, the detailed investigation of anger-provoking events in relation to attribution processes, which the anger-management method provides, can generate valuable descriptive information which can be used in the construction of theoretical models of anger and violence.

Howells promotes the formulation of anger arousal offered by Novaco (1978) as being helpful in understanding violent acts. The determinants of anger (see Figure 11.1) are seen by Novaco as a combination of physiological arousal and a cognitive labelling of that arousal. These cognitions are themselves influenced by internal and external factors and the behavioural responses to the situation. Hence, Howells suggests that cognitive restructuring of a violent person's perceptions of social events, and their relationships with others, can help in reducing aggressive behaviour and hostility.

Chapters 8 and 9 are concerned with violence in domestic contexts. Kevin Browne considers the study of family violence, first concentrating on problems of definition and incidence, then causal models, and finally the most appropriate methods for studying this form of 'hidden' violence. In considering the social interactions of families in which abuse has occurred, he outlines the uses of a naturalistic observational method derived from ethology (cf. Chapter 4 by Peter Smith) for the recognition and treatment of violent families. However, as is almost always the case when studying behavioural problems in a naturalistic setting, a multi-method approach will prove more fruitful than relying on a single means of investigation, and Kevin Browne

Figure 11.1 Determinants of anger arousal

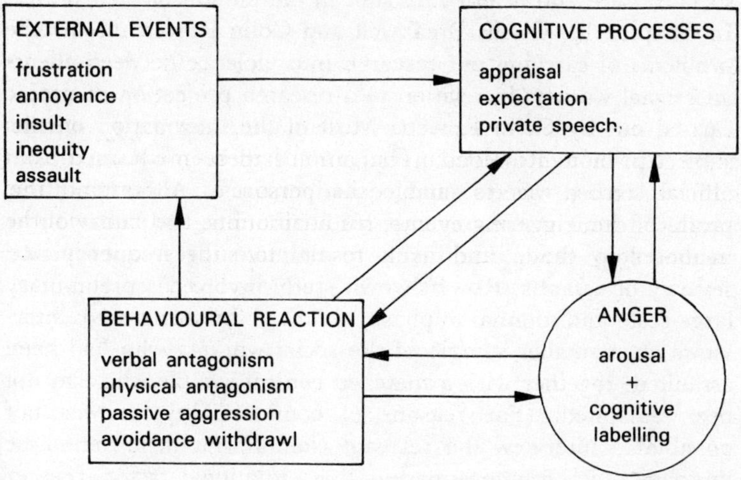

Source: From Novaco, 1978.

recommends a combination of observations and interviews (cf. a similar point about the usefulness of a combination of different approaches made earlier in this discussion, and in other chapters, for example those by Peter Smith and Kevin Howells).

In Chapter 9, Mervyn Eastman, a practising social worker, considers violence and other forms of abuse to elderly people in family and institutional contexts. First, he discusses definitions of 'old age abuse' and the lack of current awareness of the extent of the problem (when compared with other forms of domestic violence). The information on the subject is therefore fragmentary, being obtained largely from case histories, letters from relatives written to Mervyn Eastman during the course of his work, and his own survey of British social work departments. We have included a chapter on this topic in order to outline a problem involving violent behaviour which requires systematic research in the future, and which would be amenable to the sorts of naturalistic methods of enquiry discussed in this book.

Another problem which has, over the last few years, been highlighted in isolated newspaper reports and in concern shown by the relevant professional organizations is violence towards social service and health care staff in the pursuit of their duties. In Chapter 10, Glynis Breakwell and Colin Rowett discuss the problems of carrying out research into violence between clients and social workers in relation to a research project on this topic carried out by Colin Rowett. Most of the information on this subject prior to Rowett's investigation had been obtained from official record sheets and questionnaires. Although these produced some interesting case-study accounts, the nature of the methodology made it difficult to estimate the frequency and severity of assaults. Rowett's own study involved a preliminary large-scale questionnaire phase, followed by structured interviews on a smaller sample of the social workers who had been assaulted, together with a matched control sample who had not been assaulted. (For reasons of confidentiality, it was not possible to interview the relevant clients as well.) From these interviews, it became apparent that situational factors, rather than specific characteristics of the social worker or client, were the most important determinants of assault by the client. However, when questioned, social workers – whether they were the victims of assault or not – appeared unaware of the contextual nature of the assaults, attributing them instead to specific qualities of the assaulted individual. Not only does this research highlight the circumstances in which assault is likely but it also reveals the stigmatization within the profession of the victims of assault.

The work described in the last part of the book indicates some of the topics to which naturalistic methods have been, or are beginning to be, applied. However, the research carried out so far is limited. We therefore end this chapter with a discussion of some of the topics which could usefully be studied in the future using naturalistic methods.

FUTURE DIRECTIONS

So far, the study of aggressive and violent behaviour in naturalistic settings has been largely confined to certain forms which are more readily seen, such as the aggressive behaviour of schoolchildren in the playground (see Frude and Gault 1984), and to others which present legal, social, and personal problems, such as assault leading to criminal proceedings (see Hollin 1989). However, these represent only part of the violent and aggressive behaviour that occurs in many different community settings. In the last two chapters we covered two areas which have caused some concern but have been neglected both in terms of media interest and research, when compared, for example, to child and spouse abuse. To these topics we can add a long list of circumstances which have only aroused fragmentary public or research interest.

The topic of violence towards people in pursuit of their occupations, introduced in Chapter 10, is a wide one, ranging from such obvious targets as the police (cf. Toch 1969), security staff, court officials, and prison officers, to the caring and health professions who may be carrying out unwelcome legal obligations, to those who are targets only because of their vulnerability, such as late-night transport workers. This is one area which could be systematically researched in the future, and is incidentally one which in the UK has recently aroused considerable concern among trade unions and professional organizations representing occupations such as nurses, teachers, DHSS (welfare) staff, and bus crews. In the UK, it has also been highlighted by the news of the murder of a court official and solicitor's clerk while serving a house repossession order in · October 1987.

The majority of violent acts committed against people in pursuit of their occupations arise from the exercise of authority towards someone who perceives the action as threatening their welfare, status, or self-esteem. Of course, violence also occurs *by* those in authority towards people in a less powerful position. This usually occurs in the closed world of the institution or family and it is particularly difficult to research, both because it is hidden from view and because it is carried out by people in authority over others. Thus, violence by police or prison officers towards prisoners, by social workers towards clients, or by teachers towards pupils, presents particular problems for the researcher.

Information on violence by the police or prison officers is at present restricted to newspaper allegations and court reports, together with the autobiographical accounts of famous ex-prisoners such as Jimmy Boyle and John McVicar in the UK

269

(see, for example, McVicar 1982). In relation to social workers, Breakwell and Rowett point out in Chapter 10 that it is most unlikely that any social services department would allow a researcher access to clients and staff if it were known that they were researching violence by staff to clients. One would expect a similar prohibition to apply to teacher violence. Of course, as John Beynon showed in Chapter 6, however, if the researcher is engaged in a wider study of the social context in which the violent acts occur, it then becomes possible to include accounts of such violence within this wider framework which may prove acceptable to the authorities who grant access to the researcher. This was the way in which John Beynon was able to research violence by teachers to pupils, and it may prove suitable for other cases involving violence by people in authority towards those in their charge.

The two broad categories of violence towards people in the course of their occupations, and violence by those in authority over others, provide a way of considering different forms of violence in relation to the occupational, institutional, or family context in which it occurs. An alternative way of considering the context of aggression and violence is to concentrate on the psychological rather than social context in which it occurs. Thus in Chapters 4 and 7, it was argued that anger-induced (as opposed to instrumental) aggression occurred when the person's planned activities, or expectations, were not fulfilled, or when sources of self-esteem or accepted rules were challenged. Together, these cover a wide range of potentially aggression-evoking situations, and in the majority of cases outcomes other than physical assault result. Thus, for example, challenges to self-esteem may produce other emotional states, such as anxiety or depression, and when anger does occur it may be suppressed or channelled into more constructive directions than inter-personal aggressive actions. Nevertheless, the value of describing aggression-evoking situations in *psychological* terms would be to aid the understanding and prediction of when people are likely to react violently to circumstances, and hence to alert potential victims beforehand.

When the context of anger and violence is considered from a psychological viewpoint, there is a wide range of situations involving threats to a person's identity and self-esteem in which anger is known to be a likely outcome. In some of these circumstances there is a readily identifiable source to which to attribute blame. In others, blame cannot be so readily attributed to a single individual, but may be applied more widely – for example, to a particular profession – to authority figures, or to God.

One class of circumstances which produces a threat to a person's identity involves the loss of a significant part of the personal world, such as the loss of a spouse through bereavement or marital separation, the loss of a job, the loss of a bodily function, or the loss of property through crime. The 'loss' framework has been applied to these and a range of other circumstances in research and clinical literature dating back to Lindemann (1944). Anger and overt physical aggression have been described as an important component of people's responses to loss, for example in the case of bereavement (Parkes 1986), marital separation (Weiss 1976; Jacobson 1983), and job loss (Archer and Rhodes 1987). Where there is a clearly identifiable source to which to attribute blame for the event, aggressive feelings may be intensified. Thus, for example, in an interview study of separating couples at a crisis centre in Los Angeles, Jacobson (1983) reported that hostility towards the spouse was widespread, with 12 per cent of the respondents reporting that the spouse had tried to kill them at some stage. Similarly, in a discussion of the victims of automobile accidents, Dlugokinski (1985) referred to the strong anger felt by a man who lost his mobility – this was directed towards the drunken driver of the vehicle involved. The diverse circumstances involving loss can all be linked by a common framework (Parkes 1971) and therefore the anger shown in these different social contexts can be linked together by a common psychological explanation.

In future, it may be fruitful to combine the approach of studying aggression in terms of its social context (for example, child abuse, violence towards social workers) with an approach which seeks to understand the psychological antecedents, as does the 'loss' framework. This suggestion echoes that of Frude (1980), who argued that the application of psychological theories of aggression had been neglected in the study of child abuse (see Chapter 8). By stressing psychological antecedents in naturalistic studies of aggression, links can be made across the different

271

ERTEN

types of social contexts in which violent acts occur, raising the possibility of a wider theory of aggression, which may be useful in violence prevention.

REFERENCES

Archer, J. (1976) 'The organization of aggression and fear in vertebrates', in P.P.G. Bateson and P. Klopfer (eds) *Perspectives in Ethology, 2*, New York: Plenum Press, pp. 231–98.

Archer, J. and Rhodes, V. (1987) 'Bereavement and reactions to job loss: a comparative review', *British Journal of Social Psychology* 26: 211–24.

Bandura, A., Ross, D., and Ross, S.A. (1961) 'Transmission of aggression through imitation of aggressive models', *Journal of Abnormal and Social Psychology* 63: 575–82.

Blurton Jones, N. (1972) 'Characteristics of ethological studies of human behaviour', in N. Blurton Jones (ed.) *Ethological Studies of Child Behaviour*, London: Cambridge University Press, pp. 3–33.

Davies, W. (1982) 'Violence in prisons', in M.P. Feldman (ed.) *Developments in the Study of Criminal Behaviour, Vol 2: Violence*, Chichester: Wiley.

Dlugokinski, E. (1985) 'Victims of auto accidents: the quiet victims', *American Psychologist* 40: 116–17.

Frude, N. (1980) 'Child abuse as aggression', in N. Frude (ed.) *Psychological Approaches to Child Abuse*, London: Batsford, pp. 136–50.

Frude, N. and Gault, H. (1984) *Disruptive Behaviour in Schools*, Chichester: Wiley.

Hollin, C.R. (1989) *Psychology and Crime: Introduction to Criminological Psychology*, London: Routledge.

Jacobson, G.F. (1983) *The Multiple Crisis of Marital Separation and Divorce*, New York and London: Grune & Stratton.

Lindemann, E. (1944) 'Symptomatology and management of acute grief', *American Journal of Psychiatry* 101: 141–8.

McVicar, J. (1982) 'Violence in Prisons', in P. Marsh and A. Campbell (eds) *Aggression and Violence*, Oxford: Blackwell, pp. 200–14.

Marsh, P., Rosser, E., and Harre, R. (1978) *The Rules of Disorder*, London: Routledge and Kegan Paul.

Novaco, R.W. (1978) 'Anger and coping with stress', in J.P. Foreyt and D.P. Rathjen (eds) *Cognitive Behavior Therapy*, New York: Plenum, pp. 135–73.

Parkes, C.M. (1971) 'Psychosocial transitions: a field for study', *Social Science and Medicine* 5: 101–15.

—— (1986) *Bereavement: Studies of Grief in Adult Life*, London and New York: Tavistock.

Tinbergen, N. (1963) 'On the aims and methods of ethology',

Zeitschrift fur Tierpsychologie 20: 410–33.
Toch, H. (1969) *Violent Men*, Chicago: Aldine.
Weiss, R.S. (1976) 'The emotional impact of marital separation', *Journal of Social Issues* 32: 135–45.

AUTHOR INDEX

274

AUTHOR INDEX

White, J.W. 32
Whiting, B. 33
Whitman, R. 237
Williamson, A. 242
Wilson, E.O. 8, 74, 101, 102

Wittig, B.A. 200
Wolfe, D.A. 206
Woods, P. 127, 129, 132, 144

Zillmann, D. 154

SUBJECT INDEX

teacher's 122–38, 140–8, 270
towards children *see* abuse, child:
  violence, teacher's
towards old people *see* abuse, elder

weapons
  animal 98, 103

human 54–6, 141, 190, 246–7,
  250
'weapon's effect' 55–6
Women's Aid Centre *see* women's
  refuges
women's refuges 34, 186–7; *see also*
  National Women's Aid Federation